Heidegger's Metaphysics

Also Available from Bloomsbury

The Time of Revolution, Felix Ó Murchadha
Heidegger and Theology, Judith Wolfe
Heidegger and Nietzsche, Louis P. Blond

Heidegger's Metaphysics

The Overturning of "Being and Time"

Aengus Daly

BLOOMSBURY ACADEMIC
LONDON • NEW YORK • OXFORD • NEW DELHI • SYDNEY

BLOOMSBURY ACADEMIC
Bloomsbury Publishing Plc, 50 Bedford Square, London, WC1B 3DP, UK
Bloomsbury Publishing Inc, 1359 Broadway, 12th Floor, New York, NY 10018, USA
Bloomsbury Publishing Ireland, 29 Earlsfort Terrace, Dublin 2, D02 AY28, Ireland

BLOOMSBURY, BLOOMSBURY ACADEMIC and the Diana logo are
trademarks of Bloomsbury Publishing Plc

First published in Great Britain 2024
This paperback edition published 2026

Copyright © Aengus Daly, 2024

Aengus Daly has asserted his right under the Copyright,
Designs and Patents Act, 1988, to be identified as Author of this work.

For legal purposes the Acknowledgments on p. vii constitute
an extension of this copyright page.

Series design by Charlotte Daniels
Cover image: Philosopher in Meditation (1632), Rembrandt.
(Contributor: Universal Images Group North America LLC / Alamy Stock Photo)

All rights reserved. No part of this publication may be: i) reproduced or transmitted in
any form, electronic or mechanical, including photocopying, recording or by means of
any information storage or retrieval system without prior permission in writing from
the publishers; or ii) used or reproduced in any way for the training, development or
operation of artificial intelligence (AI) technologies, including generative AI technologies.
The rights holders expressly reserve this publication from the text and data mining
exception as per Article 4(3) of the Digital Single Market Directive (EU) 2019/790.

Bloomsbury Publishing Plc does not have any control over, or responsibility for,
any third-party websites referred to or in this book. All internet addresses
given in this book were correct at the time of going to press. The author
and publisher regret any inconvenience caused if addresses have changed or
sites have ceased to exist, but can accept no responsibility for any such changes.

A catalogue record for this book is available from the British Library.

A catalog record for this book is available from the Library of Congress.

ISBN: HB: 978-1-3504-1733-5
       PB: 978-1-3504-1736-6
       ePDF: 978-1-3504-1734-2
       eBook: 978-1-3504-1735-9

Typeset by Integra Software Services Pvt. Ltd.

For product safety related questions contact productsafety@bloomsbury.com.

To find out more about our authors and books visit www.bloomsbury.com
and sign up for our newsletters.

Contents

Acknowledgments	vii
List of Abbreviations	viii

Introduction: Heidegger's Turn to Metaphysics ... 1
    1   The Unity of Heidegger's Thought in the Period 1927–9 ... 3
        (a) Did the Project of Fundamental Ontology Fail? ... 3
        (b) The Metaphysics of Dasein ... 5
        (c) The Unity of Heidegger's Thought in the Period 1927–9 ... 9
    2   The Question of the "Transcendental Framework" of Heidegger's Investigation ... 12
    3   Initial Methodological Considerations ... 15

1 The Turn in *Being and Time* ... 31
    1   Dasein's "Essence" between Facticity and Projection ... 32
    2   Always Already Thrown: Mood and Turning Back ... 35
    3   Always Already Ahead-of-Itself: Going Forth Understandingly ... 38
    4   Standing between Nature and History ... 41
    Conclusion ... 45

2 Temporality and the *A Priori* ... 51
    1   Letting-Be Involved and the *A Priori* ... 52
    2   The Problem of the *A Priori* ... 57
        (a) Heidegger's Indebtedness to a Productive Paradigm? ... 57
        (b) Time and a Priority ... 60
        (c) Temporalität *and the Turn to the Metaphysical-Ontic* ... 62
    3   Time and Concept Formation in Heidegger's Interpretation of Kant ... 66
        (a) Movement and Ontic and Ontological Productivity ... 67
        (b) Ontic and Ontological Subsumption in Heidegger's Interpretation of the Critique of Pure Reason ... 69
    Conclusion ... 74

3 Metaphysics and the Turn to the Origin ... 81
    1   Anxiety, World, and the Origin of Metaphysics ... 83

	2 Nothingness, Negation, and the *Kehre*	88
	3 Metaphysics and "*die 'verkehrte Welt'*"	93
	Conclusion	97
4	Birth and the Primal Time of Myth	103
	1 The Mythical World as an Outstanding Problem in *Being and Time*	104
	2 Birth and the Darkness of Facticity	110
	3 A Phenomenology of the Mythical World	112
	(a) *The Mythical Understanding of Being and Temporality*	113
	(b) *The Mana-Representation, Dasein's "How" and the Wish*	117
	(c) *The "Factical Ideal of Dasein" and the Problem of Historicality*	120
	Conclusion	122
5	Transcendental Philosophy and Historicism?	129
	1 Historicism or Transcendental Philosophy?	130
	(a) *Crowell's Critique of Historicist Readings of Heidegger*	131
	(b) *Transcendental Philosophy and Normativity*	133
	(c) *Heidegger's Metaphysics and Metapolitics*	136
	2 Transcendental Philosophy and Dasein's Temporal Transcendence	138
	(a) *The Essential Equivocations in Ontological Concepts*	139
	(b) *Facticity and a Priority*	141
	(c) *Contingency, Necessity, and Factical History*	143
	(d) *History and Politics*	145
	Conclusion	147
6	The Native Soil or Historical Basis of Heidegger's Transcendental Philosophy	151
	1 An Interpretative Aporia—Philosophy or Politics?	152
	2 *Gemeinschaft* and *Volk* in the Existential Analytic	157
	3 Heidegger's Appropriation of Yorck von Wartenburg	161
	(a) *Yorck on Becoming-Historical*	162
	(b) *Heidegger's Appropriation of Yorck and Its Implications*	167
	4 The Political and the Alien	169
	Conclusion	174
	Conclusion: Metaphysics and Misgivings	183
	Bibliography	189
	Index	196

Acknowledgments

I am grateful to the late László Tengelyi for his intellectual and personal generosity and for his encouragement in pursuing this project. Over the years, I have also benefited from engagement with the work of, advice from, or discussions with Alexander Schnell, Inga Römer, Tim-Florian Steinbach, Irene Breuer, Stefan Schmidt, Matthias Wunsch, Giovanni Jan Giubilato, Emily Hughes, Pat O'Connor, and Felix Ó Murchadha. Manfred Baum's seminars and reading group have impressed upon me the need for careful, close readings of philosophical texts. A research grant from the DAAD allowed me to begin this project back in 2012. Translation work for Gerald Hartung and Smail Rapic in no small part helped to create the conditions for writing this work. The reports of anonymous reviewers made clear important points that needed to be addressed. To all these I express my thanks.

For discussions, comments on translation issues, and her friendship I thank Sabine Müller. I owe much to conversations with Leo Keohane, Emmet O'Cuana, and Rachel Coventry. This work would not have been possible without my family and extended family: Gabrielle Kyne, Frank Daly, Colm Daly, Una and Frank Daly, Karl and Olive Bödeker, Karla Bödeker, Seamas and Teenie Gerathy. Finally, I thank Corinna Janz for her love and support.

Abbreviations

I have used the following abbreviations for Heidegger's works and their English translations.

GA 3   *Kant und das Problem der Metaphysik*, edited by Friedrich-Wilhelm von Hermann. Frankfurt am Main: Vittorio Klostermann, 1991. KPM: *Kant and the Problem of Metaphysics*, 5th edition. Translated by Richard Taft. Bloomington: Indiana University Press, 1997.

GA 9   *Wegmarken*, 3rd edition, edited by Friedrich-Wilhelm von Hermann. Frankfurt am Main: Vittorio Klostermann, 1976. PM: *Pathmarks*, edited by William McNeill. Cambridge; New York: Cambridge University Press, 1998.

GA 14   *Zur Sache des Denkens*, edited by Friedrich-Wilhelm von Hermann. Frankfurt am Main: Vittorio Klostermann, 2007.

GA 18   *Grundbegriffe der aristotelischen Philosophie*, edited by Friedrich-Wilhelm von Herrmann and Ingrid Schüßler. Frankfurt am Main: Klostermann, 2002. BC: *Basic Concepts of Aristotelian Philosophy*. Translated by Robert D. Metcalf and Mark B. Tanzer. Bloomington: Indiana University Press, 2009.

GA 19   *Platon: Sophistes*, edited by Ingrid Schüssler. Frankfurt am Main: Klostermann, 1992. PS: *Plato's Sophist*. Translated by Richard Rojcewicz and André Schuwer. USA: Indiana University Press, 2003.

GA 22   *Die Grundbegriffe der Antiken Philosophie*, edited by Franz-Karl Blust. Frankfurt am Main: Vittorio Klostermann, 1993. BCA: *The Basic Concepts of Ancient Philosophy*. Translated by Richard Rojcewicz. Bloomington: Indiana University Press, 2008.

GA 25   *Phänomenologische Interpretation von Kants Kritik der reinen Vernunft*, edited by Ingtraud Görland. Frankfurt am Main: Vittorio

Klostermann, 1991. PIK: *Phenomenological Interpretation of Kant's Critique of Pure Reason*. Translated by Parvis Emad and Kenneth Maly. Bloomington: Indiana University Press, 1997.

GA 26 *Metaphysische Anfangsgründe der Logik in Ausgang von Leibniz*, 2nd edition, edited by Klaus Held. Frankfurt am Main: Vittorio Klostermann, 1990. MFL: *The Metaphysical Foundations of Logic*. Translated by Michael Heim. Bloomington: Indiana University Press, 1992.

GA 27 *Einleitung in die Philosophie*, edited by Otto Saame and Ina Saame-Speidel. Frankfurt am Main: Vittorio Klostermann, 2001.

GA 77 *Feldweg-Gespräche (Erdachte Gespräche 1944/45)*, edited by Ingeborg Schüßler. Frankfurt am Main: Vittorio Klostermann, 1995. *Country Path Conversations*. Translated by Bret Davis. Bloomington: Indiana University Press, 2010.

GA 82 *Zu eigenen Veröffentlichungen*, edited by Friedrich-Wilhelm von Hermann. Frankfurt am Main: Vittorio Klostermann, 2018.

H *Sein und Zeit*, 19th edition. Tübingen: Max Niemayer Verlag, 2006. *Being and Time*. Translated by John Macquarrie and Edward Robinson. Cornwall: Blackwell, 2000. *Being and Time*. Translated by Joan Stambaugh and revised by Dennis J. Schmidt. Albany: State of New York University Press, 2010.

Introduction:
Heidegger's Turn to Metaphysics

Shortly after the publication of his major work *Being and Time* (1927), Heidegger begins to refer to his project as a *metaphysics* of Dasein. At the core of this project lies a concern with those moments in which a gap between our habitual ways of making sense of ourselves, others, and things and our underlying sense of the strangeness and incomprehensibility of the world emerges. We always live within a tacit awareness of this difference between beings and our understanding of their being (the ontological difference in one of its senses) but it only becomes manifest at certain times in our existence. Heidegger's use of the term "metaphysics" plays on the double sense in which we experience a kind of transcendence in such moments. On the one hand, beings themselves transcend or surpass our possibilities of understanding them, we feel overwhelmed or overcome by the strangeness of the world. On the other hand, such experiences make clear that we transcend or are always more than any one particular way of making sense of the world. What Heidegger calls "temporality" is this interplay between being brought back to the strangeness of the world and taking up a particular and necessarily limited possibility of understanding it within a historical community.

Heidegger speaks of a metaphysics of Dasein for both substantive and historical reasons. Substantively, this project is concerned with Dasein's transcendence, that is, its surpassing or going beyond beings by virtue of being temporal. In terms of historical background, Heidegger, like Kant, claims that metaphysics or transcendence belongs to our "nature." This use of the term metaphysics also signals a critical retrieval of Aristotle's double characterization of philosophy as πρώτη φιλοσοφία, concerned with being as such, and as θεολογεῖν, concerned with τὸ θεῖον, the overwhelming, what takes us by surprise.[1] In the following study, I will be chiefly concerned with the former, substantive sense of the term "the metaphysics of Dasein" although, as we will see, the thematization of Dasein's transcendence also has an irreducible historical dimension.

The basic thesis of this book can be summed up simply: Heidegger's works in the years 1927–9 constitute a single, unified *metaphysical* investigation into the temporal conditions for the revelation of the ontological difference. These investigations do not so much abandon the fundamental ontological inquiry into the meaning of being developed in *Being and Time* as carry out a turn, entailed by the nature of the investigation itself, from the question of the meaning of being to the metaphysical event in which the ontological difference emerges. The interpretation of this period of Heidegger's work that I develop in the following is not so much concerned with the oft-discussed question of how, why, and when Heidegger's project in these years failed as with the positive philosophical possibilities of the "metaphysics of Dasein."

Central to Heidegger's investigations here is the problematization of the temporal conditions of the traditional *a priori* and, indeed, for philosophical concept formation generally. Exploration of this issue shows, contrary to a widespread and long-standing line of interpretation, that neither *Being and Time* nor subsequent works in this period can be said to be a kind of Kantian transcendental philosophy that, instead of seeking the *a priori* conditions for the region of being called nature, undertakes a wider inquiry into the *a priori* conditions for the understanding of being. Rather the very theme of Heidegger's investigation demands a transformation of transcendental philosophy and the traditional notion of the *a priori*. A key question here is how this transcendental philosophy is to be conceived and whether it is philosophically defensible.

Investigating how the project of *Being and Time* was further developed does not mean setting out to reconstruct the missing Third Division of *Being and Time*.[2] With the disclosure of more original phenomenological domains, it is indisputable that Heidegger's project undergoes a transformation or an overturning in both its method and its aims, the most important being the shift from investigating the temporal conditions for understanding the meaning of being to those for revealing the ontological difference. This study claims that it is through the thematization of a temporality of thrownness, itself unthematized but presupposed in *Being and Time*, that the ontological difference becomes central to the investigation. This development also shows how and why the temporality of concept formation in such a phenomenological investigation must be distinct to the formation of concepts in the ontic sciences.

1 The Unity of Heidegger's Thought in the Period 1927-9

How does Heidegger's metaphysics relate to the fundamental ontology of *Being and Time*? Should be it conceived as a break with the earlier work, as some commentators have argued, or its continuation? I will answer this question in three steps. I first consider a long-standing line of interpretation that claims the failure of the project of *Being and Time* occurred in the lecture course *The Basic Problems of Phenomenology* in 1927, thus immediately prior to the development of the metaphysics of Dasein *(a)*. Then I examine the correlated thesis that the metaphysics of Dasein constitutes a new phase in Heidegger's thinking, separate to that of fundamental ontology *(b)*. Against this background I will then outline the main points of the argument to be developed over the course of the following work: The metaphysics of Dasein is not a break with *Being and Time* but a transformation and continuation of its project *(c)*.

(a) Did the Project of Fundamental Ontology Fail?

Did the project of fundamental ontology, the project of *Being and Time*, fail? Heidegger's seemingly unambiguous later remark on *Being and Time* suggests an affirmative answer to this question: "Thinking failed in the saying of this turning [*Kehre*] and did not succeed with the language of metaphysics" (PM 250 [GA 9 328]). When we take this claim at face value, it leads to the further questions: *Why* did the project of fundamental ontology fail? When, where, and for what reasons was this project abandoned? In what sense did *Being and Time* remain indebted to the language of metaphysics? In what does the "turn" or *Kehre* away from *Being and Time* consist?

A significant interpretative hurdle in answering these questions lies in the fact that the extant portions of *Being and Time* give scant indications as to what "*Kehre*" and "metaphysics" could mean. According to one interpretation, given that the failed saying of the turn was to take place in Division III of *Being and Time* and that the lecture course *The Basic Problems of Phenomenology* is a new attempt at Division III, it is this latter text that shows why Heidegger's project failed. And central to this lecture course is the development of the *Temporalität* of being which Heidegger defines as "the horizon from which we understand being" (BPP 228 [GA 24, 324]). This turn to *Temporalität* can also be said to be a failure: The analysis of *Temporalität* as the "upon which" of the understanding of being runs up against three fundamental problems: the finitude of time, the root of the "not" in nullity, and the relation between time and nothingness. Read in this light, the dramatic closing hours of this lecture course document the failure of the project of fundamental ontology. And provided we read *Temporalität* as the transcendental condition for the understanding of being and take talk of the transcendental to belong to metaphysics, it seems clear this project and its metaphysical, that is, Kantian transcendental, language failed.[3]

However, this line of interpretation is, I think, problematic on the textual and philosophical levels. With respect to the former, the lecture course *The Basic Problems of Phenomenology* is itself incomplete and can by no means be seen as the full record of a new attempt on Division III of *Being and Time*. Of its projected three parts (each consisting of four chapters), only the first part and the first chapter of the second part were delivered. This raises a basic question for the preceding interpretation of the failure of the project of fundamental ontology. Are the three fundamental problems that the analysis of *Temporalität* runs up against really difficulties fatal to Heidegger's project? Or do they rather open questions that were to be further investigated and developed?

And on the philosophical level, it is difficult to see how this alleged turn to *Temporalität* is in any sense a *turn* rather than the continuation of a linear line of investigation into ever more original conditions of the possibility of the understanding of being, moving from everydayness to Dasein's temporality to *Temporalität*. And we can further ask: Is the *Kehre* really a turn to *Temporalität*? Heidegger nowhere discusses the *Kehre* in *The Basic Problems of Phenomenology* and it is first mentioned in the 1928 lecture course *The Metaphysical Foundations of Logic* where Heidegger claims that analysis of *Temporalität* "is at the same time the *turn* [*Kehre*], where ontology itself expressly runs back into the metaphysical-ontic in which it implicitly always remains" (MFL 158 [GA 26 201]). So according to the 1928 lecture course, the turn is not *to Temporalität* but *from Temporalität*. It is a turn *to* what Heidegger refers to as the metaphysical-ontic, which designates the *factical* presupposition of the understanding of being, namely the "factical existence of Dasein" and "the factical presence-at-hand of nature," so the sheer fact we exist in the midst of beings other than ourselves (MFL 156 [GA 26 199]). And this turn to facticity—and not a supposed turn to *Temporalität*—is alluded to in *The Basic Problems of Phenomenology* among the projected but unwritten topics of the lecture course as "the ontical foundation of fundamental ontology" (BPP 24 [GA 24 32–3], cf. H. 436–7).[4]

If it is questionable that the turn in Heidegger's project is to be found in the analysis of *Temporalität*, it is also far from certain that "the language of metaphysics" that Heidegger refers to in the "Letter on Humanism" is the quasi-Kantian transcendental language of *Being and Time* and *The Basic Problems of Phenomenology*. For one thing, these texts hardly speak of metaphysics at all and, as I will argue in the following section, there are good reasons to doubt that Heidegger *ever* intended his work to be understood as a transcendental philosophy akin to that of Kant. To take one of many examples, in *The Basic Problems of Phenomenology* Heidegger explicitly demarcates his investigation over against that of Kant, speaking of "the *more original concept of transcendence*" tacitly presupposed in "the Kantian idea of the transcendental and of philosophy as transcendental philosophy" (BPP, 323 [GA 24 460]). Here it should be noted that "*the more original concept of transcendence*" is the main issue treated under the heading of the "metaphysics of Dasein." In other words, it is not that Heidegger here simply takes over the purportedly metaphysical language of Kantian transcendental philosophy but instead signals his intent to carry out a *metaphysical critique* of its presuppositions.

A further reason to question the above reading of the project of fundamental ontology lies in the fact that Heidegger's claim in the "Letter on Humanism" about the failure of fundamental ontology is more equivocal than it appears at first reading. In Heidegger's work and especially in *Being and Time*, failure does not imply running up against fatal philosophical difficulties but has an important methodological significance. The failure of an item of equipment reveals the surrounding totality of significance and the failure of the everyday in anxiety is crucial to the disclosure of Dasein's ownmost temporality. In other words, failure has the positive methodological sense of opening up more original phenomenological horizons or domains. Although Heidegger's retrospective self-interpretations need to be treated with a measure of skepticism, such a sense of failure is compatible with Heidegger's claim in his 1936 auto-critique of *Being and Time* that this work was too *successful* in answering the question of being.[5]

(b) The Metaphysics of Dasein

The preceding section suggested that the project of fundamental ontology did not come to an end in 1927. And on one level, the metaphysics of Dasein does continue the project of *Being and Time* in that it deals with a presupposition of this work. *Being and Time* begins with a "fact [*Faktum*]"—that of our "vague understanding of being"—and then seeks the conditions for its possibility, that is, the horizon upon which anything like being becomes meaningful (H. 5). *The Metaphysical Foundations of Logic* (1928), on the other hand, focuses on the flip side of this inquiry, the "factual" presuppositions of this investigation. The fact of understanding being presupposes that there are *in fact* beings and that we ourselves *in fact* exist: "Being is there only insofar as beings are there." (MFL 156, [GA 26 199]).⁶

Yet the seemingly distinct natures of the fundamental ontological inquiry (into conditions for the possibility of ontological understanding) and the metaphysics of Dasein (which is concerned with special factual or "factical" conditions for ontological understanding) raise the question of whether there really is a continuity between these inquiries. Matters are not helped by Heidegger's own cryptic remarks on their supposed relation. He speaks of "the latent tendency toward fundamental, metaphysical transformation" in fundamental ontology, of a turn, a movement, a μεταβολή, that "resides in the essence of ontology itself" and that opens the metaphysical domain of questioning (MFL 156–7, [GA 26 199], cf. (MFL 158 [GA 26 200–2])). Yet because Heidegger leaves the nature of this turn and movement extremely vague and because he scarcely mentions metaphysics in *Being and Time*, the reader could well suspect that we are dealing less with a continuity than a break. For what could connect an idealistic investigation into the conditions for the possibility of ontological understanding to the thematization of real or factual presuppositions of phenomenological ontology?

The absence of a clear account of how one project unfolds from the other would seem to support the separability thesis according to which Heidegger's work in the late 1920s can be divided into two distinct periods: a fundamental ontological phase which ends with failed investigation into *Temporalität* as the transcendental condition for the meaning of being in *The Basic Problems of Phenomenology* and a metaphysical period in which the hitherto neglected problem of facticity (the fact that Dasein and nature are there) is explicitly thematized. On such a reading, Heidegger does indeed take up and treat anew problems under the heading of the "metaphysics of Dasein" that were outstanding in the project of fundamental ontology but in so doing he breaks with his earlier, one-sided approach.⁷

Several considerations seem to support such a reading. For one, in the metaphysical period, the concern with ecstatic temporality and with *Temporalität* as an ultimate condition for the understanding of being recedes and a metaphysics of facticity sensitive to the different domains of beings is foregrounded. And unlike *Being and Time*, in this latter the world is no longer only an existential of Dasein's but is considered in its independence from Dasein,⁸ a theme that is, at best, only marginally present in *Being and Time* and *The Basic Problems of Phenomenology*. Further still, several significant terminological shifts take place in Heidegger's work in the metaphysical period that are not compatible with the use of the same terms in *Being and Time*, another apparent indication of the very different character of Heidegger's thought in this period. Perhaps most notably, the term "metaphysics" takes on a positive meaning in the late 1920s, a fact likely influenced by Heidegger's discussions with Max Scheler in December 1927.[9] In contrast to this, there is no positive conception of metaphysics in *Being and Time* and the uses of the term "metaphysics" in texts and writings that precede this work are rare and largely negative.[10]

As against this reading, I want to suggest that there are reasons internal to Heidegger's texts between 1927 and 1929 that render the separation of the "fundamental ontological" and "metaphysical" periods questionable. First, the absence of the positive use of the term "metaphysics" in *Being and Time* does not establish that to which this term refers is also absent. Key concepts in *Being and Time* such as guilt, death, repetition, and the notion of temporal ecstases are largely absent in Division I in name but acquire significance with the repetition of this Division in Division II. Further, there is a thematic continuity between the fundamental ontological period of Heidegger's work (understood as encompassing *Being and Time* and *The Basic Problems of Phenomenology*) and the metaphysics of Dasein on several important points. The earlier work flags a number of issues as requiring further investigation including the incompleteness of the concept of the world (H.65, 82), the "complicated structure" of Dasein's facticity (H. 56), the problem of access to the present-at-hand as such or nature (cf. H. 45, 144–5), carrying out "a non-deductive existential genealogy" of different ontological regions (H. 11), the "factical *a priori* character of Dasein" (H. 229), the distinction between curiosity and wonder (H. 170–1), the "factical ideal" or "definite ontical way of taking Dasein's existence" that underlies the investigation (H. 310), Dasein's transcendence (H. 366), the relation between the ontic totality of beings (nature) and the understanding of being (H. 314, cf. H. 403), the temporality of thrownness or of birth (H. 373–4), and the ontic foundation of fundamental ontology (H. 436–7). As these concerns are taken up again in the metaphysics of Dasein, the latter can certainly be read as treating difficulties that Heidegger came to realize were fatal to his earlier project using a new approach. However, given that Heidegger himself insists on the continuity of his investigation, there is the strong possibility, which will be explored in this study, that we are dealing with the unfolding of a single unified problematic in the years 1927–9.

Second, like *Being and Time*, the lecture course *The Basic Problems of Phenomenology* does not neglect but explicitly and implicitly signals the problem of the ontic at key points. Its projected table of contents lists "the ontic basis of ontology" as the topic of Part Three, Chapter One of the lecture course (which was never delivered). The final pages of Part One of this lecture course also speak of a "repetition" of fundamental ontology "on a higher level" which would treat the problem of the different regions of beings (BPP 223-4 [GA 24 319-20]).[11] I will argue later that the problem of the ontic is also implicitly signaled in the aforementioned problems that analysis of *Temporalität* runs up against: the origin of the "not," the finitude of time, and the relation between time and "nothingness."[12] So rather than neglecting or ignoring the problem of the ontic, there is another possibility: This lecture course simply did not arrive at it.

Third, *The Basic Problems of Phenomenology* cannot be regarded as the highwater mark of Heidegger's concern with ecstatic-horizonal temporality or even of *Temporalität*. Ecstatic temporality remains a central theme of 1928 course *The Metaphysical Foundations of Logic* and is referred to in other texts in this period.[13] The 1928 lecture course arguably constitutes the furthest advance into the investigation of *Temporalität* and evinces a concern with both the relation between the *a priori* and horizontal-ecstatic temporality *and* with themes characteristic of the metaphysical period such as facticity and the turn to the metaphysical-ontic. This suggests that the interpretation in which Heidegger's investigation into *Temporalität* is abandoned in the metaphysical period is at the very least questionable.

Finally, the claim that Heidegger's discussions with Max Scheler in December 1927 were a central factor in the development of the metaphysics of Dasein cannot be lightly dismissed by saying that if the concern of phenomenology is with the matters themselves, then contingent biographical considerations must be bracketed. Heidegger's positive conception of metaphysics is arguably directly informed by Scheler, further the appearance of the term "metaphysics" postdates *Being and Time* and seems to respond to Scheler's criticisms of this work. Yet this consideration does not decisively indicate that there is in fact a separation between the fundamental ontological and metaphysical periods of Heidegger's work. Even if the term "metaphysics" was introduced owing to the influence of Scheler, that to which the term metaphysics refers, namely, the double conception of philosophy as encompassing the investigation of being and the problem of beings as a whole is already discussed in the summer semester course of 1926 on the basic concepts of ancient philosophy in terms very similar to those used in 1928.[14] These considerations support the interpretative possibility that the project of *Being and Time* was continued and transformed rather than abandoned.

(c) The Unity of Heidegger's Thought in the Period 1927–9

The foregoing argued for the interpretative possibility that Heidegger's work in the period 1927–9 constitutes a unified investigation. Yet it is obviously insufficient to maintain, based on both Heidegger's self-interpretation and on the fact that problems signaled in *Being and Time* are taken up anew in the development of the metaphysics of Dasein, that we can interpret Heidegger's investigations in the late 1920s as having a fundamental continuity. The key question is: What brings about or necessitates the turn from the investigation into existential-temporal conditions for the possibility of ontological understanding to an inquiry into the factical conditions for ontological investigation, namely the fact that Dasein and other beings are there?

My proposed answer is that the factical presuppositions of fundamental ontology, the being there of Dasein and nature, become manifest in a distinctive mode of Dasein's temporality, the temporality of thrownness. This means the antithesis between the "idealistic" investigation of the temporal conditions for understanding being and the "real" or factical conditions for this investigation is only apparent since it is in a distinctive mode of its temporality that Dasein is brought back to its facticity. A distinctive kind of understanding belongs to this mode of temporality: an understanding of our incapacity or powerlessness in the face of the overwhelming, incomprehensible fact of existing, of being in the midst of beings. We are confronted with the sheer fact of being there, with the reality of the Real, in those moments when all possibilities of understanding have withdrawn, where we find ourselves overpowered and overwhelmed by things and unable to "get a grip" on them. Read in this light, the thematization of this distinctive mode of temporality thus brings about a turn from fundamental ontology's focus on the *meaning* of being and toward the *ontological difference* (the difference between beings and being).

Unpacking the implications of this thesis is the task of the work that follows. But to show that it is plausible, I want to first look more closely at how Heidegger characterizes the turn in *The Metaphysical Foundations of Logic*. Heidegger describes this turn to facticity as a turn to the metaphysical-ontic:

"Fundamental ontology is this whole of founding and developing ontology; the former is 1) the analysis of Dasein, and 2) the analysis of the *Temporalität* of being [*Temporalität des Seins*]. But the *temporale* [*temporale*] analysis is at the same time the *turn* [*Kehre*], where ontology itself expressly runs back into the metaphysical-ontic in which it always implicitly remains. Through the movement of radicalizing and universalizing, the aim is to bring ontology to its latent overturning [*Umschlag*]. Here the turn [*Kehre*] is carried out, and it is turned over [*Umschlag*] into the metontology."[15]

The analysis of Dasein clearly refers to the existential analytic of *Being and Time* and the "analysis of *Temporalität*" or the "*temporale* analysis"—these terms are more or less synonymous (BPP 228 [GA 24 324])—refers to the thematizing of the horizon upon which being becomes understood, a task begun in *The Basic Problems of Phenomenology*. The key to understanding the transition to the metaphysics of Dasein lies in three terms—*Kehre*, *Umschlag*, and metontology. Turning is a kind of movement and the term *Umschlag*, overturning, is a literal translation, Heidegger points out, of μεταβολή, movement.[16] Similarly the prefix "met-" of metontology itself refers to a μεταβολή which already "resides in the essence of ontology itself" and which opens up the metaphysical domain of questioning (MFL 156–7 [GA 26 199]). How, then, could this movement from fundamental ontology to the metaphysics of Dasein occur?

Here it should be noted that in *Being and Time*, Heidegger refers to different modes of temporality as *movements* of Dasein's existence: "falling is conceived ontologically as a kind of motion," as are dealing with equipment, historizing, and seizing hold of existence resolutely. Even the problem of understanding being upon the horizon of time is "haunted by the enigma of being, and … by that of motion" (H. 180, 388, 348, 392). What remains in the background of the 1927 work, however, are the interrelations between the phenomena of facticity, temporality, and movement. There the term "facticity" refers to the fact *that* Dasein exists as delivered over to the world. Yet despite the importance of this notion—fallenness, existentiality, facticity are the three essential constituents of Dasein's being as care—facticity is not thematized at any length in *Being and Time* while fallenness and existentiality are central to Divisions I and II respectively. The discussion of facticity was postponed in the existential analytic because, Heidegger claims, it "has a complicated structure which cannot even be grasped as a problem until Dasein's basic existential states have been worked out" (H. 56). Heidegger does, however, signal that it is linked to a distinctive mode of temporality and thus to a distinctive existential movement: "The primary existential meaning of facticity lies in the character of 'having been'" (H. 328), in a manner akin to how the primary meaning of existentiality is the ecstasis of the future and that of fallenness, making-present.

If "the primary existential meaning of facticity lies in the character of 'having been'" (H. 328) and if it is in its moods that Dasein's having been thrown becomes manifest to it (H. 326, 340), then this suggests that it is in the discussion of moods in *Being and Time* that we can find some indications as to what the *Kehre* spoken of *The Metaphysical Foundations of Logic* means. And central to these analyses is the distinction between Dasein's turn from [*Abkehr*] its *having been* thrown into the world (for example, in moods such as anger, elation, fear) and Dasein's turn toward [*Hinkehr*][17] its factical being-there in anxiety (see *Being and Time* §§§29, 40 and 68 (b)).[18] In the latter, Dasein is turned toward "the pure 'that-it-is' of [its] ownmost individualized thrownness," toward its being delivered over to the world (H. 343 cf. H. 328, 135). By holding on to the present of anxiety (rather than seeking to escape it or losing its head in bewilderment), Dasein allows its everyday possibilities of being to withdraw such that it is brought before the "empty mercilessness" of its having been thrown into the world. It experiences the oppressive reality of beings other than itself; they press in upon it in their strangeness (H. 343).

Being and Time foregrounds one aspect of this experience of the brute reality of being in the midst of beings: It individualizes us and opens up the possibility of an authentic potentiality-for-being, that is, of taking over our possibilities as our own. The existential analytic largely focuses on this futural moment of seizing hold of this authentic being-toward-death rather than the moment in which Dasein is turned back to its sheer being in the midst of beings. Bearing this in mind, my interpretative proposal is that while the fallen present and the authentic future are respectively treated in Division I and Division II of *Being and Time*, the metaphysics of Dasein develops a temporality of thrownness.[19] Read in this light, the lecture "What Is Metaphysics?" foregrounds what was left in the background of *Being and Time*, namely the "first moment" of anxiety in which worldly significance withdraws and Dasein finds itself in the midst of beings as a whole (cf. H. 343). This mode of temporality brings Dasein before its factical being there, situated in the midst of beings other than itself, and so provides phenomenological access to the ontic basis of fundamental ontology. The further development of the investigation into temporality brings to the fore Dasein's transcendence—in the double sense of Dasein's transcending of beings by virtue of its temporality and their being transcendent to it by virtue of their strangeness and irreducibility to its finite possibilities of understanding.

The movement from the project of fundamental ontology to the metaphysics of Dasein, however, also changes the nature of the investigation. I characterized this change above as a shift from focusing on the meaning of being to the opening up of the ontological difference between being and beings. It is through the temporality of thrownness that the autonomy and otherness of beings can be revealed and that the ontological difference can emerge. The two moments discussed in the preceding, the futural moment of Dasein's taking over understandingly of a possibility of its being (resolute being-toward-death) and the moment of experiencing the withdrawal of worldly possibilities, of being turned back to strangeness of beings (the temporality of thrownness), are two aspects of the movement of temporal transcendence. They refer respectively to Dasein's understanding of being and to the revelation of beings in themselves in their strangeness. This movement reveals the difference between beings themselves and Dasein's finite, historical understanding of being. To say that Dasein is metaphysical is to say that this transcendence characterizes its being. It is to say that when it becomes essentially itself—that is, is open for this temporal movement—it exists within the ontological difference (GA 27, 210).

The ontological difference is thus not an arbitrary Heideggerian presupposition but rather the *emergence* of this difference and the temporal conditions for its emergence are, on this reading, the central theme of his work in the period 1927–9. The terminological inversions in the metaphysical period are, I will argue, necessitated by this movement.[20] Metaphysics in this positive sense does not mean covering up the difference between beings and being. Rather, metaphysics belongs to Dasein's existence and the *metaphysical event* of Dasein's transcendence makes the ontological difference and truth as unconcealment possible.

2 The Question of the "Transcendental Framework" of Heidegger's Investigation

This brings us to a further critical issue regarding the interpretation of this period of Heidegger's thought: the extent to which *Being and Time* can be said to have a "transcendental framework" inspired by Kant. *Being and Time* often employs the language of transcendental philosophy, referring frequently to various existential "*a priori*," to "conditions of the possibility," to time "as the transcendental horizon for the question of being" and to temporal schemata. Heidegger also explicitly connects this investigation with that of Kant, claiming that the latter is "the first and only person who has gone any stretch of the way towards investigating the dimension of *Temporalität*" (H. 23). In the discussion of *Temporalität* itself, he aims at a retrieval of Kant, claiming that his own investigation puts him in the position "to explicate by means of the *more original concept of transcendence* the Kantian idea of the transcendental and of philosophy as transcendental philosophy" (BPP 232 [GA 459–61]). And in *Kant and the Problem of Metaphysics*, Heidegger seeks testimony to and corroboration of his own approach through an interpretation of the role of the transcendental imagination in the *Critique of Pure Reason* (KPM 141–2 [GA 3 203]).

In the face of the apparently abundant textual evidence and the wide consensus in the research literature, it seems absurd, on the face of it, to deny that *Being and Time* is a type of transcendental philosophy in the Kantian mold. Indeed, the only essential philosophical question that remains, it would seem, is that of whether this Kantian concern with conditions of possibility has enabled discussing or distorted the phenomenon at issue. Theodore Kisiel has pointed out that the "Kantian draft" of *Being and Time* occurred relatively late and that one of Heidegger's key insights, that of the "it worlds," was present in his early War Emergency Semester lecture course, thus raising the question of whether this Kantian transcendental framework is needed at all.[21] Several interpreters have credited this framework as responsible for the most problematic aspects of the investigation into *Temporalität*.[22] On the other hand, Steven Crowell has argued that the shift away from a phenomenological concern with transcendental conditions of intelligibility and to an investigation of Dasein's facticity generates insurmountable philosophical and political problems.[23] Chad Engelland has advocated a middle way, arguing that the transcendental is not so much an aberration in Heidegger's early work as a necessary step in the disclosure of the phenomenologically more original domain thematized in the 1930s under the heading of being-historical thinking—which disclosure, however, makes the earlier transcendental framework untenable.[24]

All these interpretations, despite their differences, remain committed to the thesis that *Being and Time* is a work of transcendental philosophy akin to that of Kant but perhaps broader in its scope. Yet this reading is problematic on several levels. On the most general level, while it is indisputable that Heidegger does frequently use terms such as "condition of the possibility," "*a priori*," "schematism," and "transcendental," what can and I think should be disputed is whether Heidegger's use of terms from Kantian philosophy signals a commitment to a Kantian framework. For there is little reason to think that Heidegger's appropriation of Kantian concepts entails this any more than Kant's own use of terms such as apperception, analysis, and representation suggests a commitment to the tenets of Leibniz's mature philosophy.[25] And given Heidegger criticizes neo-Kantian attempts to expand the Kantian framework to different ontological domains without due consideration of the phenomena at issue,[26] it would be downright bizarre if he himself adopted this procedure in tackling the question of being in general.

This interpretation becomes more problematic when we look at Kant's own characterization of the transcendental in the *Critique of Pure Reason*. In the B edition, Kant writes: "I call all cognition transcendental that is occupied not so much with objects but rather with our mode of cognition of objects insofar as this is to be possible *a priori*" (B 25).[27] There are two crucial *a priori* conditions for the possibility of such object cognition: the forms of intuition, time and space, and the *a priori* categories of the understanding. Both are *a priori*, they are subjective, universal, and necessary (A 1–2, B 1–2). The difference between Kant and Heidegger's inquiries is not that Kant's investigation is narrower and Heidegger's broader. It is that every single Kantian term here is problematic from the perspective of *Being and Time*. Heidegger does not share Kant's conception of the object, the subject, intuition, understanding, time, space, universality, necessity, or possibility. Equally, he does not subscribe to the Kantian account of judgment nor of the schematism nor of metaphysics. Further, Heidegger criticizes Kant's philosophical focus on the "'pure I' and … a 'consciousness in general'" and his neglect of "the *a priori* character of that merely 'factual' subject, Dasein."[28] Most seriously of all for this Kantian interpretation of *Being and Time*, Heidegger does not subscribe to the Kantian notion of the *a priori* but problematizes its temporal basis.[29]

I will focus on this last issue here as it seems to me the most decisive. For the question of the alleged transcendental framework of *Being and Time* must, it seems to me, be examined in terms of Heidegger's existential-genealogical attempt to uncover the temporal presuppositions of the traditional notion of the *a priori*. For reasons that will be considered in detail in Chapter 2 and further developed in Chapter 5, Heidegger claims that the existential origin of the traditional *a priori*—the *a priori* perfect[30]—lies in the everyday horizon of meaningfulness, specifically in Dasein's productive comportment. This notion of the *a priori* has, he contends, dominated the philosophical tradition from Plato and Aristotle down to Kant. It ultimately, he insists, rests on a derivative mode of the temporalization of temporality.

Bearing this point in mind, we can see how *Being and Time* and subsequent texts in the late 1920s problematize the temporal basis of the Kantian *a priori*.[31] That Heidegger was aware of the difficulties surrounding this issue is signaled at the close of the lecture course *The Basic Problems of Phenomenology*. There Heidegger claims an *a priori* status for his own investigation into temporality, then notes that the "*a priori* is patently a time determination," before saying that it is to be disclosed "in conceptual labor of a specific sort" that is completely distinct to the concept formation of the positive sciences (BPP 324, 327 [GA 24,

461, 465]). To assume that Heidegger's understanding of the *a priori* provides either a welcome connection to Kant's critical philosophy or that it is a remnant of the "metaphysical tradition" and a kind of foreign body in Heidegger's thought that distorts his fundamental insights is to miss precisely what this movement of thinking accomplishes: the *problematization* of this notion in the light of the investigation into temporality.[32] Insofar as the traditional notion of the *a priori* is made into a philosophical problem over the course of the investigation into Dasein's temporal transcendence, it can be said that Heidegger carries out *a metaphysical critique of temporal presuppositions of Kantian transcendental philosophy*.

The problem of the *a priori* thus hangs together with the further investigation of temporality and the concomitant development of a metaphysics of facticity. Two texts from the vicinity of *Being and Time* suggest that the phenomenon of the mythical world provides clues for this further development in the account of temporality. The first text is the series of notes and drafts for the unpublished Division III of *Being and Time*. Heidegger again refers to the traditional interpretation of the being of beings as deriving from readiness-to-hand and productive comportment and then refers, in parentheses, to mythology as providing a clue for overcoming this interpretation.[33] The second is the 1928 course on Leibniz, where Heidegger again brings the problem of the mythical environment into connection with a fuller treatment of the problem of temporality. He writes that "a region of problems must be developed which we are today beginning to approach with greater clarity, the region of the mythic" and further claims that this is to be understood "with the aid of a metaphysical construct [*metaphysichen Konstruktion*] of [the] primal time [*Ur-zeit*]" of the world-entry of beings (MFL 209 [GA 26 270]). The phenomenology of the mythical world outlined in two subsequent texts[34] shows, as will be seen in Chapter 4, that this primal time is nothing other than the temporality of thrownness or birth essential to the emergence of the ontological difference.

3 Initial Methodological Considerations

The approach taken in what follows is to read Heidegger's texts in the late 1920s with a view to unfolding the problematic therein on its own terms.[35] My claim that taking these texts as developing a single unified investigation is a viable interpretative option is not intended to exclude other interpretative possibilities or the appropriation of Heidegger's work from the perspective of questions very different to his own. However, I think the kind of historicized transcendental philosophy Heidegger develops at this time is of interest both as a systematic continuation of the project of *Being and Time* and in its own right.[36]

One key limitation should be noted. Heidegger continued to be preoccupied with the problem of metaphysics well into the 1930s. Why, then, limit the discussion to the texts up to 1929? And why exclude seemingly key texts on the metaphysics of Dasein such as the 1929–30 lecture course *The Fundamental Concepts of Metaphysics*? In *Being and Time* Heidegger describes anxiety as "*a* [*eine*] distinctive way in which Dasein is disclosed" (H. 184, my emphasis), thus acknowledging the disclosive possibility of other, as yet unexplored moods. And I read the lecture course *The Fundamental Concepts of Metaphysics* as marking a new beginning in this respect. Boredom there takes on a central significance that was absent in previous texts and the temporality of this mood is distinct to that of anxiety and to the everyday attunements analyzed in *Being and Time*. Moreover, the problematic Heidegger treats in this lecture course is informed by his dialogue with the Philosophical Anthropologies of Scheler and Plessner as regards the being of the organic and living beings other than Dasein.[37] These themes were not wholly absent in Heidegger's previous work, but both with respect to the underlying fundamental attunement and the problems it focuses on, this lecture course can, I think, be seen as a departure from the investigations of *Being and Time* and the previous articulation of the metaphysics of Dasein. This is not to deny that the analyses in *The Fundamental Concepts of Metaphysics* and subsequent texts do repeat, transform, and critique *Being and Time* and the metaphysics of Dasein developed in its aftermath. But getting clear as to the nature of this repetition or critical transformation would mean first having got to grips with the first articulation of the metaphysics of Dasein, which is the task of the present work.

The scope of this study is thus delimited by its task, which is showing how the metaphysics of Dasein develops from and is necessitated by the exposition of fundamental ontology in *Being and Time* and in *The Basic Problems of Phenomenology*. Heidegger indicates the considerable difficulties involved in getting to grips with his inquiry at the close of the introduction to *Being and Time* when he writes of "the harshness of our expression … and … the minuteness of detail with which our concepts are formed [*Begriffsbildung*]" (H. 39). On the existential-phenomenological level, these linguistic difficulties are occasioned by the attempt to speak of what is alien or strange within experience, an attempt that already puts the investigation at a far remove from our usual ways of expressing ourselves, including in philosophy. This requires close attention not just to the terminology Heidegger uses but how his concepts function and their meanings shift, why they do so, and what this suggests about the experiences underlying his work. A further level of difficulty concerns the historical context of Heidegger's work. It was written from out of a factical existentiell situation that is not our own, whatever similarities we might detect or underlying shared and general structures that come into view through our appropriation of it. This requires attention to the hermeneutic context of Heidegger's work, the figures he was in dialogue with and appropriates as well as the complex temporality of this appropriation.

Regarding the first issue, central to *Being and Time* and subsequent texts is a problem of forming concepts appropriate to the matter under investigation. Heidegger frequently stresses the linguistic demands this makes, claiming "it is one thing to give a report in which we tell about *entities*, but another to grasp entities in their *being*. For the latter task we lack not only most of the words but, above all, the 'grammar'" (H. 38–9). This task requires "*liberating* grammar from logic [which itself] requires *beforehand* a positive understanding of the basic *a priori* structure of discourse in general as an existential" (H. 165–6). In the first three chapters of this book, I track how the development of Heidegger's inquiry demands linguistic formulations and concepts that are grounded in the problem of time. My interpretative proposal is that we read Heidegger's apparent terminological changes in terms of one of the major issues he introduces in *Being and Time*: "mak[ing] the possibility of concept-formation ontologically intelligible" based on the investigation of temporality (H. 349). Although this task was reserved for the unpublished Division III, Chapter 2 of *Being and Time* (H. 349 xiii), it lies in the background, on the interpretation developed here, of the *Kehre* or turn to the metaphysics of Dasein and is necessitated by the project of fundamental ontology.

Chapter 1 argues, through a close reading of Heidegger's phenomenology of attunements, how the much-discussed turn or *Kehre* in Heidegger's thinking is already in the background of the account of temporality in *Being and Time*. The background presupposition for Dasein's authenticity lies in its being turned toward (*hinkehren*) the sheer fact of its being in the midst of beings in anxiety. I maintain that this provides the key to interpreting Heidegger's discussion of the *Kehre* in his project in 1928.

Chapter 2 discusses how the underlying temporal movement here between facticity and projection raises a basic difficulty for Heidegger's project that comes to the fore in the lecture course *The Basic Problems of Phenomenology* regarding the formation of ontological concepts. Heidegger's investigation lays claim to an *a priori* status but also problematizes the relation between the traditional conception of the *a priori* and temporality. I argue the difficulties this creates are insufficiently accounted for in the interpretations of this point by Chad Engelland and Sacha Golob. Heidegger's engagement with Kant aims at untangling the transcendental from its intertwinement with the logical—in this lies the core of Heidegger's critique of Kant—and rethinking it based on Dasein's temporal transcendence. This chapter concludes by explaining how Heidegger here opens up avenues for conceiving the *a priori* more originally.

My understanding of the conceptual innovations of Heidegger's metaphysical period (1927–9) owes much to the scholarship of François Jaran, László Tengelyi, Inga Römer, Stefan Schmidt, and Matthias Wunsch but, unlike these scholars, it stresses the continuity in Heidegger's investigation. For as temporality occurs or temporalizes itself in movements that shift between prioritizing reciprocally implying but distinct ecstases, it should not surprise us that Heidegger's concepts do not involve a subsumption under a central meaning but rather exhibit a kind of multi-dimensionality, that is, they have a plurality of different but reciprocally implying senses. A case in point, which I explore in detail in Chapter 3, is seeing how the concepts of *Welt*, *Verweisung*, and *Augenblick* are used in a different sense, as compared to *Being and Time*, in "What Is Metaphysics?" and in other texts from the metaphysical period. Bearing in mind Heidegger's remark about the minuteness of detail with which his concepts are worked out, we can attend to how the terminology of this text repeats the concepts developed in *Being and Time* while also asking after what underlies the shifts in their meaning. If Heidegger's thought is fully in flux in this period, I argue, there is good reason to think the flux belongs not to a change in his philosophical standpoint but rather that the matter itself, which demands a terminological upheaval and overturning. Underlying the use of key terms from *Being and Time* in "What Is Metaphysics?" in an inverted or "turned around" sense is a temporal movement in which beings as a whole can emerge in their *non-identity* or *otherness* to Dasein's understanding of being (a key sense of the ontological difference). It thus reveals a dimension implicitly presupposed but not thematized in *Being and Time*.

In Chapters 4, 5, and 6 I seek to clarify disputed interpretative questions about the nature of the transcendental philosophy Heidegger's work develops in this period and its relation to history and to politics. I do so in part by drawing upon some key texts he refers to in developing his arguments. But two factors familiar to every reader of *Being and Time* complicate such an undertaking. First, Heidegger's work is on dialogue in almost every paragraph with numerous philosophers and approaches and it seeks to interrogate basic assumptions underlying much of the philosophical tradition. What justifies the selection of some sources over and above others? Second, *Being and Time* does not uncritically receive or passively take up its influences but "*replies* [*erwidert*] to the *possibility* of that existence which has-been-there" (H. 386, second emphasis mine), that is, it retrieves possibilities in the light of a question that Heidegger contends has been forgotten for over 2000 years. Given that it would be naïve to simply ascribe to Heidegger theses from authors that he refers to, how then can we take his influences as a guide in dealing with problems and questions in his texts?

As Chapters 4 and 6 especially examine Heidegger's appropriation of Ernst Cassirer, Jacob Grimm, and Paul Yorck von Wartenburg, I will here provide the hermeneutic justification for exploring problems in Heidegger's work with respect to these authors. I refer the reader to these chapters themselves for a more detailed discussion of the texts concerned. Ernst Cassirer is undoubtedly one of Heidegger's key interlocutors in the late 1920s. Heidegger refers to his work in *Being and Time*, in his notes on the unpublished Third Division of *Being and Time*, and in lecture courses and texts in the late 1920s. But what bearing does Cassirer have on Heidegger's continuation of the project of *Being and Time* after 1927 and his attempt to develop a novel kind of transcendental philosophy under the heading of the metaphysics of Dasein?

We saw previously that Heidegger's project post-*Being and Time* involves three central, closely correlated concerns: (i) the development of a temporality of thrownness, (ii) which exposes the limits of a Kantian transcendental framework, (iii) and highlights the more basic problem of a phenomenological a priori. And in exploring these topics Heidegger draws upon Cassirer's interpretation of mythical thinking in the second volume of the latter's *The Philosophy of Symbolic Forms*, while also criticizing what he perceived as the limitations of Cassier's investigations. Heidegger claims the temporality of thrownness is the key to interpreting the mythical world, but argues Cassirer does not see that a transcendental framework indebted to Kant is incapable of thematizing this phenomenon as he neglects the relation between the *a priori* and time. *In other words, it is through an interpretation of Cassirer that Heidegger develops the three central concerns of his own work post-*Being and Time. This means *an analysis of Heidegger's Cassirer interpretation brings to light fundamental issues in Heidegger's rethinking of transcendental philosophy in the late 1920s and shows what kind of phenomena cannot be accounted for within a Kantian understanding of transcendental philosophy.*

These points also underpin my critique of interpretations of *Being and Time* that claim its philosophical achievement lies in its phenomenologically reinterpreted Kantianism. For such interpretations, I argue, overlook points (i)–(iii) and thus misunderstand the nature of Heidegger's project post-*Being and Time*. I develop this point in Chapter 5 by examining the sophisticated conception of a phenomenological transcendental philosophy and of the *a priori* defended in Steven Crowell's interpretation of *Being and Time*. I argue this attempt to separate Heidegger's transcendental philosophy from his claims about Dasein's essential historicality, metaphysics, and from his politics fails because it neglects the historical conditions for the manifestation of essential structures of Dasein's being, because the notion of the *a priori* it employs is based on an incomplete understanding of temporality (namely, one that emphasizes our having a future and neglects our thrownness), and finally because it gives rise to an oversimplified understanding of the problem of the political in Heidegger's work.

I tackle this last problem in Chapter 6. I am aware that some readers might view the inclusion of this topic with skepticism and may think it detracts the exploration of the philosophical approach that Heidegger develops in the late 1920s. Could not the problem of the political be simply omitted in examining Heidegger's contributions to transcendental philosophy? Such an interpretative decision, however, tacitly assumes the philosophical in Heidegger can be demarcated from the political, which is a position as simplistic, I believe, as reducing Heidegger's work to his politics. For Heidegger's language, even at its seemingly most abstract and theoretical, often has political overtones or implications that are part and parcel of his understanding of philosophy. For instance, in his seminars on ancient philosophy, Heidegger emphasizes that philosophy takes within a political space, where it also finds its motivation in combatting sophistry (PS 151–2 [GA 19: 217–8]). The political space of the Greek polis—its *Boden*—enabled a particular way of addressing beings that underpinned the development of Greek ontology (BC 35 [GA 18 49], BCA 197 [GA 22 254]). And Heidegger argues that the resultant conceptuality stands in need of a fundamental critique as it is incapable of thinking the existential of dwelling and Dasein's historicality. Heidegger's terminology in his interpretation of Kant in *Kant and the Problem of Metaphysics* accords with this reading. Although it concerns highly theoretical topics (mostly especially the relation between time and concept formation), it does so using the politically loaded language of rootedness and claims that the transcendental imagination is *heimatlos*, so "without a homeland," in the first *Critique* and not the more innocuous "homeless" as the English translation renders it (KPM 95 [GA 3 136]).

Texts from the 1920s also show that Heidegger was interested in the political as such, and not merely as a by-product of purely theoretical considerations. For in addition to his emphasis on the philosopher's being situated in a political space, his lectures and seminars prior to *Being and Time* show a marked interest in the disclosive possibilities of political speech. And in the 1924–5 *Plato's Sophist* lecture course, Heidegger renders a phrase from an anti-democratic speech in Thucydides by the demagogue Cleon, who is advocating the massacre of a people under Athenian rule accused of a wartime betrayal,[38] into his own terminology.[39] It would be naïve, I think, to overlook the sinister overtones of this reference in the political atmosphere of 1920s Germany.

Such considerations suggest that Heidegger's reference to the community and the people in Division II, Chapter 5 of *Being and Time* is by no means extraneous or politically neutral. To ignore this hermeneutic context is to tacitly carry out a questionable separation of the philosophical and the political in Heidegger's work. For these reasons, I believe that any adequate interpretation of Heidegger on this point must attempt to account for *both* the philosophical significance *and* the political overtones of some of Heidegger's terminology.

The interpretations of Jacob Grimm and Paul Yorck von Wartenburg in Chapter 6 take place within the context of exploring the problem of the political in *Being and Time*. Heidegger refers to Jacob Grimm in the second chapter of *Being and Time* when elaborating on the most fundamental distinction in the entire existential analytic, that between the existential and the categorical (H. 53–6). In discussing the sense of the "*In*" of "*In-der-Welt-sein*," he draws heavily on Grimm's texts "*In*" and "*In und bei*" from his *Kleinere Schriften*. This reference should, I argue, be understood in terms of two key methodological claims Heidegger makes in the course of the existential analytic: (1) that "the ultimate business of philosophy is to preserve the force of the most elemental words in which Dasein expresses itself, and to keep the common understanding from levelling them off to that pseudo-intelligibility which functions in turn as a source for pseudo-problems" (H. 222) and (2) that in so-called "'primitive phenomena'" a "way of conceiving things which seems, perhaps, rather clumsy and crude from our standpoint, can be positively helpful in bringing out the ontological structures of phenomena in a genuine way" precisely because they "are often less concealed and less complicated by extensive self-interpretation" (H. 51). Moreover, exploring Grimm's texts in relation to Heidegger's project allows us to bring out what is methodologically distinctive about Heidegger's phenomenology, namely its historicality, by letting us see how Dasein's appropriation of its historical and linguistic heritage takes place within the existential analytic itself. This is an aid to understanding the *theoretical* stakes of Heidegger's use of politically loaded terms such as rootedness and the *Boden* [ground and/or soil] of philosophy.

This provides, I believe, a wider context for understanding the much-discussed influence of Paul Yorck von Wartenburg on Heidegger's discourse on rootedness and *Boden*. This line of influence has attracted much attention within the controversies about Heidegger's politics for good reasons. Kisiel claims that Heidegger's discussion of Yorck in *Being and Time* effectively constitutes a co-dedication of this work to Yorck and to Husserl.[40] For §76 consists almost entirely of citations from Yorck and Heidegger's assessment of Yorck's philosophical claims is unusually, perhaps uniquely, approving. The section opens by stressing Yorck's philosophical significance and closes with the claim that "the preparatory existential temporal analytic of Dasein is resolved [*entschlossen*] to foster the spirt of Count Yorck in the service of Dilthey's work" (H. 404, 397).

Moreover, Heidegger's citations from Yorck parallel key points that Heidegger himself makes in *Being and Time*, thus making §76 a kind of summary and repetition of the entire preceding analysis and indicating his philosophical proximity to Yorck. The question of Yorck's influence on Heidegger becomes considerably more charged when we recall, as Emmanuel Faye has stressed, that Yorck's letters to Dilthey contain passages that are overtly political and anti-Semitic.[41] Clearly, Heidegger's drawing upon Yorck does not suffice in itself to establish strong conclusions about Heidegger's politics in the 1920s and it is hermeneutically suspect to ascribe apparently politically charged concepts (soil/ground [*Boden*], rootedness, etc.) an exclusively political meaning.[42] For Heidegger does not cite Yorck's anti-Semitic remarks and, given the philosophical complexity of *Being and Time*, it would be oversimplifying to privilege one source in isolation from others. Nonetheless, consideration of the influence of Yorck does, I think, *corroborate* arguments about the political overtones of some of Heidegger's claims and terminology made in Chapter 6 by drawing on other sources: Heidegger's seminars on ancient philosophy, the aforementioned sinister translation of a line from Thucydides into his own terminology, and his use of Grimm.

Yet acknowledging the political dimension to Heidegger's work presents a problem for the retrieval of the possibility of transcendental philosophy from this work. For if the political and the philosophical are closely intermeshed in Heidegger's work, are not attempts to separate them misconceived? I take it that simply dropping elements of Heidegger's vocabulary that are politically problematic or denying their political implications does not present an adequate solution to this problem. At the conclusion of Chapter 6, I instead propose an immanent critique of Heidegger's claims on this point. The upshot of this analysis is that Heidegger's own procedure is at odds with his attempt to identify the historical background against which philosophizing takes place with an actual or potential national space. I argue Heidegger's own development of his concepts and the supporting historical evidence he uses have a far more complex and tangled genealogy than he allows and that cannot be given the political interpretation that he provides. I illustrate this by discussing two of Heidegger's references, the early German text *Der Ackermann* and his interpretation of the mana-representation, which is central to his critique of Cassirer and the development of a temporality of thrownness. My suggestion is that the achievement of the kind of historicized transcendental philosophy that Heidegger develops in this period concerns the temporality underlying the movement of de-familiarization and historical appropriation and that this is developed using the resources of his historical situation. His understanding of the *a priori* and of concept formation is thought from out of this movement.

Notes

1   MFL 11 [GA 26 13]. See François Jaran, *La Métaphysique du Dasein: Heidegger et la possibilité de la métaphysique (1927–1930)* (Bucharest: Zeta Books, 2010), 105–13, a work which provides a pioneering interpretation of this period of Heidegger's work. For the abbreviations used in citing Heidegger's work, see the first section of the bibliography.
2   For recent considerations on this issue, see Lee Braver, ed., *Division III of Heidegger's Being and Time: The Unanswered Question of Being* (Cambridge, Massachusetts: MIT Press, 2015).
3   Versions of this argument can be found, for instance, in Jean Grondin, *Le tourant dans la pensée de Martin Heidegger* (Paris: Presses Universitaires de France, 1987), Thomas Sheehan, "'Time and being', 1925-7" in *Martin Heidegger: Critical Assessments*, ed. Christopher McCann (London: Routledge, 1992), 29–67, Daniel Dahlstrom, "The End of Fundamental Ontology" in *Division III of Heidegger's Being and Time: The Unanswered Question of Being*, ed. Lee Braver (Cambridge, Massachusetts: MIT Press 2016), 83–103.
4   The claim that the turn to be carried out in Division III is to *Temporalität* could be defended by arguing that (1) there are two turns in Heidegger's thought in this period, namely, (a) the turn to *Temporalität* in *The Basic Problems of Phenomenology* and (b) the turn to the metaphysical-ontic in *The Metaphysical*

Foundations of Logic, (2) Heidegger's thought is in a state of fluctuation and indecision in this period and that terminological inconsistences are frequent and to be expected, and (3) when Heidegger states in the "Letter on Humanism" that the turn in *Being and Time* was said in the language of metaphysics, he was in fact confusing two distinct periods of his thought: the fundamental ontological phase and the metaphysical period. In the following I argue that a more plausible interpretative option is that there was one turn, that to the metaphysical-ontic.

5   GA 82 133–135. Heidegger identifies the shortcoming in not sufficiently awakening an understanding of the question.
6   See László Tengelyi, *Welt und Unendlichkeit: Zum Problem phänomenologischer Metaphysik* (Freiburg: Verlag Karl Alber, 2014), 228–36.
7   See Stefan Schmidt, *Grund und Freiheit: Eine phänomenologische Untersuchung des Freiheitsbegriffs Heideggers* ([Cham]: Springer, 2016), 74–81.
8   See Jaran, *La Métaphysique du Dasein*, 166–74, Tengelyi, *Welt und Unendlichkeit*, 229–36, 257 and Matthias Wunsch, *Fragen nach dem Menschen: Philosophische Anthropologie, Daseinontologie und Kulturphilosophie* (Frankfurt am Main: Vittorio Klostermann, 2014), 137–51.
9   Otto Pöggeler credits Heidegger's discussion with Max Scheler with transforming Heidegger's thinking. See Pöggeler, "Ausgleich und anderer Anfang. Scheler und Heidegger" in *Studien zur Philosophie von Max Scheler*, ed. Ernst Wolfgang Orth and Gerhard Pfafferott (Freiburg/München: Verlag Karl Alber, 1994), 166–203, especially 181–9. Rather more cautiously, Jaran speaks of the influence of Scheler in Heidegger's introducing a metaphysical *vocabulary* into his investigation. See Jaran, *La Métaphysique du Dasein*, 57–67. For a highly critical assessment of Scheler's influence on Heidegger, see Steven Galt Crowell, *Husserl, Heidegger and the Space of Meaning* (Evanston: Northwestern University Press, 2001), 222–43, especially 230.
10 See Jaran, *La Métaphysique du Dasein*, 70 and 74–5.
11 Jaran also notes these passages. See Jaran, *La Métaphysique du Dasein*, 160–1, 173.
12 See Chapter 2 for discussion of this.
13 Nor does the absence of this theme in "On the Essence of Ground" speak against this interpretation. A footnote there claims that the *temporale* interpretation of transcendence is set aside [*beiseite*], not abandoned (PM 370 [GA 9 166]). Heidegger's own marginalia to this text indicate that the analysis of transcendence was to be interpreted in terms of *Temporalität* (PM 123, 132 [GA 9 159, 171]). Notably, Heidegger's interpretation of Kant in *Kant and the Problem of Metaphysics* centers on the notion of horizon and of the schemata, that is, two terms that are also central to the investigation into ecstatic temporality. My own view, which will be developed in what follows, is that beings as a whole are revealed when Dasein's understanding is overwhelmed, that is, the "understanding" of being as overpowering in the temporality of thrownness is less characterized by a horizon of its own as by the collapse of horizons of meaningfulness. This brings about a

shift in Heidegger's investigation from the meaning of being to the ontological difference.

14 "*Ontologisches Problem schlägt um! Metontologisch*; θεολογική; das Seiende im Ganzen" (GA 22 106, cf. 263). Note how the language here in the context of a discussion of Plato, and from a text that predates the publication of *Being and Time*, strongly resembles that of the metaphysical transformation of fundamental ontology in MFL 158 [GA 26 201] (discussed in the following subsection).

15 MFL 158 [GA 26, 201], translation modified cf. GA 22 106. Michael Heim's English translation of the cited passage renders "*Temporalität des Seins*" and the associated term "*temporale*" as "temporality of being" and "temporal" respectively which effaces the distinction between these terms and Dasein's "*Zeitlichkeit*," which is also translated as "temporality." My modification follows the practice of Macquarrie and Robinson, who retain these Latinate terms in their translation of *Sein und Zeit*. Very broadly, *Temporalität* and the *temporale* analysis refer to the horizon upon which we understand the being of things. For instance, in dealing with the things in my immediate environment, I have a pre-understanding not only that they are available but also present. This can be modified by discovering something is non-present or missing. See Chapter 2 for further discussions of this point.

16 See also BPP 234 [GA 24 332]. It reads: "For κίνησις Aristotle also says μεταβολή. This is the most general concept of motion; literally it means the same as the German *Umschlag*, overturning" (translation modified). Heidegger gives the same translation in GA 22 263. An interesting perspective on this claim is opened up by the 1926 summer semester course on the basic concepts of ancient philosophy. There Heidegger translates κίνησις and μεταβολή with "*Umschlag*" and "*Bewegung*." But what is referred to specifically is the movement by which different Platonic ideas distinguish themselves from each other (GA 22 263). Heidegger's existential understanding of movement is clearly informed by this Platonic background: what concerns him is the movement from bringing the idea of existence into view (authentic being-toward-death) to that which makes manifest the idea of the Real or of beings as a whole (the temporality of thrownness, Dasein's factically finding itself in the midst of beings). In other words, it concerns the existential genesis, the γένος, of our understanding of two fundamental regions of being (existence and nature). See H. 314.

17 In addition to these three primary senses of the term *Kehre* and its cognates, several secondary but closely associated uses can be detected. There is the aforementioned (inauthentic) turn of Dasein from the enigma of its facticity [*Abkehr*] toward everyday possibilities of its being. Similarly, "What Is Metaphysics?" speaks of our pushing ourselves into the public superficialities of existence by turning toward beings and turning from the nothing (PM 92 [GA 9 116]). *Einleitung in die Philosophie* refers to another derivative sense of turn when discussing the sense of

the word κόσμος in Paul as "*einer gottabgekehrten Gesinnung*" (GA 27 242), that is, a turned-ness from God. This reference to turning to the world and so turning from God clearly parallels Heidegger's own talk of turning from the nothing in turning toward the public, superficial world. Yet, as we will see in what follows, the parallel is more complex than it initially appears, as Heidegger on the one hand considers theology as akin to the ontic, positive sciences while also signaling that religion (and science, for different reasons) cannot be equated with fallen everydayness and further hinting at the possibility of a phenomenological grounding of theology, saying that God's eternity may possibly be understood on the basis of "a more primordial temporality which is 'infinite'" (H. 427 xiii). This temporality, as will be argued in Chapter 3, is the temporality of thrownness in which Dasein finds itself overwhelmed or overpowered by beings as a whole.

18 Heidegger's 1936 remarks on *Being and Time* also refer to this connection between *Stimmungen* and the *Kehre*. See GA 82 76.
19 See also H. 373. I owe my understanding of the significance of the passages in *Being and Time* on birth to Felix Ó Murchadha, "Future or Future Past: Temporality Between *Praxis* and *Poiesis* in Heidegger's *Being and Time*." *Philosophy Today* (1998): 262–9 and *The Time of Revolution: Kairos and Chronos in Heidegger* (London; New York: Bloomsbury, 2013). My interpretation of this theme differs from his in that I stress how it is taken up in the metaphysical period to refer to the world entry of beings. On this point my interpretation draws on the work of Inga Römer, "Zeit und Kategoriale Anschauung: Heideggers Verwandlung eines Husserl'schen Grundbegriffes." *Archiv Für Begriffsgeschichte* 55 (2013): 251–62 and Alexander Schnell, *De l'existence ouverte au monde fini: Heidegger 1925–1930* (Paris: Vrin, 2005), 173–88.
20 See also the different emphases in the accounts of anxiety in *Being and Time* §68 (c) and "What Is Metaphysics?" respectively. While the former stresses Dasein's holding on to the present in anxiety and its readiness to seize hold of its ownmost potentiality-for-being (H. 344), the latter emphasizes anxiety's taking hold of Dasein and bringing it before its already being in the midst of the totality of beings affectively (PM 88 [GA 9 111–2]). This is surely why Heidegger describes this lecture as providing insight into a problematic that had been implicitly operative in the background of *Being and Time* (GA 14, 139, cf. H. 56).
21 Kisiel speaks of "the spell of the Kantian transcendental philosophy" as inducing Heidegger "to believe that something like a Kantian schematism of human existence is capable of definitively articulating the evasive immediacy of the human situation." See Theodore Kisiel, *The Genesis of Heidegger's Being and Time* (Berkeley; London: University of California Press, 1995), 457.
22 See Grondin, *Le tourant dans la pensée de Martin Heidegger*, Sheehan, "'Time and being', 1925–7," Dahlstrom, "The End of Fundamental Ontology."

23 See Crowell, *Husserl, Heidegger and the Space of Meaning*, especially 222–43, "The Middle Heidegger's Phenomenological Metaphysics" in *The Oxford Handbook of the History of Phenomenology*, edited by Dan Zahavi (New York: Oxford University Press, 2018), 229–50, "Facticity and Transcendental Philosophy" in *From Kant to Davidson: Philosophy and the Idea of the Transcendental*, ed. Jeff Malpas (London: Routledge, 2005), 100–21, and *Normativity and Phenomenology in Husserl and Heidegger* (New York: Cambridge University Press, 2013), 10, where he claims "phenomenology transforms transcendental philosophy by expanding its scope to embrace all experience, not just the cognitive, axiological, and practical 'validity spheres' addressed in Kant's three *Critiques*." I discuss Crowell's position in detail in Chapter 5, particularly how this expansion also involves a phenomenological reinterpretation of transcendental philosophy.

24 As Chad Engelland puts it: "Even though Heidegger keenly felt the need to do so, for good reason he could not extricate himself from the transcendental tradition. His difficulty is irresolvable: either *affirm* transcendental philosophy and thereby distort his goal or *deny* transcendental philosophy and thereby occlude his point of departure." See Engelland, *Heidegger's Shadow: Kant, Husserl and the Transcendental Turn* (London, New York: Routledge, 2017), 208. See Chapter 2 for a discussion of Engelland's reading.

25 This parallel is suggested by Heidegger himself, see KPM 141 [GA 3 201–2].

26 See for example his critiques of Cassirer at H. 51 xi, KPM 186–7 [GA 3 265–6].

27 This characterization modifies that of the A edition: "I call all cognition transcendental that is occupied not so much with objects but with our *a priori* concepts of objects in general" (A 11–12).

28 Kant is not explicitly named in this passage, but it is clear that he and Husserl are among Heidegger's targets here.

29 These considerations accord with Heidegger's later characterization of a "transcendental" reading of *Being and Time* that sees it as simply an expansion of the Kantian project as a "disastrous misinterpretation" of his work. "*Darum wäre es eine verhängnisvolle Mißdeutung eines Denkens, wollte man es auf den Bezirk des Transzendentalen (und gar im Sinne Kants) festlegen und nur als eine Modifikation oder als eine 'Erweiterung' desselben sehen.*" (GA 82 381).

30 See the influential discussions in Kisiel's *The Genesis of Heidegger's Being and Time*, 392–3, 402, 404, 509, where he notes ambiguities in Heidegger's conception of the *a priori*. Recent examples include Sacha Golob, *Heidegger on Concepts, Freedom and Normativity* (Cambridge: Cambridge University Press, 2016), 84, 107–13, Thomas Sheehan, "Heidegger's New Aspect: On *In-Sein, Zeitlichkeit*, and *The Genesis of 'Being and Time'*," *Research in Phenomenology*, Volume XXV (1995): 219, 217 and his *Making Sense of Heidegger: A Paradigm Shift* (London; New York: Rowman & Littlefield, 2015), 171–3, Engelland, *Heidegger's Shadow: Kant, Husserl*

and the Transcendental Turn, 175–6. Crowell, "Facticity and Transcendental Philosophy," 100–21. I discuss Golob and Engelland's positions in Chapter 2 and Crowell's, which draws on Sheehan's 1995 analysis, in Chapter 5.

31 Heidegger's *Selbstanzeige* of Part I of *Being and Time*, written for the publisher for publicity purposes, signals that the problem of the relation between temporality and the *a priori* was to be treated (GA 14 123–26), presumably in Division III. See also his letter to Karl Löwith of August 20, 1927, where he refers to the "critique of the customary doctrine of the *a priori*" through attaining access to facticity, published as "Two Letters" in Karl Löwith (ed. Richard Wolin), *Martin Heidegger and European Nihilism*, translated by Gary Steiner (New York; Chichester: Columbia University Press, 1995), 242.

For the original German text, see "Drei Briefe Martin Heideggers an Karl Löwith" in *Zur philosophischen Aktualität Heideggers II: Im Gespräch der Zeit*, ed. Dietrich Papenfuss and Otto Pöggeler (Frankfurt am Main: Vittorio Klostermann, 1990), 27–39.

32 The same can be said of other such seemingly metaphysical terms in *Being and Time*, most notably concerning Dasein's "existence" and "essence," but also the terms idea and horizon (H. 41-4, 314).

33 See Martin Heidegger. "Aufzeichnungen zur Temporalität (Aus den Jahren 1925–7)" ed. Claudius Strube. *Heidegger Studien*, Volume 18, (1998): 11–23, especially 19.

34 Specifically, Heidegger's 1928 review of Cassirer's work and in the lecture course *Einleitung in die Philosophie*. See KPM 180–90 [GA 3 255–70], GA 27 357–66.

35 Occasionally and generally in footnotes, I refer to Heidegger's later self-interpretations of this period. As these self-interpretations, however interesting they may be, are not always reliable or consistent, they do not form the basis of my reading of his earlier work.

36 My interpretations are informed by several recent important studies, most notably Jaran's pioneering *La Métaphysique du Dasein*, Tengelyi's *Welt und Unendlichkeit*, Römer's "Zeit und Kategoriale Anschauung," Schmidt's *Grund und Freiheit*, and Wunsch's, *Fragen nach dem Menschen*. In contrast to the interpretation developed here, these studies tend to treat Heidegger's metaphysical period as autonomous rather than its unfolding from out of and continuing *Being and Time*.

37 For an excellent discussion of the innovations of the 1929 lecture course with respect to Philosophical Anthropology, see Wunsch, *Fragen nach dem Menschen*, especially Chapter 4.

38 Thucydides, *The Peloponnesian War: The Complete Hobbes Translation*, Trans. Thomas Hobbes, introduction and notes by David Grene. (Chicago: University of Chicago Press, 1989), III.37–40.

39 PS 437 [GA 19 629].

40 See Kisiel, *The Genesis of Heidegger's Being and Time*, 324.

41 Emmanuel Faye, *Heidegger: The Introduction of Nazism into Philosophy in the Light of the Unpublished Seminars of 1933–1935*, trans. Michael B. Smith (USA: Yale University Press, 2009), 12.

42 It should be noted that Faye himself does not make either of these dubious interpretative moves. Although he emphasizes the political significance of Heidegger's terminology, he calls attention to the range of connotations of the key term "*Boden* [ground/ soil]" and related terminology as well as the wider context in which Heidegger uses these terms. See Faye, "Das Sein als Mythos oder als Begriff: Heidegger und Cassirer" in *Sein und Zeit neu verhandelt: Untersuchungen zu Heideggers Hauptwerk,* ed. Marion Heinz and Tobias Bender (Hamburg: Felix Meiner Verlag, 2019), 67–112 and "Thomas Sheehan: The Introduction of Insults into the Heidegger Debate," trans. Aengus Daly, *Philosophy Today*, Volume 66, Issue 4 (Fall 2022): 831–57. My assessment of Heidegger's philosophy differs greatly from Faye's, but I believe the hermeneutical issues he raises merit serious consideration.

1

The Turn in *Being and Time*

Heidegger claims in 1928 that: "the *temporale* analysis is at the same time [*zugleich*] the turn [*Kehre*], where ontology itself expressly runs back [*zurückläuft*] into the metaphysical-ontic in which it always implicitly remains" (MFL 158 [GA 26 201] translation modified). As we saw in the Introduction, this claim is notable because Heidegger does not speak of a turn *from* the *temporale* analysis or that takes place *after* the *temporale* analysis. Rather, the *temporale* analysis is "at the same time [*zugleich*]" the *Kehre*, which is to say the problem of metaphysics is *already implicit* in the fundamental ontological project. This means we should be able to detect indications of the turn in *Being and Time* itself and in *The Basic Problems of Phenomenology*.[1]

We do find a shift within the 1927 work from the claim on the first page of the first chapter—"We are ourselves the entities to be analyzed" (H. 41)—to programmatic questions in the final section of the work—"Can one provide *ontological* grounds for ontology, or does it also require an *ontical* foundation? and *which* entity must take over the function of providing this foundation?" (H. 436). This shift is entailed by the fact that who we are is always bound up with the space of the world, a given history, our finding ourselves with others and before beings other than ourselves. Existing and the understanding of being presuppose certain distinctive facts—the fact of history and the fact of nature—that, as László Tengelyi has emphasized, are, in an important sense, *necessary* facts as they essentially belong to being-there.[2] They are the metaphysically necessary ontic or factual conditions for the existential analysis.

What do these necessary factical presuppositions imply about the kind of transcendental philosophy Heidegger develops in the 1920s? This chapter broaches this question by examining (i) how the problem of facticity emerges within the account of temporality and movement in the existential analytic and (ii) why history and nature are factical but necessary conditions for Heidegger's existential analysis. A major task of the existential analytic consists in showing that Dasein's being as care—its "ahead-of-itself-being-already-in-(the-world) as being-alongside (entities-encountered-in-the-world)" (H. 192)—is made ontologically possible by temporality. The claim of temporality to function as such an *a priori* condition, however, has two peculiarities. First, there are several different but interrelated senses of the *a priori* at work therein and second, Dasein's "*a priori* character" cannot be a purely *formal* condition but is "grounded upon fact" (H. 229). The *a priori* in the existential analytic is characterized by its facticity and also by its having several different but reciprocally related senses.

I begin by discussing in general terms Heidegger's claim that temporality is a kind of existential movement in which Dasein is brought back to its facticity and goes forth to its ahead-of-itself. In so doing, I will also indicate in a provisional way how this problematizes the temporal basis of transcendental philosophy and particularly the notion of the *a priori* (**1.**). Then I examine this existential-temporal movement in more detail, focusing on Heidegger's use of terms related to the word *Kehre* in the analysis. Fallen everydayness is characterized by Dasein's turning from [*Abkehr*] its thrownness by turning-thither [*Hinkehr*] to its being-alongside the world already significant. However, while the moods of everydayness testify to Dasein's evasive turning away from its ownmost temporality, anxiety opens up the possibility of a phenomenologically interpretative turning-thither [*Hinkehr*] that makes manifest its "always already" having been thrown into the world (**2.**). Afterwards I discuss Dasein's authentic temporality, focusing on the sense in which Dasein's "always already" ahead-of-itself, its having a future, is an *a priori* constituent of its being (**3.**). With this in view, I then argue that not only does the account of temporality in *Being and Time* imply distinct but reciprocally related senses of the *a priori*, but further show that this "*a priori*" is permeated with unthematized factical presuppositions, specifically the facticity of history and the factical presence-at-hand of nature (**4.**).

1 Dasein's "Essence" between Facticity and Projection

Emphatically rejecting a substantialist ontology of Dasein—the being that we ourselves are—on the first page of the first chapter of *Being and Time*, Heidegger claims "*the 'essence' ['Wesen'] of Dasein lies in its existence.*" Our "what-it-is" or our essence is conceived in terms of how we comport ourselves toward our own being, our "'to be.'" This means the existential "characteristics which can be exhibited in [Dasein] … are not 'properties' present-at-hand of some entity which 'looks' so and so and is itself present-at-hand; *they are in each case possible ways for it to be*, and no more than that."³ Our self-understanding is always characterized by our projection of our "what" we will be from out of the "that-it-is" of our factical situation.

Dasein's "essence" thus refers to how it understands itself in terms of a possibility of itself. Such a possibility is not a free-floating possibility in the sense of something that could be or might have been or even primarily "what is *not yet* actual and what is *not at any time* necessary" but refers to its "'know[ing]' *what* it is capable of." Dasein "is primarily being-possible" in that sense that we are "always press[ing] *forward* into possibilities," that is, into a *project* of ourselves (H. 143–4). This *forward* movement of projection means that "Dasein is constantly 'more' than it factually is": We are essentially surpassing our present situation and exceed our characteristics and attributes that could be itemized at a given time (H. 145). A "not yet" is constitutive of our being. This is the approaching future, a future which underlies and enables any projection of the possible (H. 336). But despite our transcending our situation by virtue of having a future, the concrete possibilities through which the future approaches us are already found in our factical situation. Dasein has "already got itself into definite possibilities" and is a "*thrown possibility* through and through" (H. 144).

This means that Dasein's projection *forward* into its future, its throwing itself into a possibility of its being, at the same time always refers *back* to its "that-it-is," to its being already there, thrown into the world, in a concrete situation.⁴ Although facticity "is, in a specific sense, a *factum*," it does not refer to the actuality of a thing or a process (H. 55–6). It rather refers to the temporal dynamic of our "*being delivered over*" to the world, the peculiar and distinctive fact that we are always finding ourselves in the midst of beings other than ourselves (H. 134).

And while our projection of our "what" shows itself in the phenomenon of understanding, the "that-it-is" of our facticity is disclosed in mood, that is, in how beings show themselves as mattering to us, to the concerns and preoccupations that weigh on us.⁵ Such a being attuned to our situation sketches out pre-thematically and in advance the possibilities we have. And in a similar fashion to how the future makes possible our projective ahead-of-itself, Heidegger claims that our *having-been* makes possible our awareness of our thrownness into a situation:

"The thesis that 'one's disposition [*Befindlichkeit*] is grounded primarily in having-been [*Gewesenheit*]' means that the existentially basic character of mood [*Stimmung*] lies in *bringing* one *back to* something. This bringing-back does not first produce a having been; but in any disposition [*Befindlichkeit*] some mode of having been is made manifest for existential analysis."[6]

We exist, according to the existential analytic, as a thrown projection, as both delivered over to the world (facticity) and taking up our possibilities understandingly (ahead-of-ourselves). However, the claims that disposition is grounded primarily in having-been and that understanding as projection is made possible by the future conceal considerable difficulties. Why say that our disposition is made possible by having-been or that our projective understanding is made possible by the future rather than the inverse? What gives the former phenomena a claim to ontological priority over the latter? Further, what do words and phrases like "prior" and "ground" and "makes ontologically possible" mean here? Having-been and the arriving future clearly do not "ground" or "make ontologically possible" mood and understanding in the sense of being causally and (in the usual sense) temporally antecedent to these phenomena because temporality is only revealed *in and through* concrete moods and ways of understanding.

The difficulties raised by these questions will concern us over the course of this book. I will here, however, sketch out an answer by noting the sense in which the claims to originality of having-been over mood and the future as coming toward over the understanding respectively have a *somewhat similar*[7] structure. Temporality itself does not depend on any specific mood but all our specific moods are, on Heidegger's interpretation, inherently temporal in that they are attuned to the possibilities of a situation we are already in.[8] In a parallel fashion, the future as coming toward underlies any and all specific projections of our possibilities, which means the arriving future, however this is understood, is always co-given in and through these specific possibilities. The existential analytic is thus concerned with disclosing *a priori* or enabling conditions, in these cases the ecstases of having-been and the future as coming toward, as the enabling conditions for the moods we have and our taking up of any definite possibilities. Heidegger thus claims the existential analysis does not strive to "dissolv[e]" mood and understanding "into pure phenomena of temporalizing" but rather to "demonstrate that *except on the basis of temporality*, moods [or understanding] *are not possible* in what they 'signify' in an existentiell way or in how they 'signify' it" (H. 340–1). These prior or more original, enabling, or grounding phenomena are, to use a formulation that reoccurs frequently in the existential analytic, "always already" there, *a priori*, always implicitly co-given in any specific mood or way of understanding.

Yet a complication emerges once we get past the all too familiar Kantian term "*a priori.*" Essential to understanding the sense in which *Being and Time* develops a kind of transcendental philosophy is teasing out the sense or senses in which temporality is *a priori*. Because the term *a priori* refers to an enabling condition that is "always already" there, it is itself a time-determination (BPP 324 [GA 24 461–2]). A first problem, then, is that the *a priori*, as a time determination, must be understood from out of time, and not *vice versa*, or at least the relation between a priority and time must be clarified. A second problem lies in the fact that the expression "always already" has different senses in the existential analytic: We are always already *ahead* of ourselves, we have always already been *thrown* into the world and we find ourselves always already *alongside* beings other than ourselves. In other words, the term "always already" does not refer to *a* time determination but to *three* different but interrelated temporal ecstases. The following two sections focus on these different senses of "alreadiness" in the existential analytic. Bringing out these different senses and how they reciprocally imply each other[9] is critical to seeing why the *Kehre* to metaphysical-ontic was necessitated by the analyses of *Being and Time*.

2 Always Already Thrown: Mood and Turning Back

We have seen that "understanding" refers to Dasein's projecting *forth* upon possibilities and "thrownness" refers to the fact that Dasein is in its *there*, to which its moods bring it *back*. While the latter aspect of our temporality is foregrounded in *Being and Time*, Dasein's authenticity has as its precondition our having been individualized or turned back in anxiety to our always already being-there in the world. It is this backgrounded precondition for authenticity that I want to examine here.

In Heidegger's discussions of moods—especially of anxiety—we find the key to understanding the enigmatic phrase the "*Kehre* to the metaphysical-ontic." The term *Kehre* must be read in the semantic context of a series of other expressions in existential analytic, namely the references to Dasein's either turning away [*Abkehr, abkehren, abwenden*], or turning thither [*Hinkehr, hinkehren*], or a turning toward [*Ankehr, ankehren*] in its moods. It is essential to note, especially for understanding the developments of the metaphysical period and their relation to the existential analytic, that it is *only* in the analysis of mood that Heidegger consistently uses these terms to describe a movement of Dasein's existence.[10] In §29 we read that the way in which "mood [*Stimmung*] discloses [thrownness] is not one in which we *look at* thrownness, but one in which we *turn towards or turn away [An—und Abkehr]*" from it (H. 135, my emphasis). And as mood can disclose our being-in-the-world as a whole and open up the space in which worldly entities are discovered as meaningful, our either turning toward or away from our thrownness is of basic methodological significance.

For the most part we find ourselves attuned to our "there" "*in the manner of an evasive turning away [ausweichenden Abkehr]*" (H. 136). Our everyday dealings with things tend to shift between "undisturbed equanimity [*ungestörte Gleichmut*] and inhibited ill-humor [*gehemmte Missmut*]" (H. 134).[11] Despite the appearance of being mutually exclusive, both of these existentiell phenomena are characterized by a submission to the everyday horizon of significance wherein our projects can be fulfilled or frustrated, can run smoothly or go askew.

This tendency to shift between an undisturbed equanimity and disturbed ill-humor becomes clearer if we consider how the world is sighted in fallen everydayness.[12] Driven by an impatience at whatever possibility of being it is already in, Dasein tries to "run away from the awaiting in which it is nevertheless 'held' [by being immersed in a specific possibility of being], though not held on to [*ungehalten*]."[13] What we flee from is our having to put up with the arriving future as a *possibility*, we try to evade its possibility character: "In its craving, [Dasein] just desires such a possibility as something that is actual" (H. 347). The haste or impatience which underlies this craving has its basis in an implicit refusal to put up with the possible future approaching the situation we are already in.

Another kind of turning away from the possibility character of the future occurs when we turn toward a wish-world [*Wunsch-welt*] (H. 195).[14] Underlying this is again an unwillingness to endure the future as possibility. Dasein is preoccupied "with becoming rid of itself as being-in-the-world and rid of its being-alongside that which, in the closest everyday manner, is ready-to-hand" (H. 172) by "*fabricat[ing]* ... something new" so as to avoid seeing where it already is, how it is, and what factical possibilities it has (H. 347–8). The seemingly disparate everyday phenomena of a complacent well-being, ill-humor, and escapist fantasy have their basis in an *Abkehr*, a turn from our finite situatedness, from the burdensome character of being held by a specific possibility of existence.[15]

If in everydayness Dasein "turns away [*Abkehr*] from itself in accordance with its ownmost inertia of falling" (H. 184), then how can it be brought before its own being? This evasive turning away testifies to a more primordial phenomenon that is evaded, namely that our finite temporality is constituted by understanding-projection and thrown facticity. Yet the existentiell phenomenon of anxiety is distinctive for it is characterized by another and methodologically crucial kind of turning away [*Abkehr*]. It is a turn *from* fallen everydayness and a "'turning thither' ['*Hinkehr*']" *to* the sheer fact of our having been thrown into the world (H. 185).

Anxiety can reveal this because it "takes away from Dasein the possibility of understanding itself, as it falls, in terms of the 'world' and the way things have been publicly interpreted." In anxiety, entities no longer "say anything" to us, they appear in their mute enigmatic obscurity, alien to our preoccupations and preconceptions (H. 187, 343). While the space of our everyday being-in-the-world is made up of relations of significance, of things near and far to our cares and worries, in anxiety the "present-at-hand must be encountered in just such a way that it does *not* have *any* involvement *whatsoever*, but can show itself in an empty mercilessness" (H. 343). Entities show themselves as factically there prior to our concern with them, as utterly devoid of significance. Anxiety thus turns us toward the sheer "that-it-is" of the world, the sheer fact of our existing in the midst of a strangeness. What happens in anxiety is a "'turning thither' ['*Hinkehr*'] in a way which is phenomenologically Interpretative" because it turns us toward the facticity of our "there" (H. 185).

The everyday world is characterized by both being familiar [*heimlich*] and secretive [*heimlich*]—familiar because Dasein usually understands itself from out of a horizon of average intelligibility but secretive because in so doing Dasein turns away from its ownmost thrownness.[16] The experience of unmeaning, of the world as overwhelming and incomprehensible, of having no grip on things is the "first moment" of anxiety.[17] "To be anxious in-the-face-of ... does not have the character of an expecting or of any kind of awaiting" (H. 343), because anxiety takes away any possibility of understanding and any expectation. Yet it opens up the possibility of an existential movement in which another order of significance can be instituted:

> "... in anxiety there lies the possibility of a disclosure that is quite distinctive; for anxiety individualizes. This individualization brings Dasein back from its falling, and makes manifest to it that authenticity and inauthenticity are basic possibilities of its being. These basic possibilities of Dasein (and Dasein is in each case mine) show themselves in anxiety as they are in themselves—undisguised by entities within the world, to which, proximally and for the most part, Dasein clings."[18]

Anxiety discloses Dasein's "'that it is and has to be'" (H. 135). Because it "reveal[s] the impossibility of projecting oneself upon a potentiality-for-being which belongs to existence and which is founded primarily upon one's objects of concern," it reveals the "that-it-is" of our *facticity* as such, our being there alongside entities in their uncanny, mute presence that gives the lie to our everyday interpretation of them. At the same time, it reveals that Dasein "has to be," that it exists as a *potentiality-for-being* as such, that so long as it exists it has to take up a possibility of being itself (H. 343).

While we typically strive to evade this uncanniness by "turning away [*Abkehr*] from it in falling" such that "the 'not-at-home' [*das Un-zuhause*] gets 'dimmed down'" (H. 189), the phenomenologically interpretative turning hither in anxiety makes manifest the uncanniness, always already there, of our thrown facticity. And despite its focus on seemingly formal temporal conditions, the account of anxiety in Being and Time also reveals an implicit factical presupposition of the existential analytic. The revelation of the sheer that-it-is of existence presupposes the factical givenness of *other* beings as strange or alien to us (cf. MFL 156 [GA 26 199]). I will return to this point in the final section of this chapter.

3 Always Already Ahead-of-Itself: Going Forth Understandingly

The analysis of anxiety in the existential analytic—which is in an important sense one-sided—largely treats it as a preliminary to Dasein's authentic being-toward-death, as calling us to take over our care for our finitude. It awakens us to the emptiness or nullity of our previous understanding and frees us from ingrained, all-too-fixed ways of interpretation. In so doing, it individualizes Dasein, makes manifest that its possibilities are *its* possibilities, belonging to it as a finite and thrown being.

Responding authentically to anxiety entails a prior decision for and openness to the possibility of authenticity. Heidegger characterizes this as *willing-to-have-a-conscience*, a specific kind of taking action in relation to oneself, a self-restraint with regard to the interpretative tendencies of the "they" such that "one denies oneself any counter-discourse" with a view to letting to one's ownmost understanding give voice to itself.[19] This openness means bracketing or putting to one side the *personae* of our everydayness.

Willing-to-have-a-conscience is thus characterized by an openness for the mute, wordless intelligibility of the world, for how we are already attuned to our "there." In suspending our everyday interpretations of others, the world, and ourselves, we bracket our typical horizons of expectation and are ready to face the hitherto concealed strangeness of the world and the possibilities that emerge from a becoming familiar with this strangeness. Although such a self-restraint predisposes us toward anxiety—"a readiness for anxiety" Heidegger calls it (H. 296)—anxiety itself is not a matter of choice but befalls or seizes us. Interpreted from out of this prior readiness, the occurrence of anxiety acts as a call to the care for our being-in-the-world. It "summons the Self to its potentiality-for-being-its-Self, and thus calls Dasein forth to its possibilities" (H. 274). Here we need to note the interplay between the plural "possibilities" and the singular "potentiality-for-being-itself." "Possibilities" refers to the range of the possible that is in fact open to us over and beyond the self-evident "actuality" of "how things stand" and the "done thing." Yet this excess of the possible is also in an important sense restricted, for anxiety concretizes our sense of the situation not only by passing over our usual manner of interpreting things but also by putting out of play possibilities which "'count for nothing'" such as escapist distraction seeking (H. 344). It awakens us to the range of the *factually* possible, that is, what we are actually able to do. Yet of this range, we cannot choose everything but must, at any given moment, take up a way of understanding ourselves, others, and things, that is, of world-disclosure.

An authentic taking over of a potentiality-for-being implies a threefold awareness of finitude: having a finite future, choice, and a willing to return ever anew to our factical "there." Heidegger describes such a way of understanding as characterized by "anticipatory resoluteness": It allows our understanding of our being-toward-death to "acquire *power* over Dasein's *existence*," to individualize us, and it lets us think, chose, and act with an awareness of our finitude (H. 310).

Heidegger can claim that "Dasein becomes 'essential [*wesentlich*]' in that authentic existence" (H. 323, translation modified)[20] because it lets itself be brought before the essential determinants of its existence: the sheer that-it-is of its being there in the midst of beings (thrownness), the "having to be" of its always ahead of itself (projection), and the range of the possible from which it can choose (the world it is alongside). Its relation to itself, others, and things is constituted in deciding for an understanding of itself that is rooted in its "there," that is, in how it is concretely attuned to its situation and that anticipates its death and so takes cognizance of its finitude.

Authenticity is thus characterized by a particular back and forth movement: Dasein "must, in repeating, come back to its thrown 'there', but come back as something future which comes towards" (H. 343). Existential truth, the understanding of which is rooted in Dasein's factical "there" and grounds Dasein's relation to itself, others, and things, is brought forth in this distinctive existential movement (H. 297). Anticipatory resoluteness is thus a distinctive way in which temporality happens or "temporalizes itself": "Only insofar as Dasein *is* as an 'I-*am*-as-having-been' [*Ich* bin-*gewesen*] can Dasein come towards itself futurally in such a way that it comes *back*" (H. 325–26). This temporality of "I-*am*-as-having-been" is distinct from the phenomenon of expecting something:

> "By the term 'futural', we do not have here in view a 'now' which has *not yet* become 'actual' and which sometime *will be* for the first time. We have in view the arrival [*Kunft*] in which Dasein, in its ownmost potentiality-for-being, comes towards itself."[21]

The future is not an event that is awaited nor is it a projected unattainable narrative totality of Dasein's life that is seen as presently being realized. The emphasis in the account of authentic temporality falls not on what is to be realized but on the *arrival* [*Kunft*][22] of the future, its happening to us, that it arrives or comes toward us from out of the range of the factically possible and stands under the aspect of death. §65 describes anticipatory resoluteness as: "This letting-itself-*come-towards*-itself [*Sich-auf-sich-zukommenlassen*] in *the* distinctive possibility [*die ausgezeichnete Möglichkeit*] which it puts up with [*aushaltende*], is the primordial phenomenon of the *future as coming towards [Zukommen lassen]*" (H. 325, my emphasis, translation modified). The possibility spoken of here is not only distinctive but also singular and definite. It is a distinctive possibility in which we open ourselves to the range of the possible with the certainty that we exist as dying, that is, that our future is finite (H. 285).

It is against the background of these considerations that we can make sense of an apparent paradox in Heidegger's text. For, on the one hand, Heidegger claims there is "*a definite* ontical way of taking authentic existence, *a* factical ideal of Dasein" underlying the ontological interpretation of its existence (H. 310, my emphasis), thus suggesting a determinate factical ideal. Yet he also maintains such an ideal does not mean "holding up to Dasein an ideal of existence with any special 'content', or forcing any such ideal on it 'from outside'" (H. 266). The apparent paradox of describing this factical ideal as at one and the same time definite, concrete, but also *contentless* can be surmounted when we see it refers to an existentiell movement rather than a specific content, or better, that in this distinctive existentiell movement existential structures are revealed. Anticipatory resoluteness is an ontic definite, concrete way of deciding for ourselves that reveals the conditions for any authentic possibility. A corollary of this is that Heidegger's formal indicative method must be understood existentielly. The bringing to light of formal features of our existence is not to be understood primarily as a mental act or operation akin to say, abstraction in the Lockean or Kantian sense.[23] Rather, formalization or the dropping out of specific existentiell content occurs in and through an existentiell *undergoing* of the existential reduction. This distinctive way of being, underlying which is a peculiar and distinctive mode of temporality, is the point at which the method and "content" of the existential analytic show themselves in their unity. Yet the full development of this ideal only occurs with the fuller development of the temporality of thrownness, as we will see in Chapter 4.

However, for all the apparent formalism of the *a priori* of Dasein's being always-already ahead-of-itself, this structure too has an irreducibly factical dimension because any possibility of understanding, including that of existential analysis, is conditioned by the factical, historical world we are born into.

4 Standing between Nature and History

In the previous section we saw that the more original phenomena of having-been and the arriving future are "always already" there as enabling conditions that make derived phenomena of mood and understanding possible. Yet upon closer examination, this similarity is in two important respects misleading. For to say that Dasein is always already ahead-of-itself is evidently not the same as saying that it is always already thrown into the world nor, for that matter, as saying it is always already alongside entities. These are different—but co-original and co-implying—aspects of our being as care. The very characterization of our being as constituted by our projection of our "what" from out of the facticity of our "that-it-is" introduces an essential multiplicity into the notion of the *a priori* itself. The claim that "Dasein has an *a priori* character grounded upon fact" (H. 229) raises the complex problem of the movement of temporality in which different senses of alreadiness—already in the world, alongside entities, and ahead of itself—are brought together or "temporalize themselves."

This essential multi-dimensionality has immense ramifications for Heidegger's understanding of the *a priori* and of philosophical concept formation. It also explains why many of his key terms—world, moment, turn, birth, death, letting-be, being-with—cannot be pinned down as having one unequivocal meaning. In this section I want to look at why these interrelated but distinct senses of a priority are not purely formal but also have irreducible factical presuppositions. These factical preconditions were indicated at the end of the second and third sections of this chapter: the presupposition of the historical world and language on the one hand and our being factically situated in the midst of the present-at-hand as such or nature on the other.

I will broach the question of the factical presuppositions of the account of temporality in *Being and Time* through consideration of the phenomenon of existential movement. We saw in the foregoing that both inauthentic and authentic temporality are characterized by a movement forth and back between projection and thrownness. The way in which thrownness and projection are brought together or temporalize themselves occurs differently in different modes of our being. In fallenness, temporality temporalizes itself and we are given to ourselves from out of the everyday world. In anticipatory resoluteness, we take over our ownmost potentiality-for-being, that is a possibility *as* our own. In anxiety, we are brought back to the sheer "that-it-is" of our facticity.

The problem of movement is treated in *Being and Time*, Division II, Chapter 5, which discusses how "Dasein *is stretched along and stretches itself along*" between death and birth (H. 375). It concerns how being-toward-death and thrownness become unified in the temporalizing of temporality. Both birth and death, facticity and projection, are constitutive of the movement of Dasein's existence. Yet as Felix Ó Murchadha has stressed,[24] although the existential analytic foregrounds Dasein's authentic being-toward-death, we read right at the outset of the chapter on historicality that "death is only the 'end' of Dasein; and, taken formally, it is just *one* of the ends by which Dasein's totality is closed around." Not only has birth and Dasein's "being-towards-the-beginning remained unnoticed" but also "the way in which Dasein *stretches along between* birth and death" (H. 373).

> "Factical Dasein exists as born; and, as born, it is already dying, in the sense of being-towards-death. As long as Dasein factically exists, both of the 'ends' and their 'between' *are*, and they *are* in the only way which is possible on the basis of Dasein's being as *care*. Thrownness and that being towards death in which one either flees it or anticipates it, form a unity; and in this unity birth and death are 'connected' in a manner characteristic of Dasein. As care, Dasein *is* the 'between.'"[25]

The discussion of historicality in Division II of *Being and Time* thus considers how Dasein relates to its ahead-of-itself as thrown in the movement of its existence. Heidegger uses the term *Geschehen*, historicizing or happening, for this process, for how being-in-the-world occurs or happens as meaningful in the light of an appropriation of our possibilities. This authentic understanding of the historical world is made possible by facing our finitude, taking over of a possibility of being from the concrete historical situation we find ourselves in. In this sense, authenticity proves to be the existential-temporal condition for historicality: "*Authentic being-towards-death—that is to say, the finitude of temporality—is the hidden basis of Dasein's historicality*" (H. 386).

Yet as Ó Murchadha has argued, Heidegger's claim to found historicality upon temporality—in the sense that historicality comes into view in authentic being-toward-death—cannot be a one-way relationship.[26] As "those possibilities of existence that have been disclosed [in authenticity] are not to be gathered from death" (H. 383), authenticity implies a return to the concrete, historical situation we are in and the possibilities it offers. Any possibility of understanding, including "one's current understanding of being and [...] whatever possibilities and horizons for fresh interpretation and conceptual articulation that may be available" (H. 168)—and crucially these include the possibility of fundamental ontology—is historical through and through. But while this legacy is usually taken over as something self-evident and flattened out into the unthinking, one-dimensional prescriptions of *das Man*, appropriating the possibility character of the world authentically opens us to this historical field of intelligibility prior to its rigidified, one-dimensional interpretation.

This introduces an irreducible factical element into Heidegger's investigation: We must draw upon the historical past, the world we have been born into, in order to retrieve unthought possibilities for "fresh interpretation and conceptual articulation" (H. 168). In other words, taking over of a possibility of our being always presupposes and co-implies the shared social space of the world in which we find ourselves with, for, and against others.[27] While historicality is ontologically founded on authentic temporality, the latter has the former as its factical condition. We thus encounter a dynamic of reciprocal implication between the ontic and the ontological levels of the analysis.

And if Dasein's heritage, the factical legacy of possibilities, is co-implied in its authentic being-toward-death, then the factical presence-at-hand of nature in the widest sense is also co-implied in Dasein's turn toward the sheer "that-it-is" of its being-in-the-world in anxiety. For in its moods, Dasein is revealed to itself as given over to, surrounded by *other beings*. But it is in the "first moment" of anxiety, in which the everyday context of significance is nihilated, that entities within-the-world show themselves in their *otherness*:

> "Anxiety is anxious in the face of the 'nothing' of the world; but *this does not mean that in anxiety we experience something like the absence of what is present-at-hand within-the-world. The present-at-hand must be encountered in just such*

a way that it does not have any involvement whatsoever, but can just show itself in an empty mercilessness."[28]

Beings themselves in their sheer weirdness are revealed in this moment and revealed as there *prior to* Dasein's engagement with them. While *Being and Time* is concerned with the question of the *meaning* of being in general, what is encountered in this "first moment" of anxiety is *unmeaning of beings* prior to their discovery as significant to us.[29] It reveals that "all entities whose kind of being is of a character other than Dasein's must be conceived as *unmeaning* [*unsinniges*], essentially devoid of any meaning at all." This unmeaning can become evident on the everyday level when a tool unexpectedly breaks down or, more dramatically, in the power of natural events: "the present-at-hand, as Dasein encounters it, can, as it were, assault Dasein's being; natural events, for instance, can break in [*hereinbrechende*] upon us and destroy us" (H. 152).[30] In the "first moment" of anxiety, we encounter not a "senseless" accident but are brought before the *opacity of beings as a whole, of nature* as such. We encounter things in their prior unspeaking, alien presence.[31] This brings us before another sense in which the existential-temporal analysis remains implicitly embedded in the factical, namely in nature or "what is present-at-hand in the widest sense" (H. 403).

The existential analytic thus implicitly harbors factical presuppositions in the double sense of the facticity of history and of nature. And *Being and Time* sketches out "a non-deductive genealogy"[32] (H. 11) of history and nature in an original sense, in their being co-implied and given in specific movements of temporality, in the forth movement of authentic historicality and in an anxious return to the facticity of being-there. At the close of the chapter on historicality, Heidegger claims the "idea of being embraces both the 'ontical' and the 'Historical'" but "*this idea* which must let itself be 'generically differentiated.'"[33] Understanding this is possible, he writes,

"…only if we attain the following insights: (1) that the question of historicality is an *ontological* question of the state of being of historical entities; (2) that the question of the ontical is the *ontological* question of the state of being of entities other than Dasein—of what is present-at-hand in the widest sense; (3) that the ontical is only *one* domain of entities. The idea of being embraces both the 'ontical' and the 'historical.'"[34]

The problem of the relation between the ontical and the historical, between nature and historicality, is not the problem of a relation between two distinct disciplines. Rather the question of their relation concerns "the way in which man ... as the *root* of these sciences, *is*" (H. 398). Our foregoing considerations have shown how these are rooted in Dasein's being and that the idea of being is supposed to embrace both. We can also note that Heidegger signals how this thinking of the unity of these two constitutive aspects of our original temporality potentially conceals fundamental difficulties when he writes "everything is haunted by the *enigma* of *being*, and, as has now been made plain, by that of *motion*" (H. 392, cf. H 389).

It is this problem that will lead to the transformation of fundamental ontology, which focused on the meaning of being, into the metaphysics of Dasein, which thematizes the temporal conditions for the ontological difference. In *Being and Time* what is primarily historical is Dasein while "the environing nature as 'the very soil of history'" is secondarily historical (H. 381). As we will subsequently see, this relation of primacy is reversed or turned around in the metaphysical period where the focus is on the shock of being brought before beings themselves, where our understanding no longer "has a grip on things." This is made possible by a temporality of thrownness or of birth, the third temporal ecstasis which remains only in the background of *Being and Time*.[35]

Conclusion

In the preceding, I argued that we can see in *Being and Time* itself why and how "the *temporale* analysis is at the same time [*zugleich*] the turn [*Kehre*], where ontology itself expressly runs back [*zurückläuft*] into the metaphysical-ontic in which it always implicitly remains" (MFL 158 [GA 26 201]). The *Kehre* or turn-around is already implied by the account of temporality and movement in *Being and Time*. Dasein's going forth to its ownmost potentiality-for-being presupposes its having let itself turn-thither [*Hinkehr*] toward its ownmost having-been thrown, that is, toward its facticity.

Closely correlated with this, we say that the sense in which temporality functions as an *a priori* condition for ontological understanding brings two closely related problems into play that are concealed by Heidegger's use of quasi-transcendental language. First, what is called the temporalizing of temporality not only leaves the relation between a priority and temporality unclarified but introduces an essential multiplicity into the notion of the *a priori* itself. Second, Dasein's "*a priori* character" is not a purely formal condition for the possibility of understanding but is "grounded upon fact" (H. 229), it implies the facticity of nature and the facticity of the historical world. The following chapter will treat in detail how Heidegger came to critique the traditional notion of the *a priori*. This will provide the necessary background to Heidegger's attempt to ground the transcendental on Dasein's transcendence in the development of the metaphysics of Dasein.

Notes

1. The latter text will be treated in the following chapter.
2. Tengelyi has rightly stressed the significance of the factical conditions for fundamental ontology. My reading differs from his in that I argue that these factical conditions are constantly implied by the existential analytic itself, most especially by the account of temporality and movement. See Tengelyi, "L'idee de métontologie et la vision du monde selon Heidegger," *Heidegger Studies*, Volume 27 (2011): 137–53 and his *Welt und Unendlichkeit: Zum Problem phänomenologischer Metaphysik*, 228–36.
3. H. 42. The seemingly casual contrast between a present-at-hand entity "that 'looks' so and so" and Dasein's "possible ways for it to be" implicitly refers to a fundamental distinction between two different kinds of sight and two modes of temporality. The εἶδος of how things appear to us is ontologically distinct to how Dasein sights the "ideas" of its existence, the Real (the present-at-hand) and being (H. 61, 314, cf. 403). The traditional distinction between the "what" and "that" being of entities is, on Heidegger's account, existentially rooted in how Dasein views entities as having been produced, a limited ontological region. It is no exaggeration to say that this distinction is what separates the "metaphysics of Dasein" from traditional metaphysics (as Heidegger understands it). But note that in his own project Heidegger is constantly drawing upon and transforming the language of traditional metaphysics (for example, the term εἶδος), giving its terms a new sense within the context of the existential analytic.
4. "The 'that-it-is' of facticity never becomes something we can come across by beholding it" (H. 135).
5. "*Existentially, a disposition implies a disclosive submission to the world, out of which we can encounter something that matters to us. Indeed, from the ontological point of view we must as a general principle leave the primary discovery of the world to bare mood*" (H. 137–38).
6. H. 340. Translation modified. Macquarrie and Robinson use "state-of-mind," not "disposition."
7. As we will see over the course of this work, they also contain *striking differences* of enormous methodological significance.

8   For instance, in fearing we understand something as detrimental to our *being-already* in the world as coming toward us and as threatening what *already matters to us*. Or when we hope, what is hoped for is a relief from difficulties we *already have*. To take yet another example, in what Heidegger refers to as the pallid lack of mood, or a kind of existential indifference, we mindlessly give our future over to the demands and expectations of everyday world we are *already in* (H. 345). In each of these different moods, the phenomenon of temporality is co-given. However, moods in their everydayness remain tied to some specific entity or possibility of being, such as something fearsome or hoped for or whatever way of understanding is currently predominant in a given social sphere. Anxiety has a distinctive methodological significance in the existential analytic because it reveals Dasein's having-been thrown into the world *as such*. See the second section of this chapter for a discussion of this.

9   As we will see in Chapter 3, these differences ultimately make possible the ontological difference in its three senses or threefold sense.

10 Heidegger does occasionally employ such terms in a non-technical sense, such as the use of "*umgekehrt*" to mean "on the contrary" or "inversely," for example at H. 22.

11 Heidegger distinguishes this fallen equanimity and this inhibited ill-humor from their authentic counterparts, the equanimity and joy that arises from Dasein's seizing hold of its existence and putting up with the arrival of the future (H. 345, H. 325). Both the fallen and the authentic ways of being attuned to the world are, at least to some degree, self-affected through the different existentiell ways in which Dasein relates to its possibilities.

12 Everyday disclosedness is constituted by idle talk, curiosity, and ambiguity (the everyday kind of being of dispositions, understanding, and discourse) and these reveal the *specific movement of falling* (H. 180), namely as a tendency to inertia that is subject to disturbance from what befalls us from our environment. Heidegger restricts the temporal analysis of falling to curiosity "for here the specific temporality of falling is most easily seen," adding that the "analysis of idle talk and ambiguity, however, presupposes our having already clarified the temporal Constitution of discourse and of explanation (interpretation)," which task he reserves for Division III, Chapter 2 (H. 349 xiii). The temporal constitution of discourse and its implications for concept formation are a key theme of this work.

13 As Macquarrie and Robinson note, Heidegger here plays in the ordinary meaning of "*ungehalten*" as "indignant" or "unable to contain oneself."

14 In a notable turnaround, in the metaphysical period Heidegger will discuss the positive function of wishing as awakening the capacity to act in the context of the world of mythical Dasein. See Chapter 4.

15 Even moods such as elation that seem to alleviate "the manifest burden of being" (H. 134) reveal that for the most part our being is a troublesome burden we wish to be rid of. Elation does not bring alleviation by turning toward and taking over possibilities of being a self but is rather a pronounced turning-away from this, it is experienced as relief from the weight of possibilities we have taken upon ourselves (H. 135). In the authentic counterpart to this mood, Dasein is brought "without Illusions into the resoluteness of 'taking action'" and has an "unshakeable joy [*gerüstete Freude*]" in being brought face to face with its ownmost potentiality-for-being (H. 310). This joy, as we will see in Chapter 5, is connected with a creativity that essentially belongs to Dasein.

16 "When in falling we flee *into* the 'at-home' [*das Zuhause*] of publicness, we flee in the face of the 'not-at-home' [*dem Unzuhause*]; that is, we flee in the face of the uncanniness [*Unheimlichkeit*] that lies in Dasein" (H. 189).

17 See Chapter 3 for a more extended discussion of the significance of this "first moment" of anxiety.

18 H. 191.

19 *Verschwiegenheit* or the reticence that belongs to *Gewissenhabenwollen* or willing-to-have-a-conscience has connotations of closeness, reticence, discretion, secrecy. Peg Birmingham suggests translating *Verschwiegenheit* as "discretion" to capture the sense of to "show discernment or good judgment in conduct, especially in speech" and not the "'secrecy' and 'seclusion' which further connotes an isolated, separate subject." See Birmingham, "Logos and the Place of the Other," 38–9. However, I would suggest the connotations of isolation and separation are present in Heidegger's use of the term *Verschwiegenheit* given its relation to anxiety, which "individualizes Dasein and thus discloses it as '*solus ipse*.'" (H. 188). It refers primarily, as I understand it, to a refraining from giving oneself over to the interpretative tendencies of the "they" and giving oneself over to experience as one experiences it. This makes possible Dasein's authentic hearing of the call of conscience, which call brings it back to how it is already understanding its 'there'. A discreet being-with Others or one which shows good judgment is founded, then, on Dasein's own lack of secrecy before its self.

20 The Macquarrie and Robinson translation reads: "Dasein becomes 'essentially' Dasein in that authentic existence which constitutes itself as anticipatory resoluteness" (H. 323).

21 "'*Zukunft*' meint hier nicht ein Jetzt, das, noch nicht 'wirklich' geworden, einmal erst sein wird, sondern die Kunft, in der das Dasein in seinem eigensten Seinkönnen auf sich zukommt" (H. 325).

22 See Chapter 6 for a discussion of the archaic term "*Kunft*" here.

23 See Locke, John, *An Essay Concerning Human Understanding*, edited by Roger Woolhouse (London: Penguin, 2002), I, ii, 15, III, iii, 6, IV.vii.9 and Kant, *Lectures*

on *Logic*, Translated and edited by J. Michael Young (Cambridge: Cambridge University Press, 2004). I discuss Heidegger's phenomenological analysis of the Kantian account of concept formation and how it differs from Heidegger's own understanding of ontological concept formation in Chapter 2.

24 See Ó Murchadha, "Future or Future Past," 262–9 and his *The Time of Revolution: Kairos and Chronos in Heidegger*, 28–50. Ó Murchadha also stresses the importance of birth in Heidegger's analysis. See Chapter 4 for a discussion of this topic.

25 H. 374.

26 Ó Murchadha, "Future or Future Past," 262–9 and his *The Time of Revolution: Kairos and Chronos in Heidegger*, 28–50.

27 See Chapter 6 for a more detailed discussion of these issues with reference to Heidegger's philosophy and politics. See also Aengus Daly, "Deciding the Fate of the State: Heidegger, Thucydides and the Boden of Ontology," *Journal of the British Society for Phenomenology*, Volume 53, Issue 4 (2022): 440–54.

28 H. 343, my emphasis. This aspect of anxiety, which remains in the background of the treatment of this phenomenon in *Being and Time*, is foregrounded in the lecture "What Is Metaphysics?" See Chapter 3 for a discussion of the repetition of key elements of the existential analytic in this lecture.

29 In everydayness nature is encountered as serving or threatening, as impacting Dasein's concerns from a definite direction. "The wood is a forest of timber, the mountain a quarry of rock; the river is water power, the wind is wind 'in the sails'" (H. 70–1). The threat that nature poses is reckoned with and preparations are made to ward off its potentially disruptive power. "A covered railway platform takes account of bad weather; an installation for public lighting takes account of the darkness, or rather of specific changes in the presence or absence of daylight." Here the possibility of an affective relation to nature lies hidden or covered over (H. 70–1).

30 In *The Metaphysical Foundation of Logic*, Heidegger again emphasizes how the attempt to control and subjugate nature is symptomatic of an original powerlessness before it. "[Dasein's] powerlessness is metaphysical, i.e., to be understood as essential; it cannot be removed by reference to the conquest of nature, to technology, which rages about in the 'world' today like an unshackled beast; for this domination of nature is the real proof for the metaphysical powerlessness of Dasein, which can only attain freedom in its history" (MFL 215 [GA 26278–79]).

31 See also the claim at H. 212: "… Being (not entities) is dependent upon the understanding of being; that is to say, Reality (not the Real) is dependent upon care."

32 See Chapter 4 for a discussion of Heidegger's "deduction" of the categories of mythical thinking from Dasein's thrownness.

33 Similar comments can be found at H. 314. Underlying these distinctions are the different senses of the ontological difference. See Chapter 3 for a discussion of this point.
34 H. 403.
35 The account of birth in *Being and Time* is one in which Dasein's having been-born is taken over in its authenticity, in taking up a historical possibility as its own. In other words, birth is understood on the basis of being-toward-death and, as Ó Murchadha has rightly pointed out, repetition "assumes the passivity of birth as its prior condition." See Ó Murchadha, *The Time of Revolution: Kairos and Chronos in Heidegger*, 32–8, here: 37. As we will see in Chapter 4, when Heidegger speaks of Dasein's having been born in the metaphysical period, this refers not only to its inheriting possibilities from its history but also to the helplessness of its being delivered over to beings other than itself. These two aspects of birth are reciprocally conditioning.

2

Temporality and the *A Priori*

In the previous chapter, I argued that Heidegger's conception of the *a priori* is characterized both by an essential multiplicity and by its factical character. This chapter discusses what Heidegger claims are the implicit time-determinations in the traditional notion of the *a priori*. As is well-known, Heidegger frequently stresses the Kantian background to his undertaking. In the introduction to *Being and Time*, he describes his investigations as seeking *a priori* conditions: "The question of being aims ... at ascertaining the *a priori* conditions not only for the possibility of the sciences as entities of such and such a type" and which thus presuppose a prior understanding of their being, "but also for the possibility of ontologies themselves which are prior to the ontical sciences and which provide their foundations." This radicalizes the insights of Kant's *Critique of Pure Reason*. While Kant had contributed to "the working out of what belongs to any nature whatsoever" and his transcendental logic "is an *a priori* logic for the subject-matter of that area of being called 'nature,'" what is needed is an inquiry into the meaning of being in general (H. 11).

As we saw in the introduction, a key claim from many different strands of Heidegger scholarship is that Heidegger employs a Kantian transcendental framework in *Being and Time*. Yet despite its centrality to Heidegger's investigation, the *a priori* becomes a fundamental *problem* whose dimensions become ever clearer in the late 1920s. In lecture courses, unpublished manuscripts, and private correspondence from this period, Heidegger claims to problematize the traditional conception of the *a priori* in its relation to temporality.[1] This problematization or destruction can be seen especially in those sections of *Being and Time* and *The Basic Problems of Phenomenology* where Heidegger provides an existential genealogy of the traditional understanding of the *a priori*, claiming that it originates in the everyday world of productive concern and thus in a *derivative* mode of temporality. Yet this raises a basic question concerning Heidegger's own undertaking: What does he mean when he refers to ascertaining *a priori* conditions? If he is read as employing the term *a priori* in the traditional sense, then he seems to fall into a kind of category error: He takes an understanding belonging to ontic dealings with the ready-to-hand to be paradigmatic of the understanding of being as such. However, if he means something else, then how is it to be positively understood? Could it be that the very language of the *a priori* is a remnant of the "language of metaphysics" that brought about the failure of *Being and Time*?

I have already expressed my misgivings about the narrative of failure and the claim that Heidegger's fundamental ontology employs a Kantian "transcendental framework" in the introduction. However, there are three immediately outstanding tasks that my reading must tackle. First, I need to explain how and why Heidegger's investigation into temporality problematizes the traditional conception of the *a priori*. Second, I have to tease out what lines of inquiry are opened up in Heidegger's work for conceiving the *a priori* more originally. Third, the preceding topics must be explored with regard to Heidegger's interpretation of Kant. These are the tasks of the present chapter. Their implications will be explored over the remainder of this book.

1 Letting-Be Involved and the *A Priori*

Heidegger finds the existential origin of the *a priori*, as well as the origin of other basic philosophical concepts, within the horizon of everyday concern. I will first discuss how this existential genealogy is briefly indicated in an important marginal note to §18 of *Being and Time*. Then I will show how this origin is further investigated in *The Basic Problems of Phenomenology*.[2] We will thus be able to get a clear idea about how and why the temporal presuppositions of the traditional notion of the *a priori* become problematic, as will be discussed in the following section.

In §18 of *Being and Time* Heidegger refers to "a *perfect* tense *a priori*" which belongs to the letting-be characteristic of dealings with equipment. The crucial passage reads:

> "When we speak of having already let something be involved, so that it has been freed for that involvement, we are using a *perfect* tense *a priori* which characterizes the kind of being belonging to Dasein itself [*Das auf Bewandtnis hin freigebende Je-schon-haben-bewenden-lassen ist ein apriorisches Perfekt, das die Seinsart des Daseins selbst charakterisiert*]. Letting an entity be involved, if we understand this ontologically, consists in previously freeing it for its

readiness-to-hand within the environment. When we let something be involved, it must be involved in something; and in terms of this 'in-which', the 'with-which' of this involvement is freed."³

An "'*a priori*' letting-something-be-involved ['*apriorsche*' *Bewendenlassen*] is the condition for the possibility that the ready-to-hand can be encountered" (H. 85). When Dasein is oriented toward bringing forth or producing something, it encounters entities in the light of a "towards-this." The manner in which it so releases entities for involvement is clearly not through a passive contemplation of them but rather sighting them in terms of what can be done with them: "we do not let them 'be' ['*sein*' *lassen*] as we have discovered that they are, but work upon them, make improvements in them, or smash them to pieces" (H. 85).

Heidegger advances a further thesis in the above citation linking these claims with a particular sense of the *a priori*. Letting something be involved implies "a *perfect* tense *a priori* which characterizes the kind of being [*Seinsart*] belonging to Dasein itself." This brief statement alludes to a fundamental phenomenological problem, that of the existential origins of a temporal determination of the being of beings which, Heidegger claims in a handwritten note to this paragraph, has been predominant in the philosophical tradition:

> "In the same paragraph, we speak of 'previous freeing'—namely (generally speaking) of being for the possible manifestness of beings: 'Previously' in this ontological sense means in Latin *a priori*, in Greek πρότερον τῇ (Aristotle, *Physics*, A 1). More clearly in *Metaphysics*, E 1025 b 29 τὸ τί ἦν εἶναι 'what already was-being', 'what always already presences in advance (*Wesende*)', the having-been, the perfect [*das Gewesen, das Perfekt*]. The Greek verb εἶναι has no perfect tense; this is named here with ἦν εἶναι. It is not something ontically past [*ontisch Vergangenes*], but rather what is always earlier [*das jeweils Frühere*], what we are referred *back* [*zurückverwiesen*] to in the question of beings as such. Instead of *a priori* perfect we could also call it ontological or transcendental perfect (cf. Kant's doctrine of the Schematism)."⁴

Given that Heidegger's own investigation aspires to an *a priori* status, special care must be taken in interpreting this passage. Crucial to understanding the broad claim that Heidegger makes here about the determination of the being of beings in the philosophical tradition from Aristotle to Kant is understanding the link between the ontological or transcendental perfect and everyday dealings with the ready-to-hand. This link lies in the having been, the perfect, "the always earlier [*das jeweils Frühere*], what we are referred *back* [*zurückverwiesen*] to in the question of beings as such" which functions as a temporal determination of the being of beings. However, the sense in which everyday concern refers back to a having been that precedes chronological time remains enigmatic here as does the connection between this and the temporal determination of the being of beings in the philosophical tradition.

§11 of *The Basic Problems of Phenomenology* provides us with a somewhat fuller account of the emergence of a certain conception of the *a priori* within the horizon of Dasein's productive comportment.[5] It provides a phenomenological interpretation, albeit a highly condensed one, of the concepts of εἶδος, ὑποκείμενον, and οὐσία with a view to interrogating the ontological presuppositions of Kant's claim that being is not a real predicate. What is of interest to us here is not the philological accuracy of Heidegger's interpretation but rather in signaling how these claims bear on the development of his project and specifically the problem of the *a priori* therein.[6] Despite its brevity, this discussion does show us how Heidegger interprets the relation between productive comportment, the basic concepts of Greek philosophy, and the *a priori*.

At the outset of this phenomenological analysis, Heidegger reminds his listeners of the distinction between perceptually seeing and the sighting of entities in productive comportment. When we perceive something, we have the possibility of pushing through how it looks so as to arrive at its form, its what. This relation is inverted in producing or seeking to bring something about: The form, image, idea, or εἶδος precedes and grounds the thing.[7] We refer back to this image and take our guide from it in producing and in dealing with the stuff in our environment:

> "All forming of shaped products is effected by using an image, in the sense of a model, as guide and standard. The thing is produced by looking to the anticipated look of what is to be produced by shaping, forming. It is this anticipated look of the thing, sighted beforehand, that the Greeks mean ontologically by εἶδος, ἰδέα. The shaped product, which is shaped in conformity with the model, is as such the exact likeness of the model."[8]

The image that provides the standard is "*always* earlier": It precedes chronological time and refers to what the thing "already was and is before all actualization" (BPP 107 [GA 24 150–1]). It is "that from which production takes the measure for its product" and so is also "that whence what is formed properly derives" (BPP 107 [GA 24 150–1]). The letting be involved [*Bewendenlassen*] of productive comportment, shaping, forming, and making refers back to this standard. It implies a "letting-come-here, letting-derive-from [*ein Herkommenlassen, ein Herstammenlassen-aus*]" the image, model, or εἶδος that is always already given and which provides the measure for what is to be produced (BPP 108 [GA 24 152]).

Looking toward this model is at the same time the anticipation of what can be done with environing things. Producing thus not only refers to the image from which production takes its measure but also to our "wherein," what we find there and work on. "*Her*-stellen" means to place here, "to bring into the narrower or wider circuit of the accessible, here, to this place" such that "the produced being *stands for itself* on its own account and remains able to be found there and to *lie-before there* [*vorliegen*] as *something established stably for itself*" (BPP 108 [GA 24 152]). In producing, we sight the equipment and those things of nature that we make use of or have to take into account—such as "house and yard, forest and field, sun, light and heat" (BPP 108 [GA 24 153])—as present and available, as at our disposal. This is, Heidegger claims, the phenomenological horizon from which the Greek term ὑποκείμενον, that which-lies-before, derives. That which is handy and available is "reckoned by everyday experience as that which is, as a being, in the primary sense" (BPP 108 [GA 24 153]). The term οὐσία, Heidegger claims, testifies in its pre-philosophical usage to this understanding of being. In this pre-philosophical meaning, it is "still synonymous with property, possessions, means, wealth" (BPP 108 [GA 24 153]) such that "a being is synonymous with a *ready-to-hand disposable* [vorhandenes Verfügbares]" (BPP 108–9 [GA 24 153]).

Heidegger's claim is not that Greek philosophy *explicitly* drew upon the horizon opened up by productive comportment in its determination of the being of beings. Rather it *implicitly* and *naively* drew upon this horizon, upon the everyday meaning of εἶδος, ὑποκείμενον, and οὐσία in the development of its basic concepts. The philosophical employment of these terms also modifies their meaning. For one, the character of thingness is fixed by Greek ontology from within the horizon of productive comportment and the basic concepts became *formalized* and employed more widely (BPP 108 [GA 24 152]). Secondly, in their philosophical use these concepts underwent a change of emphasis. The term οὐσία in its philosophical use refers not so much to the availability of a useful *thing* as to our *finding it present* (BPP 109 [GA 24 153]). Thirdly, the meaning of these terms changed over the course of the philosophical tradition, most notably in their translation from Greek to Latin. Thus, while the term *essentia* emphasizes *what* is produced in producing, that which belongs to an available entity "due to its having been produced," οὐσία stresses the *at-handness* of a being, its availability, and presence, the "producedness of the produced [*die Hergestelltheit des Hergestellten*] in the sense of things disposably present-at-hand" (BPP 109 [GA 24 153]). Heidegger also notes that his existential genealogy of the basic concepts of Greek philosophy is itself incomplete: It does not discuss why access to the being of beings is defined through an *intuitive* finding-present, nor does it discuss Greek concept of world (BPP 109–10 [GA 24 154–5]).

Nevertheless, this phenomenological analysis, despite its limitations, does show, according to Heidegger, the necessity for going back to Dasein's productive comportment as the pre-philosophical horizon of meaningfulness from which philosophical concepts were drawn. This discussion thus partially makes good on a question raised in the introduction to *Being and Time*, namely indicating the existential origin of the distinction between temporal and non-temporal entities (H. 18–19).[9] Productive comportment looks toward a standard that is always already present, toward a past that never came into being at a specific time.

And Heidegger claims that this temporal determination of the being of beings, notwithstanding the process of formalization and translation that took place over the course of the philosophical tradition, remains determinative for the basic concepts of Kantian philosophy including the Kantian conception of the *a priori*:

> "The anticipated look, the proto-typical image, shows the thing as what it is before the production and how it is supposed to look as product. It is no accident that Kant, for whom the concepts of form and matter, μορφή and ὕλη, play a fundamental epistemological role, conjointly assigns to the imagination [*Einbildungskraft*] a distinctive function in explaining the objectivity of knowledge. The εἶδος as look, anticipated in imagination [*Einbildung*], of what is to be formed gives the thing with regard to what this thing already was and is before all actualization."[10]

Understanding in the Kantian sense means looking back to *a priori* forms of unity for the sensibly given: "the εἶδος as look, anticipated in imagination, of what is to be formed gives the thing with regard to what this thing already was and is before all actualization" (BPP 207 [GA 24 150–1]). Unlike the empirically given, these forms of unity are not subject to coming to be and passing away. The Kantian understanding of thinking remains within the productive paradigm in that it is characterized by an *a priori* letting-be-involved [*Bewandenlassen*], a previously freeing of the given for certain forms of unity, a "letting-come-here, letting-derive-from [*ein Herkommenlassen, ein Herstammenlassen-aus*]" (BPP 108 [GA 24 152]).[11] I will examine how these themes are taken up anew in Heidegger's lecture course *Phenomenological Interpretation of Kant's Critique of Pure Reason* and in *Kant and the Problem of Metaphysics* in the final section of this chapter. But first I want to consider how the *a priori* becomes a problem for Heidegger's own work.

2 The Problem of the *A Priori*

We have seen how and why Heidegger claims that the traditional conception of the *a priori* originates in productive comportment. However, this poses a particular difficulty for Heidegger's own project. What do the expressions "always already" and *a priori* mean in the context of *his* work? Does the term *a priori*, as a large number of commentators have maintained, have the same sense as this "ontological or transcendental perfect" (Heidegger's note to H. 85)?[12] If so, it would seem that Heidegger at best fails to show what legitimates this use of the term and at worst falls into a kind of category error in that he takes the understanding of being that belongs to the discovery of the ready-to-hand to be paradigmatic of our understanding of being in general. I will explore these issues by first examining two interesting recent interpretations of the *a priori* as the *a priori* perfect in *Being and Time*: that of Chad Engelland, who argues that Heidegger's work in the 1920s and 1930s implies an aporetic transcendentalism and that of Sacha Golob, who argues for the centrality of temporal "prototypes" to the project of *Being and Time* ((a)). I will then argue that Heidegger is in fact criticizing this conception of the *a priori* ((b)) and this critique motivates the turn from fundamental ontology to the metaphysics of Dasein ((c)).

(a) Heidegger's Indebtedness to a Productive Paradigm?

In *Heidegger's Shadow: Kant, Husserl and the Transcendental Turn*, Engelland describes a shift that takes place between *Being and Time* and the being-historical thinking of the 1930s as a shift from an investigation that focuses on an analytic *a priori* to historical affectivity.[13] Heidegger's early work, on this reading, is characterized by a "transcendental framework" that cannot accommodate the dynamic of *Ereignis*.[14] The former involves a unilateral movement, initiated by Dasein in heroic authenticity, of transcendence while the latter is a bilateral and reciprocal movement that takes place between historical need and Dasein. Engelland also detects this shift in Heidegger's interpretation of Kant. In the late 1920s Heidegger maintains Kant "shrank back" from the time-forming power of the transcendental imagination, while in the lectures of the 1930s what interests him is the reciprocity between condition and conditioned in making possible the "between" in which entities, self, world can show themselves.

On Engelland's reading the transcendental is not an aberration that blocks Heidegger's view of the "things themselves" but it remains Heidegger's point of access to the underlying dynamic of what Engelland aptly describes as a "'post-subjective, affective transcendentalism.'"[15] In other words, the transcendental approach opens up the way to a more original condition that cannot be accommodated within its "framework." The transcendental is thus not a brief, misleading phase of Heidegger's thought in the 1920s but is rather the indispensable way into the matter of Heidegger's thinking, hence his "quandary" or "irresolvable" difficulty, as Engelland characterizes it:

> "Even though Heidegger keenly felt the need to do so, for good reason he could not extricate himself from the transcendental tradition. His difficulty is irresolvable: either *affirm* transcendental philosophy and thereby distort his goal or *deny* transcendental philosophy and thereby occlude his point of departure."[16]

Clearly, a key issue for this interpretation is what the expressions "transcendental philosophy" and "*a priori*" mean. It is clear from the above that Engelland sees these as bound up with voluntarism, authenticity, and a unilateral movement of transcendence. Engelland broaches the *a priori* in fundamental ontology by citing a passage in *The Basic Problems of Phenomenology* where Heidegger refers to the Platonic good beyond being as both rendering truth and knowledge possible while remaining itself mostly unseen.[17] Engelland claims: "Rather than enter more deeply into the text, he [Heidegger] simply offers the thesis that Plato's conception *somehow remains mired within the productive ontology of ancient thought*."[18] Heidegger's question, Engelland continues, concerns the conditions for the possibility of understanding being and his answer is time. Time is *a priori* in the sense of being "earlier than any possible earlier." Engelland argues:

> "Now, Plato is the discoverer of the *a priori*. Plato, according to Heidegger, recognized in the doctrine of anamnesis that the possibility for clarifying being can be pursued only as a coming back to what was earlier and already understood."[19]

It is against this background that Engelland contends that Heidegger retrieves two theses from Plato, namely (1) seeing the truth is the condition for taking on human form and (2) "learning itself is nothing but recollection."[20] What is interesting about this reading of Heidegger's philosophy in the late 1920s is that a cluster of different issues are brought together: an implicit indebtedness to the productive paradigm, an intellectualistic understanding of the *a priori*, and a voluntarism.

It is also clear that this reading sees Heidegger's *Being and Time* as indebted to a productive metaphysics that has characterized philosophy from Plato down to Kant. In other words, we find no radical break with or critique of the metaphysical tradition in Heidegger's early work. The understanding of the *a priori* here is that of the *a priori* perfect, always already there, and capable of being brought to light by Dasein in its authenticity. Given this understanding of the *a priori*, Engelland sees *Being and Time* and Heidegger's work in this period as an aporetic path that opens up the more original domain of being-historical thinking, which latter, however, makes the former approach untenable.

We can find similar considerations regarding the productive paradigm and the *a priori* in Golob's *Heidegger on Concepts, Freedom and Normativity*. I cannot hope to do justice to the richness of Golob's analyses here, which to my mind signal the fertility of readings of Heidegger from the perspective of analytic philosophy. I instead want to focus simply on his reading of the relation between the problem of the *a priori* and the productive paradigm in *Being and Time* and *The Basic Problems of Phenomenology*. Golob characterizes the project of unveiling time as the horizon for the understanding of being as involving a prototype approach and argues that it motivates Heidegger's readings of both Plato and Kant. It is in the context of this reading that Golob draws the reader's attention to the aforementioned passages in *The Basic Problems of Phenomenology* where Heidegger discusses the implicit temporal horizon of the Platonic εἶδος and the Kantian *a priori*.[21] Briefly put, Golob claims that different modes of temporalization function as the prototypes for different modes of ontological understanding or knowledge. We sight and implicitly conceive of entities in terms of different temporal prototypes and this makes possible their showing themselves as entities of a specific kind.[22]

Golob's understanding of the prototype refers, as the name suggests, back to a productive paradigm. A prototype functions as schemata for our understanding of the being of entities—for taking them "as" this or that—in a manner analogous to how a physical object can function as the model for producing further entities. Golob asks us to imagine a hat that acts as a prototype that guides the production of other, similar hats. The prototype hat functions as a *normative standard*: It shows us what the hats to be produced should look like. It defines *extension*: It tells us what counts as a hat of this kind and what does not. The prototype can, but does not have to, be *described in propositional terms*. The sighting of temporal prototypes occurs in an analogous fashion. It is because of my implicit pre-understanding of the temporal schema of the "in-order-to" that I understand something as being ready-to-hand. It prescribes the norm for what can and cannot be counted as ready-to-hand. It prescribes the extension of readiness-to-hand—a teabag can be used "in-order-to" make a cup of tea while a pile of stones cannot. I can describe this in-order-to structure in propositional terms, as Heidegger's phenomenological description of dealings with the ready-to-hand shows.[23] The prototype of the "in-order-to" is the antecedent temporal condition for the "being in itself" of the ready-to-hand manifesting itself as ready-to-hand.

These temporal prototypes, sighted in advance, allow entities of different kinds to show themselves as meaningful.[24] They are the ultimate, *a priori* conditions for ontological understanding.[25] On Golob's reading, we should expect three such prototypes to be brought to light by Heidegger's analysis. §69 (c) of *Being and Time* refers to three horizontal schemata: the "in-order-to," which is the horizontal schema for the present, the "for-the-sake-of-which" is the schema for the future and "that *in the face of which* it has been thrown and that *to which* it has been abandoned" is the horizontal schema of what has been. Yet, as Golob notes, Heidegger's project remains radically incomplete.[26] Both the prototype for Dasein's "for-the-sake-of-which" remains outstanding as does that of "Reality."[27] The former is a prototype for Dasein's pre-understanding of the temporality of its existence, the latter is "a type of time, in virtue of which Dasein has familiarity with the properties that define real entities," that is, the "distinctive manner" in which such entities can be revealed in their independence from Dasein.[28] In these valuable considerations, Golob also highlights an oft over-looked aspect of Heidegger's fundamental ontology: the use of quasi-Platonic language to characterize its undertaking. As we previously saw, Heidegger refers to "the idea of being [that] embraces both the 'ontical' and the 'historical'" (H. 403) or to the "formal idea of existence" and the "idea of 'Reality'" that "'presuppose' an idea of being in general" (H. 314).

(b) Time and a Priority

What both of the above interpretations have in common is that they identify the ontological or transcendental perfect with the *a priori* sought in Heidegger's work in the late 1920s. But is this reading correct? For one thing, such a straightforward identification of the "always already" drawn from the domain of production would be surprising given that Heidegger signals that it is in no way proven these basic concepts drawn from the domain of productive comportment apply to every being whatsoever (BPP 110–11 [GA 24 156–7]), let alone that they can function as the paradigm for the understanding of being in general. Rather than reading the passages discussed above as providing an existential genealogy of the notion of the *a priori as such*, I want to suggest that they provide an existential genealogy of a notion of the *a priori* that Heidegger is concerned to *call into question* with a view to developing a fuller and phenomenologically more appropriate conception through the investigation and thematization of the relation between the *a priori* and time. Several considerations support this reading.

First the claim that the "a *perfect* tense *a priori* … characterizes the kind of being [*Seinsart*] belonging to Dasein itself" is qualified by the context in which this claim is made. The perfect tense *a priori* belongs to Dasein's letting an entity be involved, "in previously freeing it for its *readiness-to-hand within the environment*" (H. 85). This itself is interpreted in terms of the "in-which" and the "with-which" of this involvement and ultimately in terms of the temporality of everyday concern (H. 353–4). In other words, the perfect tense *a priori* belongs to Dasein's being in its *everyday circumspection*, to how it previously understands the being of beings discovered *in everyday concern*.

Second, the letting entities be involved [*Bewandenlassen*] of everyday concern presupposes other more fundamental modes of letting be. For Dasein sights them in terms of its potentiality-for-being, its primary for-the-sake-of-itself, "which it may have seized upon [*ergriffenen*] either explicitly or tacitly, and which may be either authentic or inauthentic" (H. 86). Letting-be-involved, in other words, presupposes either Dasein's "letting-itself-come-toward-itself in that distinctive possibility which it puts up with [*die ausgezeichnete Möglichkeit aushältende, in ihr sich auf sich* Zukommen-*lassen*]," that is, its *letting itself* come toward itself from out of its ownmost finitude (H. 325, cf. H. 106, 298) or the bogus *Gelassenheit* of fallen everydayness where Dasein "liv[es] along [*Das Dahinleben*] in a way which 'lets' everything 'be' as it is ['*sein lässt', wie es ist*]," that is, "forgetting and abandoning oneself to one's thrownness" (H. 345).[29] Further, while these latter two modes of letting-be refer to the authentic future and the fallen present respectively, a third kind of letting-be, discussed in the development of the metaphysics of Dasein after 1927, is entailed by Dasein's turn toward its facticity: "*das Sichloslassen in das Nichts*," Dasein's releasing itself into the nothing, in which it is brought before beings as a whole affectively (PM 96 [GA 9 122]). A full treatment of *Bewandenlassen* must contextualize it within the other more original modes of letting-be (those of authentic futurity, the fallen present, and the turn to Dasein's ownmost facticity in which the world entry of beings occurs). That is to say, a phenomenologically appropriate conception of the *a priori* would have to be developed on the basis of a further investigation of the problem of temporality.[30]

Further still, although Heidegger does indeed criticize ancient philosophy as "*somehow remain[ing] mired within the productive ontology of ancient thought*"[31] and also signals his intent to repeat or appropriate a kind of productive paradigm in his own approach, this does not necessarily lead to an aporia regarding the transcendental. For there are two different senses of productivity in Heidegger's own philosophy and his reading of ancient philosophy. The first is ontic productivity, from which the fundamental concepts of Greek philosophy were drawn, as *The Basic Problems of Phenomenology* makes clear. However, there is also a middle voiced ontological or temporal productivity which he refers to in both the 1927 lecture course and *The Metaphysical Foundations of Logic*. It is this latter productivity that interests Heidegger. And Heidegger explicitly claims that the Platonic good beyond being refers to this original temporal productivity. This suggests that despite some of the less cautious formulations in *Being and Time* and elsewhere, a close reading of Heidegger's texts between 1927 and 1929 shows that at no point was he doing transcendental philosophy in Kant's sense but was rather carrying out a critique of the temporal basis of Kant's transcendental philosophy.

(c) *Temporalität* and the Turn to the Metaphysical-Ontic

I want to suggest that the preceding interpretation is also borne out by the second Part of *The Basic Problems of Phenomenology* in which Heidegger broaches *Temporalität* as the condition for the possibility of the understanding of being. It may seem surprising to attribute this aspect of Heidegger's lecture course such a role with regard to his conception of the *a priori*. Despite Heidegger's having described the lecture course as a reworking of Division III of *Being and Time*, the course is incomplete as it only tackles the *temporale* condition for the possibility of one derivative ecstasis of Dasein's temporality. This discussion of *Temporalität* has been described by one commentator as "a very meagre advance" that "hardly represents any notable progress" into the Third Division of *Being and Time* and another characterizes it as "colossally disappointing," "more a label for the gap in Heidegger's argument than the completion of it."[32] Yet I want to suggest there is significantly more at stake in this discussion concerning Heidegger's transcendental philosophy than has been generally recognized.

In the closing hours of the lecture course, Heidegger states that the "always already" or the *a priori* "is patently a time-determination." While traditionally "it is not seen how the interpretation of being necessarily occurs in the horizon of time [and] the effort is made to explain away the time-determination by means of the *a priori*" (BPP, 324 [GA 24 461]), for the phenomenological approach "*it is only by means of the* Temporalität *of the understanding of being that it can be explained why the ontological determinations of being have the character of apriority*" (BPP, p. 325 [462]). In other words, what the lecture course *The Basic Problems of Phenomenology* ultimately accomplishes is the *temporale problematization* of the *a priori* and *not* the acceptance of the traditional conception.

On this interpretation, the lecture course *The Basic Problems of Phenomenology* also points the way toward the attempts in texts from 1927 to 1929 to develop a conception of the *a priori* that includes Dasein's facticity and the factical being there of beings as a whole. This interpretation is at odds with a widespread reading of Heidegger's work according to which the 1927 lecture course *The Basic Problems of Phenomenology* is in fact the record, in real time as it were, of the failure of the project of fundamental ontology.[33] On the latter reading, it is here, in his concern with *Temporalität* as the "horizon from which we understand being" (BPP 228 [GA 24 324]), that Heidegger's analyses are at their most formal. The different temporal ecstaces—future, making present, and having been—each have their horizon or *temporale* condition upon which the respective understandings of being are projected. This account is said to be beset by three difficulties that Heidegger signals in the closing hours of the lecture course: (1) the origin of the "not," (2) the finitude of time, and (3) the relation between time and "nothingness."[34] This reading is seemingly supported by the fact that the concern with *Temporalität* largely recedes after 1927.

Yet bearing in mind the methodological transformations that Heidegger's investigation undergoes, we can see the transition to the metaphysics of Dasein precisely in these analyses.[35] The analysis of *Temporalität* and specifically of *praesens* in *The Basic Problems of Phenomenology* not only discloses, on Heidegger's account, the horizon upon which the meaning of being in traditional ontology is implicitly understood (H. 8), but it also points toward the problem of the ontological difference, a term that is introduced for the first time in this lecture course.[36] The development of the problem of *Temporalität* and the emergence of the ontological difference entail not so much a break with the fundamental ontology of *Being and Time* as rather a transformation internal to it.[37]

I will focus here on how and why several outstanding difficulties in the discussion of *Temporalität* indicate the necessity of the turn toward facticity and what Heidegger will call the metaphysical-ontic in 1928. I will outline Heidegger's account of this horizonal schema before discussing why this, for Heidegger, is not an original horizon of meaningfulness. In so doing, I will highlight several problems concerning the horizonal-schema of *praesens* that point beyond the analysis of this lecture course and toward the metaphysics of facticity developed thereafter.[38]

The analysis in the final sections of *The Basic Problems of Phenomenology* focuses on one mode of *Temporalität*, *praesens* as the (for the most part) non-conceptual pre-understanding or schematic pre-designation of the being of ready-to-hand beings. This analysis parallels and supplements the preliminary analysis of worldhood in *Being and Time* by unveiling the *temporale* horizon upon which it is implicitly understood. Heidegger follows the methodological prescription of bringing a positive phenomenon into view by way of a negative[39] by again considering disturbance to the equipmental totality. However, in this instance this disturbance is not considered as revelatory of the surrounding everyday with-world but of the horizon of *praesens*.

This disturbance to the course of our usual dealings with things "*proceeds from the being itself [vom Seienden selbst] with which we are dealing*" (BPP 310 [GA 24 440], my emphasis). It frustrates our previous expectations and our implicit understanding of what we are dealing with. The being itself shows itself as irreducible to the horizon of our previous understanding. According to the aforementioned methodological prescription, it is when this pre-understanding breaks down that it can be thematized in its ontological—that is to say *temporale*—presuppositions: "this means that the *temporale*[40] interpretation of handiness in its sense of being must be clearly attainable in is orientation towards non-handiness" (BPP 309 [GA 24 439]).

Heidegger focuses on an item of equipment as *missing* or not showing itself as expected in the equipmental context. To miss something implicitly refers back to and becomes possible against a tacit horizon of expectation: The missing thing is expected to be there, to be present and available. Only on this basis of this expectation can it be discovered as absent or missed. One might think here of the shock of discovering the non-presence of one's wallet or house keys. The missing of something "is the not-finding of something that we have been expecting *as needed [als eines Benötigten]*" (BPP 310 [GA 24 441], my emphasis).[41] This antecedent understanding of the needed as present and available, as presencing, underlies our dealings with the ready-to-hand.

Without a "*schematic pre-designation* of the *where out there* [of] this specific 'beyond itself'" (BPP 306 [GA 24 435]), we could not discover anything as missing or absent. This schematic pre-designation Heidegger calls *praesens*. Finding that something is missing is "*a specifically modified horizon of the present, of praesens*" (BPP 311 [GA 24 442]). The discovery of something as missing modifies "*praesens* into *absens*, [...] presence into absence." *Absens* "has the character of negativity, of the not, of not-presencing ..." (BPP 311 [GA 24 442, 443]). It is through this privation of *praesens* that it becomes visible as the condition "on the basis of which the specific presence of the ready-to-hand [*Zuhandenen*], in distinction, say, from what is merely at hand, present-at-hand [*Vorhandenem*], becomes antecedently intelligible" (BPP 309 [GA 24 440]).

Several points must be noted here. First, the analyses presuppose the ontological difference in the narrower sense as the distinction between beings and their being. For *praesens* is the understanding of the *being* of ready-to-hand *beings* and this understanding of being can itself be disordered by the beings *themselves* that are factically present in Dasein's environment. In other words, beings are not reducible to a prior horizon of understanding but this latter can be modified by "a disturbance which *proceeds from the being itself with which we are dealing*" (BPP 309 [GA 24 440], my emphasis). Any schematic pre-designation of the being of beings occurs within the limits of facticity and is subject to modification by factical beings or events that lie outside of this horizon. For a prior horizon of meaningfulness can be disturbed not only by factical beings themselves but it can also collapse entirely as in anxiety, which reveals beings as a whole, and not just particular factical beings, as other to Dasein's understanding. A first outstanding task that becomes apparent here, then, is the thematization of *facticity* and showing how the *ontological difference*, wherein beings and the understanding of being are given as belonging together but non-identical, can be disclosed to or carried out by Dasein (BPP 120–1, 319–20 [GA 24 170–1, 454–5]).

Second, the three problems against which Heidegger's analysis runs up—(1) the origin of the "not," (2) the finitude of time, and (3) the relation between time and "nothingness"—do not so much signal a fatal weakness that led to the abandonment of the project of fundamental ontology. Rather, they are a threefold index of the need for the turn to facticity. *Praesens* is the *temporale* condition for concernful dealings with the ready-to-hand. In being so concerned, Dasein is already absorbed in a possibility of its being and is oriented to a specific "towards which" that has *not yet* been attained. This "not yet" is constitutive of everyday concern and it is indicative of Dasein's finite, *futural* temporality. Further, the methodological prescription that "everything positive becomes particularly clear when seen from the side of the privative" (BPP 309 [GA 24 439]) is a further index of finitude of Dasein's temporality. Dasein is also finite in the sense of being *thrown* into the midst of beings other than itself. This finitude is revealed in the withdrawal of the possible in *anxiety* when Dasein is brought before the "nothing" of its being-in-the-world, brought back to its factical being in the midst of beings as a whole.

Third, as should be clear from the above analysis, the traditional conception of the always already or the *a priori* has its existential origin in dealings with the ready-to-hand and it presupposes *praesens* as the (derivative) horizon of its meaningfulness. This is the point Heidegger is making in the final hours of the lecture course: The *a priori* "is patently a time-determination" and must be investigated in terms of its temporality (BPP 324–5 [GA 24 461]). These points are especially important for understanding why the transition to the metaphysics of Dasein is entailed by the project of fundamental ontology.

3 Time and Concept Formation in Heidegger's Interpretation of Kant

The implications of these claims for ontological concept formation are pursued in Heidegger's 1927–8 lecture course *Phenomenological Interpretation of Kant's Critique of Pure Reason*. On Heidegger's interpretation, at the heart of the *Critique of Pure Reason* is a tension between two modes of temporality, between a derivative and an original productivity of time. Heidegger claims that while Kant's indebtedness to the logico-metaphysical tradition prevents him from thematizing the latter, it nonetheless shows itself at key moments in the first *Critique*: "Kant, for the first time, came upon this primordial productivity of the 'subject'" and this constitutes "the first moment in the history of philosophy in which metaphysics endeavored to liberate itself from logic" (MFL 210–11 [GA 26 272], cf. H. 23–4). This project of developing a metaphysics freed from logic—the "metaphysics of Dasein" in Heidegger's terms—entails developing the "original and authentic concept-formation [*ursprüngliche und eigentliche Begriffsbildung*]" particular to this undertaking (KPM 78 [GA 3 110]). Such a concept formation is one in which temporality does not follow and accord with *a priori* logical forms of unity but rather in which *a priori* concepts must follow and be in accordance with the unity specific to temporality.

The problem of the *a priori* and concept formation coalesce in the 1927–8 lecture course *Phenomenological Interpretation of Kant's Critique of Pure Reason*. This course (1) criticizes the intertwinement of the transcendental with the logical in Kant's first *Critique* with a view to unveiling the time as an ultimate, but unthematized enabling condition, (2) argues that the conceptualizing of temporality as *a priori* is of a different order to that which belongs to the logico-transcendental determination of the *a priori* conditions for object relatedness, (3) thereby also calls into question the priority of the understanding over facticity, and (4) understands the first *Critique* as exhibiting a tension between a derivative and an original temporal productivity. In other words, in this lecture course we find a sustained attempt to show how the Kantian understanding of the transcendental presupposes Dasein's transcendence and find crucial indications for a phenomenological thematization of the *a priori* and for what Heidegger describes as the "original and authentic concept-formation as such" (KPM 78 [GA 3 110]).

In what follows, I first contextualize Heidegger's Kant interpretation within some general considerations about movement and ontic and ontological productivity in his phenomenology (*(a)*). Against this background, I then draw out these considerations with respect to the temporality of concept formation, focusing largely on Heidegger's Kant interpretation of the 1927–8 lecture course (*(b)*). These will provide us with essential background to understanding subsequent developments, discussed in the chapters that follow, concerning the *a priori*, concept formation, and temporality as well as concerning Heidegger's politics.

(a) Movement and Ontic and Ontological Productivity

In interpreting Heidegger's 1927–8 lecture course on Kant's first *Critique*, I will be guided by two theses. The first is the claim that what is essential to the phenomenological investigation of *Being and Time* is not so much its results but its movement character. The problem of movement in an originary sense emerges at numerous points in *Being and Time*, for instance in the claim as to the circularity of the investigation, in the *Kehre* from Dasein's understanding of being to its finding itself in the midst of beings, and in the accounts of truth and historicity. This movement, as was argued in the previous chapter, concerns the relatedness back and forth between facticity and projection. Second and closely connected with this, Heidegger's interpretation of Kant problematizes the priority accorded to the understanding over facticity. For Heidegger aims to retrieve a sense of the *a priori* that encompasses Dasein's facticity (H. 229). A reoccurring theme of the 1927–8 lecture course is the implicit primordial strife between facticity and projection.

The problem of movement and the question of the transcendental are also intimately related. Heidegger contends that Kant had seen that motion is reducible neither to the logical forms of thought nor to the forms of intuition alone but "'unites' 'both elements of space and time'" (A 41, B 58) and further recognizes the phenomena of "'motion as an act of the subject'" (B 155, cf.

B 250 and A 404f.)." However, Kant's logico-transcendental investigation of the conditions for object-relatedness obscures or covers over this fundamental "presupposition" of movement, hence Heidegger's claims that what must be done is to bring into view that "motion in an original sense is the presupposition [*Voraussetzung*] for time as Kant understands time" (PIK 97–9 [GA 25 141–4]).

It is in the phenomenon of production, more specifically the aforementioned distinction between ontic productivity and "the peculiar [*eigentümliche*] productivity intrinsic to temporality" (MFL 210 [GA 26 272]), that we can see the connection between the problem of motion and the temporal critique of Kantian philosophy. Both these forms of productivity stand, on Heidegger's interpretation, in an uneasy tension in the *Critique of Pure Reason*. On the one hand, the Kantian conception of the *a priori* moves within the horizon of "the ancient ontological difference ὕλη-εἶδος" which itself comes forth from "the *productive horizon*" (KPM 178 [GA 3 254]). On the other hand, implicit in the *Critique of Pure Reason* and especially in Kant's account of the transcendental imagination, is an attempt to free metaphysics from logic, to bring to light the movement of Dasein's transcendence. Yet this liberation is only partial and, in Heidegger's view, ultimately unsuccessful. (MFL 210–11 [GA 26 272], cf. H. 23–4).

The implicit drama of the *Critique of Pure Reason* is thus, on Heidegger's reading, the tension between these two modes of temporality, between a derivative and an original productivity of time. This problematic runs throughout the lecture course of the winter of 1927–8. Heidegger claims that the intertwinement of the logical and the transcendental in Kant's work constantly circles around the problem of the temporality of concept formation (PIK 116, cf. 53, 64, 123 [GA 25 170, cf. 78, 93, 180]). His interpretation of the first *Critique* seeks to show that the sense in which temporality is *a priori* is more fundamental than the *a priori* conditions for object relatedness, that it moves or takes place on a more basic level. What is at issue is a tension between two senses of temporal productivity, one derivative and one original, and the attempt to bring out an implicit understanding of transcendence that underlies Kant's conception of the transcendental.[42]

By spelling out the relation between the transcendental and the logical and examining the deleterious efforts of the alleged pre-eminence of the logical in the first *Critique*, it becomes clear how and why this problem is bound up with Heidegger's problematization of the temporal conditions of the Kantian *a priori*. The focus of Heidegger's interpretation lies on the production of concepts, specifically of *a priori* concepts, and of showing how it differs from ontic productivity. In other words, at the heart of this lecture course is the problem of "mak[ing] the possibility of concept formation ontologically intelligible" (H. 349), which had originally been reserved for Division III, Chapter 2 of *Being and Time*. In the following subsection I do not make an attempt at an exhaustive critical examination of Heidegger's reading of Kant in this period nor to defend it as a plausible interpretation. Instead, in accordance with my aim of drawing out the implications of this interpretation for Heidegger's own philosophy, I will focus on the tension between these two types of temporal productivity.

(b) *Ontic and Ontological Subsumption in Heidegger's Interpretation of the* Critique of Pure Reason

Heidegger makes two general criticisms of Kant's position that are relevant to the present context. First, although Kant aims to lay the foundation for metaphysics as "the science of beings," he equates "beings with what is present-at-hand [*Vorhandenen*]" thus meaning "his posing of the problem suffers a significant contraction [*Verengung*]" (PIK 30 [GA 25 44], translation modified). Second, Kant's focus in determining the *a priori* principles of this regional ontological understanding of being is on pure reason, as a human faculty. Because "reason as well as understanding is a *faculty of concepts*," "*a priori* knowledge means knowledge gained from concepts; it is a knowledge which the 'thinking I' achieves by itself and in advance, without the assistance of experience" (PIK [GA 25 41]). This closes off the dimension of facticity or of the manifestation of the ontic totality of beings (MFL 164 [GA 26 210], H.144–5). Kant "misconstru[es] the primary transcendence" because he "conceives thinking as more originally *a priori* than intuition instead of taking intuition—time—as *a priori* over against thinking." (PIK 168 [GA 25 247]).[43]

The unity that belongs to empirical concepts is not given in the sensible manifold itself but is the result of a *conceiving*, an activity of thinking as a spontaneous power.[44] When Kant speaks of concepts being made or "brought about [*gemacht*],"[45] this refers, on Heidegger's interpretation, to a type of production: "'Brought about' in the sense of *gemacht* means: made, shaped, engendered, produced ['*Gemacht*' *meint*: '*gebildet, erzeugt*']" (PIK 156 [GA 25 228]). This process has three interrelated structural moments: reflection, comparison, and abstraction. Of the three, reflection has the key role on Heidegger's reading: it is the unthematic bringing into view of that unity wherein objects can be seen as agreeing or having a something in common. While the *content* or *matter* of an empirical concept is given in experience, the *form* of its unity "does not already exist in the individuals who make up the many of the objects" but is "made transparent in individual objects and first [...] brought into view and held therein" by the activity of thinking (PIK 157 [GA 25 230]). By looking in advance toward ways in which the objects given can agree, this view looks toward bringing out what is common to the manifold.

As the term "rendering transparent" suggests, this procedure is analytic: It does not introduce any new content to the given but simply makes visible a unity wherein the given plurality of different particulars can be seen as agreeing. Only in the light of this looking toward a form of agreement can objects be compared and their differences noted and abstracted. The concept is a "*product* [Gebilde] of thinking" (PIK 156 [GA 25 229], cf. BPP 106 [149–50]) in the sense that agreement or generality is brought out in the particulars given, these latter are given to a look that seeks unity among them. What this process shares with the account of productive comportment outlined in *Being and Time* and *The Basic Problems of Phenomenology* is the implicit looking back to forms of unity that are already there. Such conceptualizing temporalizes itself as a retention which awaits (cf. KPM 105–09 [GA 3 149–55]).

However, while in empirical subsumption, the content of the concept—greenness, tree-ness, animality for instance—is homogenous with the content of that which is subsumed, in ontological subsumption which concerns *a priori* concepts or categories, the problem is precisely the non-homogeneity of the content of these concepts—causality, substantiality, reciprocity, for example—with that which is subsumed under them. Neither the form nor the content of these categories is given in the pure sensible manifold itself. Heidegger sees the difference between the two ways of bringing forth concepts as revealed in Kant's text in the distinction between the process of bringing particulars "*under* [unter]" concepts in empirical concept formation, wherein sensible representations, which provide the content of the concept, are seen in terms of pre-given forms of unity, and the bringing of the manifold of sensibility "*to* [auf]" concepts in temporal synthesis that allows *a priori* categories to refer to sensibility and thus to have meaning (A 78–9, B 104, my emphasis, cf. PIK 194 [GA 25 285–86], KPM 44–5, 77–80 [GA 3 62–3, 108–13]).

In the latter, the "original and authentic concept-formation [*Begriffsbildung*] as such" (KPM 78 [GA 3 110]), the schematizing action of the transcendental imagination [*Einbildungskraft*] plays the crucial role. The imagination has the function of representing *a priori* concepts in pure sensibility. It carries out a pure temporal synthesis that provides both a pure image [*Bild*] of the category in time, a schema, while at the same time providing the rule for applying this concept within experience. For example, the schema of substance is "the persistence of the real in time, i.e., the representation of the real as a substratum of empirical time determination in general, which therefore endures while everything else changes," that of causality is "the real upon which, whenever it is posited, something always follows" and that of community or the reciprocal causality of substances with regard to their accidents is the "simultaneity of the determinations of the one [of their accidents] with regard to another" (A 144, B 183-4). These act as criteria or norms for judging what does and does not count as substance, a causal relation, or reciprocal interaction. The essential point here, however, is that the categories are realized in terms of temporal predicates—permanence, succession, and simultaneity in the above examples—and this allows them to be meaningful to us.

This means that on the one hand the understanding is *ontically* the master of the action of the transcendental imagination. Schematizing is in this sense a logical operation in which a pure form or category of the understanding is realized in pure sensibility. The understanding's *a priori* forms of unity underlie and guide the imagination's temporal synthesis. On the other hand, Heidegger claims that the *ontological* dependence of the understanding on intuition lies in the fact that the origin of these *a priori* concepts cannot lie in the understanding alone because they must refer essentially to time as the condition for their showing themselves and having significance for us. The realization of these *a priori* forms of unity must look toward time as the "horizon wherein *all* empirical objects, *all* appearances are viewed *in advance*" (PIK 172 [GA 25 252-3], last emphasis mine).[46] The claim as to the priority of time over the *a priori* forms of unity lies in what Heidegger in *Being and Time* calls "the principle *a potiori fit denominatio*" (H. 329): Time can be what it is without the logical forms of unity, but these forms of unity can only be realized within the horizon of time.

It is precisely at this point that we can see an inversion or a turnaround with respect to the priority of the understanding. For in order to refer essentially to time, the imagination does not look first to the *a priori* forms of unity but to *time* as that within which the forms of thinking can be realized (A 147, B 187). The bringing forth of pure sensible categories is a secondary process that follows this prior taking into view of the horizon of time. This horizon is the *a priori* or enabling condition for the bringing forth of the categories. As the *Metaphysical Foundations of Logic* puts it, "prior to every possible 'prior to' is time!" (MFL, 146 [GA 26, 184-5]).

Standing at the center of Heidegger's interpretation is a temporal productivity in which the understanding no longer has a clear ascendency or priority but in which the "battle that surges back and forth, without a clear outcome" between the transcendental imagination and understanding "for priority as the basic source of knowledge" (PIK 198). When Heidegger identifies the transcendental schematism as "the original and authentic concept-formation as such" (KPM 78 [GA 3 110]), what must be heeded therein is the partial inversion or turnaround in the manner of production of concepts whereby the priority of the understanding becomes displaced. It is for this reason that Kant is accorded such a centrality in Heidegger's reading of the history of philosophy—an original temporal productivity comes into view in the first *Critique* which is then concealed by the logical forms of unification.

In the penultimate section of *Kant and the Problem of Metaphysics*, Heidegger inscribes Kantian forms of pure thinking within a tradition where "the ontological interpretation of the what-being of the being [that is] expressed in the τὸ τί εἶναι," of the "what always already was," contains "the moment of constant presence."[47] Yet the first *Critique* also problematizes this understanding because the type of productivity unveiled in the transcendental schematism shows that the bringing forth of "the always already was" can only take place in the light of an advance looking toward the horizon of time. It must be remembered that "time" in this context means the formal condition, always already given, for *one particular way* of encountering entities, that is, within the horizon of everydayness. The pure forms of intuition of the transcendental aesthetic are that "in which 'all the manifold of appearances is intuited in certain relations'" and appearances are "things encountered in daily life [*alltäglich begegnende Dinge*]" (PIK 70, 73 [GA 25 101, 106]). This is not, on Heidegger's account, the sole or the most original mode of the temporalization of temporality. Kant's achievement is thus to have indicated the question of "the nature of previousness" or of a more original sense of the *a priori*, of allowing this to "recur as an intensified problem" (KPM 168–9 [GA 3 240–41]). What is needed is a "'going back'" to possibilities of temporalization "whereby what has hitherto been known as the transcendental power of imagination is broken up into more original 'possibilities' so that by itself the designation 'power of imagination' becomes inadequate" (KPM 98 [GA 3 40]).

As we saw, Heidegger had himself run up against the problem of "the nature of previousness" in *The Basic Problems of Phenomenology*. Yet Heidegger's interpretation of Kant gives important clues as to how it is to be tackled. First, his reading emphasizes that forms of understanding cannot be said to be always already there but are only realized or brought forth because they essentially refer to the horizon of time (PIK 191–4 [GA 25 285–7], cf. A 147, B 187). Further, thinking is not pure spontaneity but dependent on the receptivity of pure intuition. In Heidegger's terms, it is the interplay and movement between facticity and projection that opens up the horizonal leeway or play-space [*Spielraum*] within which the forms of the understanding are able to have significance. This receptivity-spontaneous structure is middle-voiced, resting neither on the activity of thinking nor on sensible receptivity. Finally, Heidegger speaks of "more original 'possibilities'" in the plural. Thematizing the horizon of time also means keeping in view the different possibilities of temporalization. Heidegger's own concepts are characterized by their disunity as much as their unity, their having a multi-dimensionality that encompasses having-been, the future and making present without subsuming them under a form of unity.

These claims provide the essential context for understanding Heidegger's frequent use of Kantian language, mostly especially for his references to the horizonal schema that belong to the different ecstases of temporality. For in Kant schematizing is the result of the transcendental power of imagination and is a logical operation in the sense that it realizes the categories, makes them meaningful, within time as the form of our intuition. This forming, *Bilden*, of the categories in time by the transcendental imagination [*Einbildungskraft*] presupposes having previously looked toward the more original *a priori* of time. However, the "forming out [*Ausbildung*] of ontological inquiry in general lies in the bringing forth or production [*Herausstellung*] of Dasein's temporality" (BPP 327 [GA 24 465], translation modified). The concept formation [*Begriffsbildung*] that belongs to this inquiry is not guided by the understanding's forms of unity, is decidedly not a logical operation, and opens onto more original possibilities of temporalization than those of everyday concern or the determination of the objects of knowledge. This is crucial to understanding why Heidegger's critique of the priority of logic in metaphysics is not an unreflective irrationalism and to seeing how he develops a metaphysics based on the primal fact of Dasein's transcendence.

Heidegger's engagement with Kant, and *Kant and the Problem of Metaphysics* especially, is also an exercise in historical retrieval. Kant is both to provide testimony to the project of fundamental ontology and the metaphysics of Dasein and at the same time is among the historical pre-conditions for this undertaking. This act of historical retrieval, what Heidegger calls the movement of historicizing, presupposes a return to the possibilities opened up by the historical world. In *Being and Time* authenticity both conditions an authentic access to the historical past and lets the historical past speak to Dasein, lets it retrieve "the quiet force [*Kraft*] of the possible" (H. 394). Kant shrinks back before the basic possiblities of the temporalization of temporality, that is to say, from temporality in its historical occurrence, from the movement of historicizing. If the transcendental imagination is, as Heidegger repeatedly insists, the *root* of sensibility and understanding, it is itself "*heimatlos*," so not simply "homeless" but without a homeland and perhaps, given Heidegger's insistence on its being a root, without a native soil (KPM 95 [GA 3 136]). For essential to Dasein's authenticity is a taking upon itself of a given history, within a community and among a people (H. 384–5). The political implications of these claims will be discussed in Chapter 6.

Conclusion

If Heidegger does not take over the traditional conception of the *a priori*, then what understanding does he himself have of this term? Clearly, an account of this is wanting. Yet in the previous chapter, we were able to detect some features that it must have. For one, *a priori* ontological conditions do not have a simple priority over the ontic and the factically given but constantly imply these. Heidegger's existential *a priori* must have a factical and ontic character, including the facticity of Dasein's own being, of history, and of nature in the widest sense. Further, we have also seen that the *a priori* is characterized by an essential multi-dimensionality because of the different, co-implying senses of the always already that characterized different temporal ecstases.

This means that we find once again in this context a complex relation between condition and conditioned. While Heidegger does indeed refer to seeking the *a priori* ontological conditions of the particular sciences and their presupposed regional ontologies, this can in no way be seen as a foundational relationship between ontological conditions and the ontic conditioned for the very disclosure of ontological conditions has itself ontic conditions. Heidegger in fact signals this in *The Basic Problems of Phenomenology*, saying that "*the illumination of the meaning of being* and of *the horizon of the understanding*" must be regarded as "preparatory" and subject to a later repetition in an inquiry which includes both "the question of the being of beings and the being of the different regions of being" (BPP 224 [GA 24 319], cf. BPP 24 [GA 24 33]).

The sense in which the understanding of being is *a priori*, however, as well as the sense in which beings as a whole are prior to Dasein, remains at this stage of the investigation indeterminate. What must be explored are the conditions for the metaphysical recollection of the understanding of being, a recollection that is affective rather than intellectualistic in character and in which we are brought before the ontological difference, the difference between being and beings. We will thus have to explore the double sense of the prior, that both being and beings are somehow earlier than Dasein but "what is prior thus belongs neither to the order of conceptualization nor to the order of being present-at-hand [*des Vorhandenseins*]," it is neither of the order of the understanding nor of the extant, neither logically nor ontically prior (MFL 146 [GA 26 184–5]). Rather the temporal movement that encompasses both of these aspects and which allows them to emerge in their difference lies at the root of the problem of the *a priori*. After 1927, the themes of the return to facticity, the world entry of beings and the metontological, ontical conditions of fundamental ontology assume central significance in Heidegger's thinking. We will explore these themes in the following chapters.

Notes

1 See GA 14 123–6 and his letter to Karl Löwith of August 20, 1927 in Löwith, "Two Letters," 242 and "Drei Briefe Martin Heideggers an Karl Löwith" 27–37.

2 I broached some of these issues in a preliminary way in two earlier papers: Aengus Daly, "Zeitlichkeit und Geburt in Heideggers Auslegung der mythischen Umwelt" in *Die Lebensphilosophie zwischen Frankreich und Deutschland/La philosophie de la vie entre la France et l'Allemagne*, eds. Agard, O., Hartung, G., Koenig, H. (Deutschland: Ergon-Verlag, 2018), 267–78 and "Heidegger's Metaphysics of Objects: A Reply to Graham Harman" in *Phänomenologie und spekulativer Realismus/Phenomenology and Speculative Realism/Phénoménologie et réalisme spéculatif*, eds. Ferrer, G., Gourdain, S., Garrera-Tolbert, N. and Schnell, A. (Würzburg: Königshausen & Neumann, 2022), 228–38.

3 H. 85.

4 "Im selben Absatz ist die Rede von der 'vorgängigen Freigaben'—nämlich (allgemein gesprochen) des Seins für die mögliche Offenbarkeit von Seiendem. 'Vorgängig' in diesem ontologischen Sinne heißt lat. *a priori*, griechisch πρότερον τῇ, Aristot., *Physik*, A 1; noch deutlicher: *Metaphysik*, E 1025 b 29 τὸ τί ἦν εἶναι 'das was schon war-sein', 'das jeweils schon voraus Wesende', das Gewesen, das Perfekt. Das griechische Verbum εἶναι kennt keine Perfektform; diese wird hier im

ἦν εἶναι genannt. Nicht ein ontisch Vergangenes, sondern das jeweils Frühere, auf das wir *zurück*verwiesen werden bei der Frage nach dem Seienden als solchen; statt apriorisches Perfekt könnte es auch heißen: ontologisches oder transzendentales Perfekt (vgl. Kants Lehre vom Schematismus)." I have here used the translation in Stambaugh and Schmidt (2010) 83. However, I have retained "having been" for "*das Gewesen*" (Stambaugh and Schmidt have "what has been").

5   See also Golob, *Heidegger on Concepts, Freedom and Normativity*, 70–155 for a lucid discussion for these passages. Unlike Golob, I argue this is precisely the conception of the *a priori* Heidegger subjects to a temporal critique. See section 2 below for a discussion of Golob on this point.

6   In the final section of this chapter, we will see how these theses bear on Heidegger's phenomenological interpretation of Kant.

7   John Haugeland summarizes this reversal nicely: "… if we consider *seeing* a pot, then the pot itself must already have its form before the look of it can be taken in by the viewer; so *morphe* is prior to *eidos*. But if we consider, instead, *making* a pot, then the potter must *already* have the look in mind, to guide him in giving the requisite form to the clay; hence, the resulting *morphe* itself is grounded in that prior *eidos*." See Haugeland, "Letting Be" in *Transcendental Heidegger,* ed. Steven Crowell and Jeff Malpas (Stanford: Stanford University Press, 2007), 93–103, here 97. In **2.** *(b)* I argue that this kind of letting be must be understood in terms of two more fundamental ways of letting be.

8   BPP 106 [GA 24 150].

9   A footnote toward the end of *Being and Time* indicates that the distinction between the finite and the infinite is not to be equated with this distinction between the temporal and the atemporal. It claims that further phenomenological investigation might unveil "a more primordial temporality which is 'infinite'" on which basis "God's eternity can be 'constructed'" (H. 427, xiii.). See Chapters 3 and 4 for a discussion of the temporality of this "infinity."

10 BPP 207 [GA 24 150], cf. H. 26.

11 This is not to be understood as the work of a transcendental demiurge but as bringing forth the norms or standards for what counts as substance, a causal relation, and so forth.

12 See for example Kisiel, "The Mathematical and the Hermeneutical," 109–20; his *The Genesis of Heidegger's Being and Time*, 392–93, 402, 404, 509; Golob, *Heidegger on Concepts, Freedom and Normativity*, 84, 107–13; Engelland, *Heidegger's Shadow*, 175–76; Crowell, *Normativity and Phenomenology in Husserl and Heidegger*, 10 and his "Facticity and Transcendental Philosophy"; Sheehan, *Making Sense of Heidegger*, 171–73, Sheehan, "Heidegger's New Aspect: On *In-Sein, Zeitlichkeit*, and *The Genesis of 'Being and Time*,'" 219, 217 and his *Making Sense of Heidegger*, 171–73, See Chapter 5 for a discussion of Crowell's account.

13 Engelland, *Heidegger's Shadow*, 176.
14 Engelland, *Heidegger's Shadow*, 206.
15 Engelland, *Heidegger's Shadow*, 20, 213.
16 Engelland, *Heidegger's Shadow*, 208, cf. 2.
17 BPP 286 [GA 24 405].
18 Engelland, *Heidegger's Shadow*, 176, my emphasis. We will see in Chapters 5 and 6 that Heidegger's understanding of this passage from the Republic has an important political dimension.
19 Engelland, *Heidegger's Shadow*, 175.
20 Engelland, *Heidegger's Shadow*, 175.
21 Golob, *Heidegger on Concepts, Freedom and Normativity*, 117–23.
22 Golob, *Heidegger on Concepts, Freedom and Normativity*, 112–13.
23 Golob, *Heidegger on Concepts, Freedom and Normativity*, 109–13.
24 Golob, *Heidegger on Concepts, Freedom and Normativity*, 108–9, 115–6.
25 Golob, *Heidegger on Concepts, Freedom and Normativity*, 141, 173.
26 Golob, *Heidegger on Concepts, Freedom and Normativity*, 144.
27 Golob, *Heidegger on Concepts, Freedom and Normativity*, 141.
28 Golob, *Heidegger on Concepts, Freedom and Normativity*, 175, cf. 141, 144. Golob sees Heidegger's reading of Kant, which interprets substance in terms of temporality, as going in the direction of such a schema.
29 In connection with this fallen letting-be, see the *Unterlassung* of idle talk ("thus idle talk is really, in accordance with its omission [*Unterlassung*] of a return to the soil of what is talked about, a closing off" (H. 169, my translation)) and the *Sichüberlassen* of curiosity ("the care of this seeing goes not towards grasping and to being knowingly in the truth, but to possibilities of leaving the self over to the world [*Möglichkeiten des Sichüberlassens an die Welt*]" (H. 172, my translation)).
30 Correlated with this, Heidegger's account of Dasein's transcendence in the late 1920s is not voluntaristic for fundamental moods such as anxiety are not a matter of Dasein's choice. The recollection involved in this type of "transcendentalism," then, is not intellectualistic, but affective. This alreadiness has a different temporal basis to that of *mathesis* and a different mode of givenness. Further, the alleged voluntarism of *Being and Time* must be read together with the works of the metaphysical period that emphasize the event character of Dasein's being brought before its facticity. In other words, there is already a bilateral movement at the heart of the transcendentalism of *Being and Time*. Engelland does not distinguish between the fundamental ontological and the metaphysical periods of Heidegger's work. See Engelland, *Heidegger's Shadow*, 86.
31 Engelland, *Heidegger's Shadow*, 176, my emphasis.
32 See Sheehan, *Making Sense of Heidegger*, 205 and Golob, *Heidegger on Concepts, Freedom and Normativity*, 144.

33 See Grondin, *Le tourant dans la pensée de Martin Heidegger*; Sheehan, "'Time and being', 1925-7," 29-67; Dahlstrom, "The End of Fundamental Ontology," 83-103.

34 Grondin, *Le tourant dans la pensée de Martin Heidegger*, 82-3 and BPP 308, 311 [GA 24 437, 442-3].

35 This reading accords with Heidegger's remark that: "the *temporale* analysis is *at the same time* [*zugleich*] the turn [*Kehre*], where ontology itself expressly runs back [*zurückläuft*] into the metaphysical-ontic in which it always implicitly remains" (MFL 158 [GA 26 201] translation modified).

36 As we will see in the following chapter, the term "ontological difference" has three different interrelated senses, once again exhibiting the multiplicity that characterizes Heidegger's concepts in this period. The term "ontological difference" is used in the first sense in this paragraph. In this work, I generally use the term in the second sense unless otherwise stated.

37 Although in his 1936 critique of *Being and Time* Heidegger does repeatedly criticize the concern with conditions of the possibility in *Being and Time*, he does not so much claim the analysis is false as rather that the problem of the understanding of being is both solved—in that the condition for one mode of understanding being, and that which was previously predominant in philosophy, is disclosed—and surpassed (GA 82 32-9, 133-5). However, given the need to treat Heidegger's later self-interpretations with caution, I base the argument in what follows in Heidegger's texts from the late 1920s.

38 Cf. GA 27 209-12, 394.

39 This is also operative in *Being and Time*, for example in the logic of failure governing the analyses of *Being and Time*: The failure of equipment discloses the everyday social world as the precondition of concern, the failure of the everyday world in anxiety discloses the sheer that-it-is of Dasein's throwness and of Dasein's taking over its ownmost finitude. The analyses of death, conscience, and historicity proceed through a phenomenological variation in which the everyday senses of these phenomena are shown to be insufficient.

40 Note that the translations of this term and others used in this text have been modified.

41 Grondin, *Le tourant dans la pensée de Martin Heidegger*, 82: "*L'étant-á-la-portée-de-la-main, défini par la disponibilité, tombe sous le sens quand il devient indisponible.*"

42 This tension between a derivative and an original temporal productivity is not the same as the strife or back and forth movement between the understanding and facticity.

43 This criticism deepens a point already made in *Being and Time*: To understand "nature ontologico-categorically" is to overlook to how nature becomes accessible in terms of the world (H. 65, cf. H. 63, 145 and MFL 164-5, 194-5 [GA 26 210, 251-2], PM 370 note 59 [GA9 155 note 55]). In this lecture course Heidegger

again refers to the mythical world as providing indications for this understanding of nature: "the myths of nature contain a history of this struggle" and are "interpretations of an original comportment towards nature" and show that "we do not reveal nature in its might and power by reflecting on it, but by struggling against it and by dominating it." (PIK 15 [GA 25 21]). While mythical existence seeks to dominate the overwhelming power of nature by identifying with it, the philosophical stance recognizes that powerless before nature is metaphysical and can never be overcome (see MFL 215 [GA 26 279]).

44 Hence Heidegger emphasizes the distinction between conceptual unity in this sense and the "unity of the whole against the parts" of space and time (PIK 155 [GA 25 228]). The key problem that will emerge in the context of Heidegger's investigation is how to bring forth and conceive time in its originality. See section 3, below.
45 Heidegger refers here to Kant's *Logic* §1 note 1 and *Logic*, §4.
46 See the analyses in Dietmar Köhler, *Martin Heidegger: Die Schematisierung des Seinssinnes als Thematik des dritten Abscnhitts von "Sein und Zeit"* (Bonn: Bouvier Verlag, 1993), 57–61. He also points out that the actions of abstraction and comparison in empirical concept formation, because they are applied to empirical *objects*, presuppose the schematism.
47 This point is also emphasized by Köhler, *Martin Heidegger*, 120–2.

3

Metaphysics and the Turn to the Origin

The previous chapters contended that the turn to the origin, to facticity is already implicit in *Being and Time*, especially in the accounts of the movement of temporality and of the relation between history and nature. And *The Basic Problems of Phenomenology*, supposedly the highwater mark of the fundamental ontological project, in fact explicitly states that it is necessary to move beyond this project and toward a more original problematic:

> "… it is requisite that the Dasein be subjected to a *preparatory ontological investigation* which would provide the foundation for all further inquiry, which includes the question of the being of beings in general and the being of the different regions of being. We therefore call the preparatory ontological analytic of Dasein *fundamental ontology*. It is preparatory because it *alone first leads to the illumination of the meaning of being* and of *the horizon of the understanding of being*. It can only be preparatory because it aims only to establish the foundation for a radical ontology. Therefore, after the exposition of the meaning of being and the horizon of ontology, it has to be repeated [*wiederholt*] on a higher level."[1]

While Heidegger does not speak of metaphysics here, he refers to working out "a radical ontology" and "the being of the different regions of being." The table of contents for this course also testifies to Heidegger's (there unrealized) intention to a return to the ontic foundation of ontology (BPP 24 [GA 24 33]) and a later passage announced the (also unrealized) intention of working out a more original conception of transcendence (BPP 323 [GA 24 460]).

In this chapter, I will argue that we can gain a good understanding of what the repetition of fundamental ontology on a higher level means by looking at lecture "What Is Metaphysics?" Heidegger described this lecture as giving a first insight into the formation of a problematic that had been operative in the background of *Being and Time* but without being explicitly presented there. This not only means that a metaphysical problematic was already implicit in *Being and Time* but further that making it thematic as a "living event [*lebendiges Geschehen*]" entails a transformation of the earlier work (GA 14 139).

The notion of repetition is key to the analytic progression of *Being and Time* itself: Division II repeats the analyses of understanding, attunement, falling, and discourse in Division I on the basis of Dasein's finite temporality.[2] I will argue that the repetition that takes place in the metaphysics of Dasein foregrounds the problem of Dasein's facticity. The lecture "What Is Metaphysics?"—and, the following chapter will argue, other texts from 1927–9—repeats, re-inscribes, and re-interprets the analyses of *Being and Time* in terms of the turn to facticity. This repetition not only involves the development of a temporality of thrownness but also has far-reaching implications for Heidegger's understanding of philosophical concept formation.

This chapter begins by focusing on an interpretative problem: If the metaphysical problematic was *already* operative within *Being and Time*, then why do we not find the term "metaphysics" used in a positive sense in this work at all?[3] And even if it is granted that there is a continuity between fundamental ontology and the metaphysics of Dasein and that the latter is necessitated by reasons internal to the former, it is not clear why this should be described as a *metaphysical* problematic.[4] Understanding this means first seeing how *Being and Time* raises but does not answer four closely correlated problems: (1) the existential conception of the world, (2) the independence of entities from Dasein, (3) the origins of philosophy and of existential truth, and (4) the possibility of an "infinite" theological temporality. I will then examine why these can be described as problems of metaphysics (**1.**).

The first section having provided the background to Heidegger's claim in "What Is Metaphysics?" that metaphysics belongs to "human nature" or, strictly speaking, to Dasein's temporal transcendence (PM 96 [GA 9 121]), the second section then examines how "What Is Metaphysics?" takes up and transforms key aspects of the existential analytic. In this lecture, as in *Being and Time*, the question of the nothing is broached through the event of anxiety. However, whereas the emphasis in the earlier work had fallen on Dasein's projective understanding, this lecture foregrounds Dasein's facticity. And concepts first introduced in *Being and Time* are now used to characterize the recursive movement back to Dasein's facticity, back to beings as a whole as overwhelming. Specifically, this analysis repeats and transforms the meaning of the terms assignment or reference [*Verweisung*], urge or striving [*Drang*], anxiety [*Angst*], the moment of vision [*Augenblick*], fallenness [*Verfallen*], and historicality [*Geschichtlichkeit*] (**2.**).

The third and final section broaches a problem implicit in the preceding: that of the peculiarities of philosophical discourse and conceptualization in Heidegger's work at this time. Philosophical terms are characterized by an essential multi-dimensionality whose basis lies in temporality. I argue that original modes of temporality both let the ontological difference, a technical term which is itself characterized by a plurality of interrelated senses, emerge and point toward a reconceiving of the *a priori* (**3.**).

1 Anxiety, World, and the Origin of Metaphysics

In the preceding two chapters we saw that several problems remained outstanding in *Being and Time* and *The Basic Problems of Phenomenology*: the factical ideal of Dasein, the givenness of entities as independent of Dasein, facticity, and reconceiving the *a priori* on the basis of a more original mode of temporality than that implicitly presupposed in the philosophical tradition. And while these concerns are taken up in subsequent texts, thus suggesting a continuity in the investigation, it is not clear why this continuation should be described as a *metaphysical* problematic. The difficulty becomes more pressing still when we recall that Heidegger does not use the word "metaphysics" to characterize his project in *Being and Time* nor in *The Basic Problems of Phenomenology*.[5] Why, then, maintain that Heidegger's texts from 1927 to 1929 merit the title of a "metaphysics" of any kind?

In both Heidegger's own investigation and in his reading of the philosophical tradition, the metaphysical problematic is fundamentally related to questions concerning Dasein's transcendence and the world. In a programmatic statement in §11 of *Being and Time*, Heidegger writes that the task ahead "includes a *desideratum* which philosophy has long found disturbing but has continually refused to achieve: *to work out the idea of a 'natural conception of the world'* [die Ausarbeitung der Idee eines 'natürlichen Weltbegriffes']" (H. 52). Notably when, in Division I, Chapter 3, Heidegger characterizes the sense in which the term "world" will be employed in the existential analytic, he does not refer, as might be expected, to the "ontologico-existential concept of worldhood" or "the *a priori* character of worldhood in general." Instead, "world" in the existential analytic has the more restricted "ontical sense" or "pre-ontological existentiell signification" of the "'*wherein*' a factical Dasein as such can be said to 'live'" (H. 65).[6] Hence it is not only in the philosophical tradition that the *desideratum* of working out an existential conception of the world remains unachieved but also in *Being and Time* itself.

The essay "On the Essence of Ground" suggests that this was no oversight, but rather that *Being and Time* contains only "an initial characterization of the phenomenon of world" and the intention there was a "leading over into an analysis of this phenomenon and of *preparing the transcendental problem of world*" (PM 121 note 58 [GA 9 155, note 55], my emphasis). This leading over, Heidegger explains, was the sole intent of the analysis of the everyday world in sections 14–24 of Division I, sections that, as we saw in the previous chapter, are of particular significance for understanding the existential origin and phenomenological destruction of the Kantian *a priori*. And the transcendental problem of the world is the problem of *transcendence*:

> "What has been published so far of the investigations on 'Being and Time' has no other task than that of a concrete projection unveiling *transcendence*. It is on this basis that nature can first be broached in its autonomy, as independent of the ways in which it is discovered and reckoned with in the light of Dasein's concerns (cf. §§12–83; especially §69)."[7]

The development of a fuller conception of world "is directed toward an interpretation of Dasein in its relation to beings as a whole" (PM 121 [GA 9 156]). The interpretation of the temporal constitution of being-in-the-world in *Being and Time* itself *leads over to* the problem of nature or the givenness of beings in themselves. Far from being a violent, retrospective re-interpretation of the earlier work, we can find corroboration of this claim in §69 of *Being and Time*:

> "... in what way is anything like a world possible at all? in what sense *is* the world? what does world transcend, and how does it do so? how are 'independent' ['*unabhängige*'] entities within-the-world 'connected' ['*hängt* ... '*zusammen*'] with the transcending world? To *expound* these questions *ontologically* is not to answer them. On the contrary, what such an exposition accomplishes is the clarification of those structures with regard to which the problem of transcendence must be raised—a clarification which is necessary beforehand."[8]

The problem of the independence of entities from Dasein is the problem of transcendence, of the temporal constitution of being-in-the-world. And to turn toward entities in their independence from Dasein—the cosmological sense of world—is to turn toward an origin in a double sense.

First, when Dasein understands itself and takes over its ownmost potentiality-for-being in the moment of vision, this authentic disclosedness is nothing less than "the *truth of existence*" (H. 221). Yet it is anxiety that "holds the moment of vision at the ready [*auf dem Sprung*]" (H. 344). Only in being brought back to the nothing of the world, only in being brought before the sheer presence of entities themselves, without having a grip on them, can we be ready for the emergence of an authentic potentiality-for-being (H. 343). Insofar as the turn to facticity is the condition for the possibility of the emergence of existential truth, the further investigation of this turn is an investigation of the *origin of truth*.

Second, this turn to facticity is, on Heidegger's interpretation, a return to the *origin of philosophy*. In the interpretation of curiosity, Heidegger alludes to the Platonic and Aristotelian claim that philosophy arises from wondering,[9] writing: "Curiosity has nothing to do with observing entities and marveling at them—θαυμάζειν. To be amazed and wonder to the point of not understanding is something in which it has no interest."[10] Although in this passage Heidegger is seeking to clarify the phenomenon of curiosity by contrast and negation—contrasting curiosity with what it is not with a view to bringing out what it is—it implicitly also provides a positive characterization of θαυμάζειν. Unlike curiosity, wonder abides by and is astounded by the incomprehensibility of beings in themselves, their sheer being there. And this phenomenological distinctiveness also hints at a phenomenological kinship with anxiety. In the first moment of anxiety, Dasein encounters the present-at-hand "in just *such* a way that it does *not* have any involvement *whatsoever*" (H. 343). Read in the context of *Being and Time*—and this is borne out by "What Is Metaphysics?"—wonder and θεωρία are made possible by the withdrawal of significance in anxiety and by holding to this sense of the strangeness of beings.

These considerations also bear on the project of unveiling the existential conditions for the possibility of ancient ontology, specifically for why it tends to conceive being in terms of the present-at-hand: "Why does being get 'conceived' proximally in terms of the present-at-hand *and not* in terms of the ready-to-hand, which indeed lies *closer* to us?" (H. 437). At issue here is nothing less than the problems of the origin of philosophy and of how nature becomes accessible on the basis of being-in-the-world (H. 65), which latter was to have been broached in Division III of *Being and Time* (H. 100). In Heidegger's subsequent treatment of this problem, as we will see, the origin of philosophy lies in the emergence of the ontological difference—which emergence has its condition in a specific and distinctive movement of Dasein's temporality.

An enigmatic footnote in the final chapter of *Being and Time* gives a further indication concerning this distinctive kind of temporalizing and hints at an as yet undiscussed theological dimension to Heidegger's investigation:

> "The fact that the traditional concept of "eternity" as signifying the 'standing "now"' (*nunc stans*), has been drawn from the ordinary way of understanding time and has been defined with an orientation toward 'constant' presence-at-hand, does not need to be discussed in detail. If God's eternity can be 'construed' philosophically, then it may be understood only as a more primordial temporality which is 'infinite'. Whether the way afforded by the *via negationis et eminentiae* is a possible one, remains to be seen."[11]

If we read this footnote in terms of the analysis of primordial temporality in §65, it makes very little sense. The temporality at issue in the latter is finite ("Primordial time is finite" (H. 331)) and "infinite" temporality as an endless series of nows is said to derive from this primordial finite temporality (H. 330 424, 427). The reference to the possibility of understanding the divine from out of a "more primordial" "infinite" temporality is all the more bizarre because practically all references to God and to theology in *Being and Time* are critical (see H. 48–9, 92, H. 194 iv, 275, 427). Against this background, Ben Vedder's dismissal of this footnote as a "remnant" of Heidegger's early ahistorical approach to philosophy seems warranted.[12]

But there is good reason to read this passage as anticipating a key theme of the metaphysics of Dasein, namely as a provisional indication of the temporality of thrownness in which beings become manifest in their otherness. For as we will see, this mode of temporality is itself a kind of *via negationis et eminente*: We are *deprived* of our hold on things, power*less*, *lacking* understanding in the face of what surpasses and overwhelms our understanding. We are, so to speak, "in the dark," the darkness of our facticity, the origin. We are confronted with a kind of in-finite here in the sense that the horizons of our understanding break down in the face of the overwhelming, revealing our sheer being-there in the world. Such a sense of the "infinite" as what overwhelms and surpasses our understanding is clearly distinct to the "infinity" of an endless sequence of nows.

In *Being and Time*, then, the problem of the world and of the autonomy of entities within the world is a problem of origins: of truth, of metaphysics, and of the divine. It concerns the temporal problematic of not only the turn to facticity but of the belonging together of facticity and projection. Why Heidegger characterizes this as a "metaphysics" and why he claims that such a metaphysics belongs to "human nature" become clearer in the 1928 lecture course *The Metaphysical Foundations of Logic* where he claims his investigation is a re-appropriation—that is, a repetition in the sense of taking over and transforming an inherited possibility—of the Aristotelian conception of philosophy.[13] According to the Aristotelian characterization, philosophy is πρώτη φιλοσοφία, first philosophy, the striving to "explain what it is that belongs to being as such." But it is also θεολογεῖν, the science of the highest. "Τὸ θεῖον means simply beings—the heavens: the encompassing and overpowering, that under and upon which we are thrown, that which dazzles us and takes us by surprise, the overwhelming." And "beings" does not just refer to the ontic sum of entities but to the world as that which surpasses or transcends Dasein: "θεολογεῖν is a contemplation of the κόσμος," the world or beings as a whole (MLF 10, 11 [GA 26 12, 13]).[14] Dasein's striving to explain what belongs to being as such, its desire to elucidate an original horizon of meaningfulness, is now thought explicitly together with "the encompassing and overpowering, that under and upon which we are thrown" (MLF 11 [GA 26 13]).

This twofold character of philosophy as "knowledge of being and knowledge of the overwhelming" corresponds, Heidegger claims, "to the twofold of existence and thrownness" (MLF 11 [GA 26 13]). This understanding of philosophy entails a rethinking of the preliminary conception of phenomenology (§7). It involves a deeper investigation of the enigma of motion alluded to at several points in *Being and Time* and which is inherent in the phenomenological understanding of the φαινόμενον. As middle voiced the term φαινόμενον refers to the back and forth of our modes of sighting ourselves, others, things, and ultimately to the different meanings of being. What we find in the 1928 lecture course is an attempt to think the method of phenomenology in terms of the two aspects of the movement of temporality and to think this movement in its unity.

And as we will see—and this point raises considerable complexities for the Heideggerian conception of the *a priori*—the understanding of being must be "each time sought anew." Drawing on a Hegelian formulation that is repeated in "What Is Metaphysics?," Heidegger describes this venture as a "'turned-around world [*verkehrte Welt*]'" (MFL 11 [GA 26 13], cf. PM 82 [GA 9 103]).[15] The term "*verkehrte*" not only both means "to turn around" and alludes to the "*Kehre*" to facticity, but also has the sense of going about things wrongly. The philosophical endeavor is, to the tasks and demands of the everyday order of things, a disruptive movement. It places us in question and, by moving against standards and expectations of the "they," is contrary or false. Re-inscribing the Aristotelian account of the "σοφός" in this context,[16] he claims φιλοσοφία, the love of wisdom, is characterized by a trust in and striving after "the possibility of the correct conceptual [*begrifflichen*] understanding of what is essential." This is not a prudential seizing of the opportune moment—which latter presupposes the retention of a world already significant within which one's interests are meaningful and so remains within an "if-then" schema (cf. H. 359 and 390)—but rather having eyes for "the θαυμαστά, for what arouses wonder, astonishment" (MFL 11–12 [GA 26 14]). The difficult, the astonishing, and the daemonic impel philosophizing, in other words, from the perspective of the everyday, the useless and the imprudent.

Heidegger appeals to Aristotle in characterizing his conception of metaphysics and of philosophizing not just because "in ancient thought, basic philosophical problems are intelligible in their elemental originality" but more fundamentally because his work contains "a gigantic beginning, and *as such it contains within itself a wealth of truly undeveloped and in part completely hidden possibilities*" (MFL 9 [GA 26 11], my emphasis). In other words, he is broaching a *problem* in the Aristotelian understanding of philosophy, the problem of the unity of the knowledge of being and of the world, more precisely still, he seeks what makes this unity possible. The *problem of metaphysics* is the *problem of motion*, that of how projection and thrownness are united. Rather than speaking of Heidegger's "metaphysics," it would be more accurate to speak of a "metaphysics of metaphysics," or a metaphysics that belongs to human—or Dasein's—nature.

The problem of metaphysics thus ultimately leads back to the *metaphysical essence* of Dasein, who unifies projection and thrownness in its ways of being. While projection as enabling the understanding of being was emphasized in *Being and Time* and *The Basic Problems of Phenomenology*, the investigations of the metaphysical period treat the *a priori* of facticity and the problem of the transcendence of the world. However, the metaphysical period is not solely concerned with facticity but more fundamentally with the belonging together of projection and facticity. The following sections of this chapter examine how Heidegger broaches these themes in "What Is Metaphysics?"

2 Nothingness, Negation, and the *Kehre*

Like *Being and Time*, the lecture "What Is Metaphysics?" begins with everydayness. It addresses the everyday world of the university, the community [*Gemeinschaft*] of researchers, teachers, and students whose passion [*Leidenschaft*] is science (PM 82 [GA 9 103]). Although the term *Gemeinschaft* signals a link to the analyses of *Being and Time* (cf. H. 384–5), the analyses of the lecture move in an inverse direction.[17] The accent in *Being and Time* had largely fallen on Dasein's "leaping ahead"[18] of its historical community by seizing hold of its authentic potentiality-for-being, but here Heidegger shows how such a leaping ahead presupposes turning to facticity, to what he calls in *The Metaphysical*

Foundations of Logic the "primal history [*Urgeschichte*]" of the world-entry of beings (MFL 209 [GA 26 270]).

The historical community this lecture addresses has, as Heidegger characterizes it, a free-floating understanding of itself and its undertakings. The fields of scientific research are dispersed [*Zerfallen*] into a manifold of subjects and disciplines, a division whose apparent self-evidence closes off inquiry into their factical roots, that is, the existential basis of their basic concepts (PM 82–3 [GA 9 104, cf. H. 9–11). Each science takes its lead from the governing concepts of a thematically demarcated region of being, no one science can be said to have a precedence over any of the others, "neither nature over history nor inversely [*weder die Natur vor der Geschichte noch umgekehrt*]" (PM 83 [GA 9 104], translation modified).[19]

The lecture will call into question this everydayness by raising a fundamental metaphysical question. In so doing, it seeks to retrieve metaphysics as a "living event [*lebendiges Geschehen*]" (GA 14 139, cf. PM 82 [GA 9 103]). The aforementioned understanding of the scientific enterprise, in trying to exclude what is beyond the domain of beings from its consideration, draws attention, Heidegger alleges, to the phenomenologically constitutive role of this beyond. Because scientific undertaking refers to, is guided by, and is confronted with beings themselves "and nothing besides," and "nothing further," and "beyond that, nothing" (PM 84 [GA 9 105]), it seems the nothing is both presupposed by and transcends the domain of science. If this is so, then science is characterized by a split in its essence: While dependent upon the nothing, it also turns away from this and toward beings themselves, toward the ontic, and it is concerned to give these beings the first and last word.[20] The metaphysical question, by contrast, is "How is it with the nothing?" (PM 84 [GA 94 105]) and it treats both our access to beings themselves as well as the phenomenon of the nothing.

The way Heidegger introduces the question of the nothing in its supposedly constitutive role for science gives rise to the legitimate suspicion that his initial characterization of science is loaded toward his own problematic. That Heidegger takes this determination of what science is from the French positivist Hippolyte Taine[21] does little to vouch for its phenomenological legitimacy. The reference to the nothing seems entirely superfluous: It could equally be said that scientific undertaking refers to, is guided by, and is confronted with beings themselves, full stop. Yet this introduction into the question becomes less artificial when we recall its background in *Being and Time*, which not only raised the question of the existential origin of science in Dasein's authenticity but also indicated a connection between anxiety, which is about "nothing," and facing beings in themselves in their independence of us. More than a merely verbal formula, the nothing signals the existential origin of science in a fundamental attunement (cf. H. 9–11, 363).

Yet if questioning about the nothing does not result from an arbitrary linguistic formulation, tackling this question raises a problem: Even if we grant that science presupposes the nothing, Heidegger signals that there are compelling "scientific" reasons against explicitly inquiring into it: "Interrogating the nothing—asking what and how it, the nothing, is—turns [*verkehrt*] what is interrogated into its opposite" (PM 85 [GA 9 107]). Here, as throughout the text, it is especially important to pay attention to terms related to *Kehre*. The claim is that to ask this metaphysical question is already to go wrong [*verkehrt*] because we will inevitably end up speaking about what is. In interrogating we seek the *being* of the matter interrogated, which means that the question as to what and how the *nothing is* must be in principle impossible.

Rather than taking this objection as ruling out such an inquiry as impossible at the outset, the lecture seeks to call into question these implicit ontological assumptions. These assumptions will be turned over [*umgekehrt*] in a double sense (PM 86 [GA 9 108]). First, Heidegger tries to show that the nothing is more original than the "not" and negation—and indeed that the former is the condition for the possibility of these latter. For the lecture describes a basic experience that shows that speaking of what is, of beings, does not have the existential priority that the scientific understanding imagines. Second, the aforementioned objection to the question of the nothing itself presupposes Dasein's having turned away [*Abkehr*] from the nothing (PM 92 [GA 9 116]). Overturning these assumptions means looking at how we concretely experience the nothing in anxiety.

This interrogation of the assumptions underlying the scientific objection to the question of the nothing has highly significant implications for philosophical, in contrast to scientific, concept formation. The conceptualization demanded by philosophy must be fundamentally different to that of science both as regards its form and enactment sense. Heidegger underscores the difference between scientific and philosophical conceptualization with his claim that we experience the nothing in a mood, anxiety, rather than by the logical operation of negating beings as a whole.[22] The latter presupposes an initial—and impossible—conceptual grasp of beings as a whole. As we saw previously, our being able to grasp, seize, or comprehend anything at all, be it a possibility of ourselves, a being or a region of beings, our being able to intentionally direct ourselves toward anything presupposes an attuned openness to the world (H. 137).

In everydayness we are both immersed in a given possibility while also remaining dimly aware of existing amidst beings as a whole (PM 87 [GA 9 110]). Our shadowy awareness of this split between our understanding of being and beings, like that of the split in science's essence mentioned earlier, is our unthematic, pre-conceptual awareness of the ontological difference. This difference emerges explicitly in anxiety:

> "All things and we ourselves sink into indifference. This, however, not in the sense of mere disappearance. Rather, in their very receding, things turn towards us [*kehren sie sich uns zu*]. The receding of beings as a whole, pressing in on us in anxiety [*das uns in der Angst umdrängt*], oppresses us [*bedrängt uns*]. We can get no hold on things [*Es bleibt kein Halt*]. In the slipping away of beings only this "no hold on things" comes over us and remains.
> "Anxiety makes manifest the nothing."[23]

The analysis of anxiety in "What Is Metaphysics?" has strikingly different points of emphasis to *Being and Time* (see especially §41 and §68 (b)). It uses terms, phrases, and concepts familiar to readers of the latter work in an inverted or "turned around" sense. They are taken up and understood anew from out of the dimension opened up by the temporal movement back to facticity. We can see this subtle but decisive shift in emphasis in the passage just cited: It is not so much *Dasein's* turning toward [*Hinkehr*] its facticity in anxiety that is accentuated but rather *things* turning toward us ["*kehren sie sich uns zu*"] in their inherent weirdness as they recede ["*Wegrücken*"] from our usual ways of understanding of them.

Anxiety "manifests these beings in their full but heretofore concealed strangeness as absolutely other—with regard to the nothing [*offenbart es dieses Seiende in seiner vollen, bislang verborgenen Befremdlichkeit als das schlechthin Andere—gegenüber dem Nichts*]" (PM 90 [GA 9 114] translation modified). The nothing thus *refers* to beings as a whole in a peculiar way. The notion of reference [*Verweisung*] was analyzed in Division I, Chapter Three of *Being and Time*. However, the way in which the nothing refers to beings as a whole and Dasein, for its part, lets this occur is of a quite different character to letting being involved [*Bewandenlassen*] of entities discovered within a referential totality. The nothing refers to beings as turning or slipping away *from* the referential totality of significance and indicates their being *alien* or *absolutely other* to it. The referring here is an "*abweisende Verweisung*" (GA 9 114, cf. PM 90). Beings show themselves as *having themselves turned from* their everyday significance, repulsing such significance, and in their unsettling otherness.

Although facing the strangeness of beings involves a distinctive kind of letting be, the emphasis in this lecture falls more on beings themselves than on us. It is not Dasein's drive, striving or urge [*Drang*] that is emphasized here but how beings as a whole turn toward us, how in anxiety they press in on [*umdrängt*] and oppress [*bedrängt*] us (H. 194–6, H. 345, PM 88 [GA 9 112]). This emphasis on the revelatory power of the nothing also brings out a previously hidden dimension of anxiety, resoluteness, and fallenness. *Being and Time* distinguished anxiety by claiming "the Present of anxiety is *held on to* when one brings oneself back to one's ownmost thrownness [*die Gegenwart der Angst im Sichzurückbringen auf die eigenste Geworfenheit* gehalten]" (H. 344), but in bewilderment we seek some*thing*, any*thing* to seize hold of (H. 342). In "What Is Metaphysics?" the occurrence of the nothing is discussed in its equivocality: Dasein is both "*held out* into the nothing [*Hineingehaltenheit in das Nichts*]" and it "*hold[s] itself* in the nothing [*Sich hineinhaltend in das Nichts*]."[24] It both has us in its grip and is something we let happen, overcome us. And Heidegger emphasizes this point when writing of the relations between anxiety, the *Augenblick*, and readiness:

> "Original anxiety [*Die ursprüngliche Angst*] can awaken in Dasein at any moment [*Augenblick*]. It needs no unusual event to rouse it. … It is always ready [*auf dem Sprung*], though it seldom springs, and we are snatched and left hanging."[25]

The existential analytic uses the term *Augenblick* to describe the moment of our awaking to and seizing hold of our authentic potentiality-for-being but the term here refers to when anxiety awakens and seizes hold of us.[26] And previously Heidegger had spoken of how anxiety holds the *Augenblick*, the moment of vision, at the ready, "*auf dem Sprunge*," to be seized resolutely[27] but here it is anxiety itself, the nihilator of significance, that is ready to spring [*auf dem Sprung*] at every moment [*Augenblick*] to seize Dasein.[28] These shifts in emphasis indicate the turn as a temporal movement to the sheer "that-it-is" of our facticity. Anxiety holds ready the possibility of a return to the origin.[29]

The 1929 lecture seems at first to treat the role of Dasein's fallenness, its quotidian busyness, in obscuring the nothing in much the same way as in the 1927 treatise. We read:

> "We usually lose ourselves among beings in a certain way. The more we turn toward beings in our preoccupations [*in unseren Umtreiben an das Seienden kehren*] the less we let beings as a whole slip away as such and the more we turn away from the nothing [*kehren wir uns ab von Nichts*]. Just as surely do we hasten into the public superficialities of our existence."[30]

Turning away [*abkehren*] here seems to refer, as in *Being and Time*, to *Dasein*'s turn away [*Abkehr*] from the nothing to the public world. But "What Is Metaphysics?" further stresses that Dasein's losing itself in everydayness is not simply due to its own self-evasion but is a response to the nothing's self-concealment:

> "And yet this constant if ambiguous turning away [*zweideutige Abkehr*] from the nothing accords, within certain limits, with the proper significance of the nothing. In its nihilation the nothing refers us [*verweist uns*] precisely toward beings. The nothing nihilates incessantly without our knowing of this occurrence in the manner of our everyday knowledge."[31]

In everydayness, beings do not turn toward us in their otherness, but are discovered in their place as significant. In terms of the analysis of "What Is Metaphysics?," this means that, for the most part, the nothing refers us to significant environing things by not seizing hold of us and that we generally move unwittingly within it.

We are not brought before and do not seize hold of our finitude on our own initiative but this is an event which happens to us and which we can, at best, be ready for.[32] This readiness is characterized in "What Is Metaphysics?" as readiness to let oneself into the nothing. This self-letting is nothing other than what is presupposed in the wanting-to-have-a-conscience [*Gewissenhabenwollen*] described in *Being and Time*, which was characterized by a readiness for anxiety, that is, a readiness for the withdrawal of everyday meaning. Wanting-to-have-a-conscience, seen from the recursive movement of temporality thematized in this lecture, is a readiness for the nothing and a readiness to let world entry of beings occur.

3 Metaphysics and "*die 'verkehrte Welt'*"

In the opening section, we discussed four problems left open by *Being and Time*—the problem of world and of the independence of entities from Dasein, the origin of metaphysics, and a quasi-theological understanding of temporality. How are these taken up in "What Is Metaphysics?"? Heidegger cited Hegel's claim that philosophy is, for healthy human understanding, "*die 'verkehrte Welt'*" (PM 82 [GA 9 103]), the turned around or inverted world. Anxiety overturns a "healthy" or "sound" commerce with things, it places us in question and, by moving against usual standards and expectations, goes about things wrongly [*verkehrt*].

Metaphysics begins with this disruptive movement. The origin of metaphysics, the astonishment at beings as a whole, is thus, to the understanding of everydayness, characterized by this "peculiarity [*Eigentümlichkeit*]" (GA 9 103, cf. PM 82). The peculiar temporality of anxiety [*der eigentümlichen Zeitlichkeit der Angst*] (H. 343) makes this astonishment possible. In anxiety we have no hold on our usual sense of ourselves, the world we are already in, and our approaching future. We cannot get a grip on things.[33]

The temporality of anxiety is thus *fundamentally different from that of everydayness and of a scientific directedness toward objects*. The opening of the lecture had characterized science as dominating the everyday world of the university and then sought to show how and why a scientific concern with grounds presupposes the experience of the nothing:

> "Only because the nothing is manifest in the ground of Dasein can the total strangeness of beings overwhelm us. Only when the strangeness of beings oppresses [*bedrängt*] us does it arouse and evoke wonder [*Verwunderung*]. Only on the ground of wonder—the manifestness of the nothing—does the "why?" loom before us. Only because the "why" is possible as such can we in a definite way inquire into grounds and ground things. Only because we can question and ground things is the fate [*Schicksal*] of our existence placed in the hands of the researcher.
>
> "The question of the nothing puts us, the questioners, ourselves in question. It is a metaphysical question."[34]

This passage seems to present a series of conditions, starting with the most original, the total, and unconditioned strangeness of beings,[35] and moving to what is conditioned. Yet the relation between condition and conditioned is more complex than this superficial reading would lead us to believe. The unconditioned here is the abysmal, an *Abgrund* rather than a ground. The revelation of the unconditioned is not the disclosure of a sufficient reason for a historical mode of understanding but of an original groundlessness that the search for grounds strives to close off. Further, we are only able to face the strangeness of beings against the background of and subsequent to our having already submitted to a particular historical fate and subsequent to our being caught up in the destiny of our historical world.

The relation between the abyss of anxiety and the historical world is reciprocally conditioning and exhibits an essential multi-dimensionality. Dasein is always already thrown, that is, factically in the midst of beings as a whole and it is always already ahead of itself understandingly (H. 145), that is, understanding itself in terms of possibilities that are handed down. These two senses of the "always already"—which are implicit in the discussion of Dasein's essence at the beginning of the first chapter of *Being and Time*—are not mutually exclusive but rather reciprocally conditioning. Thinking the *a priori* as a time determination means thinking it in terms of the two fundamental aspects of Dasein's temporality.

We noted earlier that Heidegger characterizes philosophy as trusting in and striving after "the possibility of the correct conceptual [*begrifflichen*] understanding of what is essential" (MFL 11–2 [GA 26 14]). Such philosophical, as distinguished from scientific, conceptualization is peculiar in demanding a vocabulary, conceptuality, and "grammar" of its own (H. 38–9, cf. H. 63, 65, 100, 349). We saw how the thematizing of the phenomenon of the nothing, which was an already implicitly operative background condition for the analyses of *Being and Time*, entails a conceptual transformation of terms and concepts used in the earlier work. The afore-discussed terminological reversals or turn arounds do *not replace or supersede* the early work but rather make explicit a *further dimension* that was already implicit therein. The turn-around brings forth a new dimension of the terms such as *Angst, Augenblick, Verweisung, Verfallen*. The multi-dimensionality of philosophical concepts means that philosophy is essentially richer or more "scientific" than science.[36] The different senses of the key terms can neither be subsumed under a common characteristic nor are they subject to a dialectical reconciliation. This conceptual multi-dimensionality reflects and is made possible by Dasein's temporal transcendence. Conceptualizing this transcendence demands rethinking philosophical concept formation on the basis of temporality (cf. H. 349)[37] for this conceptual non-identity indicates a non-identity at the heart of temporal transcendence. When this temporal movement occurs, beings as a whole explicitly emerge in their *non-identity* to our factically situated understanding of being.

'What Is Metaphysics?' and other texts in this period seek to make manifest the ontological difference, by way of reference to basic experiences and by drawing upon the language of metaphysics.[38] In these texts we find a shift away from the question of the *meaning* of being to the *difference* between being and beings. And it was deepening of the investigation that brought about this shift in focus. I see this line of interpretation as supported by Max Müller's report of Heidegger's account of the ontological difference as it was to be treated in *Being and Time*, Division III. According to Müller, the term "ontological difference" has a threefold meaning encompassing: (a) the transcendental or ontological difference in the narrower sense as the difference between beings and their being, (b) the difference between beings and their beingness and being itself, and (c) a transcendent or theological difference of God from all of the aforementioned. We note that Müller does not speak of *three differences* but of *a threefold difference*, "*eine dreifache Differenz*," thus a single difference with three distinct but co-belonging aspects.[39] The multi-dimensionality we detected in other Heideggerian concepts in this period also characterizes the ontological difference itself.

And although Müller's report refers to the unpublished Division III of *Being and Time*, we can find this threefold meaning of the ontological difference in the extant texts. The horizonal-schema of *praesens* is the enabling horizon for the ontological difference in the narrower sense (a), the difference between beings and their being. In taking an entity *as* something, for example, as useful for …, I do not explicitly distinguish the entity from its being but the ontological difference is implicitly presupposed in the "as structure": I take *this* (available entity) as *that* (kind of thing). In so doing, I do not only see it as a particular *kind* of entity (hammer, cup, chair, public transport) but more fundamentally implicitly rely on its *presence and availability*, I understand it upon the horizon of *praesens*. Heidegger's reported use of the term "transcendental" to characterize this narrower sense of the ontological difference supports this reading. As we saw, Heidegger sees the existential origin of the *a priori* perfect that characterizes the transcendental in the traditional sense in productive dealings with entities.

The ontological difference in sense (b), the difference between beings and their beingness and being itself, is made possible by "the twofold of existence and thrownness" and corresponds to the twofold character of philosophy as "knowledge of being and knowledge of the overwhelming" (MLF 11 [GA 26 13]). Heidegger speaks in a similar vein in *Being and Time* of "an idea of being in general" presupposed in both the idea of existence and the idea of the Real (beings as a whole) (H. 314). The key problem here is the nature of the unity that belongs to this temporality and whether it is capable of yielding "*an idea of being in general.*"

The third sense of the ontological difference is the "theological difference" of God from beings (c). This too is broached in *Being and Time* and subsequent texts. We saw that in *Being and Time* Heidegger had referred to a more primordial "infinite" temporality as possibly opening up a way of philosophical construing God's eternity. In the metaphysical period, this theological "infinite" temporality breaks in upon Dasein when it is confronted with the overwhelming, when beings as a whole press in upon it, surpassing its finite capacity for getting a grip on things. We can recall Heidegger's claim: "Τὸ θεῖον means simply beings—the heavens: the encompassing and overpowering, that under and upon which we are thrown, that which dazzles us and takes us by surprise, the overwhelming" (MLF 10, 11 [GA 26 12, 13]). This mode of temporality is, as we will see in the next chapter, the existential origin of the divine.

Conclusion

We just saw how Heidegger's conception of metaphysics takes up anew the Aristotelian problem of metaphysics as "knowledge of being and knowledge of the overwhelming," rethinking it in terms of "the twofold in *Being and Time* of existence and thrownness" (MLF 11 [GA 9 13]). We can gain a further understanding of the philosophical challenges and conceptual inversions that Heidegger's work undergoes by considering more closely the temporality of the return to the origin, the temporality of thrownness or birth, the topic of the following chapter.

Notes

1   BPP 223–24 [GA 24 319–20].
2   See François Jaran, *Phénoménologies de l'histoire: Husserl, Heidegger et l'histoire de la philosophie* (Paris: Éditions Peeters Louvain, 2013), 81–8.
3   See Jaran, *La Métaphysique du Dasein*, 70, 74–5.
4   The readings developed in Jaran's *La Métaphysique du Dasein*, Tengelyi's *Welt und Unendlichkeit*, Schmidt's *Grund und Freiheit*, and Römer's "Zeit und Kategoriale Anschauung" have strongly influenced my understanding of the innovations of Heideggers metaphysical period but differ from the interpretation here proposed in that I again stress the continuity between the investigations.
5   Again, see Jaran, *La Métaphysique du Dasein*, 70, 74–5.
6   See Matthias Wunsch, "'Welt' in Heideggers metaphysischer Periode" in *Rostocker Phänomenologische Manuskripte*, 18, ed. Michael Großheim (Rostock, 2013) 3–28 and his *Fragen nach dem Menschen*, 18–29.
7   PM 125, note 66 [GA 9 162, note 59].
8   H. 351.
9   H. 172, translation modified. At *Theaetetus* 155d, Plato's Socrates claims that wonder is "the mark of the philosopher" and "philosophy indeed has no other origin [ἀρχή]." I have taken the English translation from Plato, *Plato's Theory of Knowledge; The Theaetetus and the Sophist*, translated, with commentary by

Francis M. Cornford (New York: Dover Publications, 2003) and the original Greek terms from *Platon: Werke VI*, ed. Peter Staudacher and translated by Friedrich Schleiermacher (Darmstadt: wbg Edition, 2019). Aristotle says "it is owing to their wonder that men both now begin and at first began to philosophize [ἤρξαντο φιλοσοφεῖν]" Aristotle, *Metaphysics* 982b 12 ff, English translation from Aristotle, *The Basic Works of Aristotle*, ed. Richard McKeon (New York: Random House. 1941), 692, and the Greek terms from Aristotle, *Aristotle's Metaphysics: A revised text with introduction and commentary. 2*, with introduction and commentary by William David Ross (Oxford: Clarendon Press, 1981), 982b 12ff. For Heidegger wonder originates in anxiety: The withdrawal of significance that occurs therein makes possible wonder and amazement at the sheer being there of things. See GA 27 163–80, 383–6.

10 "*Die Neugier hat nichts zu tun mit dem bewundernden Betrachten des Seienden, dem θαυμάζειν, ihr liegt nicht daran, durch Verwunderung in das Nichtverstehen gebracht zu werden, sondern sie besorgt ein Wissen, aber lediglich um gewußt zu haben*" (H. 172).

11 H. 427, note xiii. "*Daß der traditonelle Begriff der Ewigkeit in der Bedeutung des 'stehenden Jetzt' (nunc stans) aus dem vulgären Zeitverständnis geschöpft und in der Orientierung an der Idee der 'standigen' Vorhandenheit umgrenzt ist, bedarf keiner ausführlichen Erörterung. Wenn die Ewigkeit Gottes sich philosophisch 'Konstruieren' ließe, dann dürfte sie nur als ursprünglichere und 'unendliche' Zeitlichkeit verstanden werden. Ob hierzu die via negationis et eminentiae einen möglichen Weg bieten könnte, bleibe dahingestellt.*"

12 See Vedder, *Heidegger's Philosophy of Religion: From God to the Gods* (Pittsburgh: Duquesne University Press, 2007), 31.

13 See the lucid account in Jaran, *La Métaphysique du Dasein*, 105–28.

14 Heidegger refers to Aristotle, *Metaphysics* 1003a 21f, 1026a 18ff.

15 "The πρώτη φιλοσοφία is the ἐπιστήμη ζητουμένη: the science sought after, the science that can never become a fixed possession and that, as such, would just have to be passed on. It is rather the knowledge that can be obtained only if it is each time sought anew. It is precisely a venture, an 'inverted world [*verkehrte Welt*]'. That is, genuine understanding of being must itself always be first achieved." (MFL 11 [GA 26 13]). The expression "*eine verkehrte Welt*" can be found in Georg Wilhelm Friedrich Hegel, *Werke Band 02—Jenaer Schriften Volume: 2* (Frankfurt: Suhrkamp, 1986), 182.

16 Heidegger refers to Aristotle, *Nichomachean Ethics*, 1141a 12, 1141b 3 ff.

17 I discuss the political senses of the term *Gemeinschaft* and the correlated notions of roots and soil in Chapter 6.

18 Amongst others, Irene McMullin and Lawrence Vogel have examined the ethical possibilities of "leaping ahead." See Irene McMullin, *Time and the Shared*

World: Heidegger on Social Relations (Evanston: Northwestern University Press, 2013), 202–30 and Lawrence Vogel, *The Fragile "We": Ethical Implications of Heidegger's "Being and Time"* (Evanston: Northwestern University Press, 1994), 69–98. In this context, however, I use the term "leaping head" to highlight its ontological role in disclosing different areas of being, see H. 10, 399, cf. H. 122, 298.

19 At issue here is the question of the phenomenological origin of the different disciplines (H. 11, cf. H. 18). This question has a clearly political dimension: It concerns both pedagogy and the question of university reform. See Thomson, *Heidegger and Ontotheology*, 78–140, especially 104–14.

20 This ambiguity is signaled by a play on the word *geben* [to give]. Science has both betrayed or relinquished ["*preisgegeben*"] as well as admitted ["*zugeben*"] the nothing (GA 9 106 [PM 84]). Science, while presupposing the ontological difference, does not allow it to emerge as such. Letting the ontological difference emerge demands a specific way of being [*Haltung*] discussed in the following chapter.

21 See his handwritten note to the 1929 edition of "What Is Metaphysics?," contained in PM 84 [GA 105].

22 Cf. Kant's *Critique of Pure Reason*, A 574–6, B 602–4.

23 PM 88 [GA 9 111–12], translation slightly modified. Cf. H. 343.

24 PM 91 [GA 9 115]. Heidegger's marginal note to this passage highlights the essential ambiguity: "Who holds originarily? [*wer hält ursprünglich?*]."

25 PM 93 [GA 9 118].

26 See also the original version of "What Is Metaphysics?": "primordial anxiety happens only in rare moments [*Augenblicken*]." The passage there also refers to the "horizon [*Horizont*]" of the nothing, an expression that is not used at all in the published version. I read this terminological change as reflecting the shift in the inquiry from seeking the horizon for the meaning of being to the revelation of the ontological difference. See Heidegger, "Was ist Metaphysik? Urfassung/What Is Metaphysics? Original Version," ed. Dieter Thomä and trans. Ian Alexander Moore and Gregory Fried *Philosophy Today*, Volume 62, Issue 3 (Summer 2018): 733–51, here 741.

27 "*Wenngleich die Gegenwart der Angst gehalten ist, hat sie doch nicht schon den Charakter des Augenblickes, der im Entschluss sich zeitigt. Die Angst bringt nur in die Stimmung eines möglichen Entschlusses. Ihre Gegenwart hält den Augenblick, als welcher sie selbst und nur sie möglich ist, auf dem Sprung*" (H. 344). The Macquarrie and Robinson translation reads: "But even though the Present of anxiety is *held on to*, it does not as yet have the character of the moment of vision, which temporalizes itself in a resolution. Anxiety merely brings one into the mood for a *possible* resolution. The Present of anxiety holds the moment of vision *at the ready* [*auf dem Sprung*]; as such a moment it itself, and only itself, is possible" (H. 344).

28 In GA 27, Heidegger also uses the term *Augenblick* in discussing a shared, silent amazement of two hikers at an extra-ordinary view. "*Nehmen wir an, die beiden Wanderer kommen alsbald um eine Biegung des Pfads zu einer unerwarteten Aussicht auf das Gebirge, so dass sie beide plötzlich hingerissen sind und schweigend nebeneinander stehen. Es ist dann keine Spur von gegenseitigem Sicherfassen, jeder steht vielmehr benommen von dem Anblick. Sind die beiden jetzt nur noch nebeneinander wie die beiden Felsblöcke, oder sind sie in diesem Augenblick gerade in einer Weise miteinander, wie sie es nicht sein können, wenn sie unentwegt zusammen schwatzen oder gar sich gegenseitig erfassen und auf ihre Komplexe beschnüffeln?*" [GA 27 86]. The passage is interesting because it suggests that (i) the moment of turning toward facticity can be shared, whereas in the *Augenblick* in *Being and Time* Dasein takes over its finite being-toward-death as an individual, (ii) for its suggesting a positive account of *Miteinandersein* in contrast to the negative treatment of this phenomenon in *Being and Time*, which latter, however, presupposes an "original being-with one-another [*ursprüngliche Miteinandersein*]" (see H. 174–5). For a critical discussion of the limits of Heidegger's conception of intersubjectivity here, see Tengelyi, *Welt und Unendlichkeit*, 246–52.

29 Note how in the cited sentences Heidegger signals how anxiety brings us back to our facticity as such, to an original experience of beings as a whole, by playing on the expressions "*ursprüngliche Angst*" and "*auf dem Sprunge.*"

30 PM 91–2 [GA 9 116].

31 PM 92 [GA 9 116].

32 PM 93 [GA 118].

33 The moments of Heidegger's analysis here clearly parallel the three transcendental ideas that Kant claims are constitutive of traditional *metaphysica specialis* except that, on Heidegger's account, we face therein a basic existential rather than rational indeterminacy with regard to I, world, and possibility.

34 PM 95–6 [GA 9 121]. I have modified the translation of "*Schicksal*" to "fate" so as to preserve consistency with citations from the Macquarrie and Robinson translation of *Being and Time*.

35 GA 27 360–61.

36 See GA 27 16 where Heidegger claims philosophy is not a science, but not in the sense that it falls short of the scientific ideal but rather through an overabundance or surplus ["*Überfluß*"]. The underlying experience is both more original than science and is that in which science is rooted. See Tengelyi's clear discussion of this point in his *Welt und Unendlichkeit*, 236–8. Such an understanding underlies Heidegger's attempt in this period to "deduce" or "derive" disciplinary divisions (history, nature, the mythical) from ways in which temporality temporalizes itself or occurs. See also GA 27 382–3 on what Heidegger sees as the essential law of genesis, that the origin is richer and higher than what is formed from out of it.

37 It seems to me that central to the question of whether or not Heidegger's early work, especially *Being and Time*, is committed to conceptualism is seeing how he problematizes the relation between temporality and conceptualization in the late 1920s. For a defense of a conceptualist interpretation of *Being and Time*, see Golob, *Heidegger on Concepts, Freedom and Normativity*, for my critique of Golob, see Chapter 2.

38 I interpret this as the sense of Heidegger's much-debated comment in the "Letter on Humanism" that "thinking failed in the saying of this turning [*Kehre*] and did not succeed with the language of metaphysics" (PM 250 [GA 9 328]). See section 1 of the Introduction for my discussion of this. The turn here is clearly neither a biographical event nor a pious but vague injunction to turn to the practice of philosophizing but is to be understood in terms of the underlying account of temporality and movement in this period.

39 I am here paraphrasing the following passage: "*Bei der ersten Ausarbeitung des III. Abschnittes des ersten Teils von ‚Sein und Zeit', der, wie oben erwähnt, den Titel ‚Zeit und Sein' tragen und eine ‚Kehre' der Betrachtung vom Sein Selbst her bringen sollte, versuchte Heidegger—nach eigener Mitteilung—eine dreifache Differenz zu unterscheiden: a) die ‚transzendentale' oder ontologische Differenz im engeren Sinne: Den Unterschied des Seienden von seiner Seiendheit. b) die ‚transzendenzhafte' oder ontologische Differenz im weiteren Sinne: den Unterschied des Seienden u n d seiner Seiendheit vom Sein selbst. c) die ‚transzendente' oder theologische Differenz im strengen Sinne: Den Unterschied des Gottes vom Seienden, von der Seiendheit und vom Sein.*" See Max Müller, *Existenzphilosophie im geistigen Leben der Gegenwart*, third expanded and improved edition (Heidelberg: F. H. Kerle Verlag, 1964), 66–7.

4

Birth and the Primal Time of Myth

The present chapter will discuss how Heidegger, in critical dialogue with Ernst Cassirer's work on mythical thinking, makes several striking philosophical innovations in further developing the theme of Dasein's transcendence.[1] These include a temporality of birth, the working out of a positive account of a philosophical way of being, an explanation of how the phenomenon of the world is capable of different variations, and a critique of the temporal presuppositions of neo-Kantian philosophy, especially of the notion of the *a priori* therein.

A properly phenomenological account of mythical thought must, Heidegger claims, be understood in terms of the primal time of the world-entry of beings. He contends, however, that Cassirer's interpretation of the forms of mythical thought using a Kantian architectonic overlooks this:

> "World-entry is based on the temporalization of temporality. The primal fact [*Urfaktum*], in the metaphysical sense, is that there is anything like temporality at all. The entrance into the world by beings is primal history [*Urgeschichte*] pure and simple. From this primal history a region of problems must be developed which we are today beginning to approach with greater clarity, the region of the mythic. The metaphysics of myth must come to be understood out of this primal history, and it can be done with the aid of a metaphysical construct of primal time [*Ur-Zeit*], i.e. the time with which primal history itself begins."[2]

I will argue that by following the guiding thread of the temporality of thrownness or birth, we can, despite the scattered nature of much of Heidegger's comments on Cassirer's work, see how his critique of Cassirer is both coherent and central to his own investigation into the temporal conditions for ontological understanding.[3]

I begin by discussing how and why the problem of the mythical world, which Heidegger mentions at several points in *Being and Time*, highlights issues that are unresolved in the existential analytic as well as their significance for his overall project (**1.**). I then examine Heidegger's treatment of the temporality of birth in *Einleitung in die Philosophie*. This theme not only provides crucial background to the phenomenological interpretation of the mythical world but also to the further development of Heidegger's investigation of temporality (**2.**). The third section then examines how these problems are taken up in subsequent texts, especially Heidegger's 1928 review "Ernst Cassirer's Philosophy of Symbolic Forms. Part Two: Mythical Thought (Berlin 1925)" and the 1928-9 lecture course *Einleitung in die Philosophie*. At stake in Heidegger's projected metaphysics of myth is what he calls a metaphysically primal temporality—the temporality of birth or of thrownness—, the "factical ideal of Dasein" referred to in an open ended way in *Being and Time* (H. 310), and understanding of thinking and of truth underlying his investigation (**3.**).

1 The Mythical World as an Outstanding Problem in *Being and Time*

Far from being of marginal significance, the phenomenology of the mythical world, inspired by the second volume of Cassirer's *The Philosophy of Symbolic Forms*, is a reoccurring theme in Heidegger's work between 1926 and 1929. In *Being and Time*, Heidegger claims Cassirer's work "contained clues of far-reaching importance" but suggested its foundations were not sufficiently transparent and need to be subject to a "*repetition* [Wiederholung]" on the ontological level.[4] These clues, it emerges from other texts, bear on a cluster of fundamental problems in Heidegger's own work. The notes for Division III of *Being and Time* hint at a connection between the problem of the mythical world and the *a priori*[5] and in *The Metaphysical Foundations of Logic* Heidegger refers to a "primal time" of the world entry of beings, that is, a mode of temporality still outstanding in the extant divisions of *Being and Time*, and claims this allows us to understand "metaphysics of myth" (MFL 209 [GA 26 270]).

Before turning to Heidegger's most sustained engagement with Cassirer's work in his 1928 review of *The Philosophy of Symbolic Forms* and the 1928-9 lecture course *Einleitung in die Philosophie*, I first want to look at how the phenomenon of mythical or "primitive" world[6] indicates the limits of and outstanding difficulties in the treatment of the relation between temporality, world, the *a priori*, and historicity in *Being and Time*. In §11, Heidegger first refers to the everydayness of primitive or mythical Dasein, an everydayness that he claims both differs from that of our historical Dasein as well as being of positive significance for an analytic of Dasein. In a footnote to this section,

Heidegger questions whether Cassirer's approach to the mythical world, directed by the architectonic of the *Critique of Pure Reason*, can accommodate such a task or whether the phenomena in view demand a "more primordial approach" (H. 51 xi). The seeds of Heidegger's critique of Cassirer, developed in texts from 1928 and 1929, can be found here: The phenomena brought to light in an investigation of mythical Dasein point toward an original mode of temporality, which latter demands a methodological and temporal transformation of the presuppositions of Kantian philosophy. This critique also strikes directly at a problem central to Heidegger's own undertaking that we discussed in Chapter 2: that of reconceiving the *a priori* through an investigation of temporality.

And in *Being and Time* §17, Heidegger highlights several features that distinguish the use of signs in the fetishism and magic of the mythical world from the character of signs in the world of our historical Dasein. For mythical Dasein, "the sign coincides with what is indicated": It is not merely a substitute for what it indicates but "the sign itself always *is* what it indicates." Further, this coincidence between sign and thing does not rest on mental processes of abstraction: It is "not an identification of things which have hitherto been isolated from one another" and the sign "is not based on a prior Objectification." Unlike our everyday use of signs and concepts,[7] "the sign has not as yet become free from that of which it is the sign" because "such a use of signs is completely absorbed in what is indicated" and so incapable of detachment from this (H. 81–2).

Heidegger is alluding to passages in the second volume of *The Philosophy of Symbolic Forms* where Cassirer stresses that an implicit, pre-conceptual understanding of the boundedness of all beings, events, and forces and the lack of differentiation between different levels of being is fundamental to the use of images, signs, and rituals in the mythical world. In this world, a dancer is not merely representative of the god but *is* the god, the rites surrounding the death and resurrection of vegetative life do not imitate the gods but *are* the gods. Equally, the image of a person, or a part of them such as a hair or a nail, or even their shadow does not represent a person but *are* the person. To bore arrows or needles into the image of an enemy or to damage something of theirs immediately impacts, in a magical way of thinking, the enemy themselves. The same holds of the name of a person or a thing—the word does not have a representative function and it does not have a meaning or a signification that is independent of that which it stands for. Rather, to possess the word, the name, is to possess the thing as it contains the real powers of the person, thing, or god it names.[8]

Although Heidegger's intention in *Being and Time* §17 is to bring into relief the work world of our Dasein, the considerations also point toward a positive problematic that will be further developed in subsequent texts. Hence in his remarks on the mythical world, Heidegger not only refers to the possibility, on the basis of "work[ing] out the 'formal' idea of worldhood," of providing both a phenomenological interpretation of the mythical world but also to the possibility of "an understanding of being that is constitutive for primitive Dasein and the primitive world in general" (H. 82).[9] To work out the formal idea of worldhood means thematizing that which makes the different existentiell concepts of world existentially possible, for instance the existential-temporal basis for the differences between the world of mythical Dasein and our historical Dasein.

How does the world of mythical Dasein differ from our own? First, Heidegger notes that the use of signs in the mythical world "always remains completely within a being-in-the-world which is *'immediate [unmittelbaren]'*" (H. 81, my emphasis). Second, Heidegger raises the possibility that for mythical Dasein "ultimately what is 'ready-to-hand' within-the-world just does not have the kind of being that belongs to equipment" and even, as the use of scare quotes around "ready-to-hand" indicates, that readiness-to-hand and equipment may "have nothing to contribute as ontological clues in Interpreting the primitive world." Thirdly, central to this task is the elucidation of the phenomenal meaning of "what is not" (H. 82).

While these three issues seem to signal three different fields of problems—the immediacy of mythical being-in-the-world, the problem of the ready-to-hand therein, and the problem of the "not" in general—they are phenomenologically connected. In a mode of being that is entirely absorbed in what is immediate, signs are not discovered as equipment or as having an in-order-to structure. This is because dealings with the ready-to-hand refer to a future implicitly or explicitly expected and awaited, which is *not yet*. A being in the world that is "immediate," however, is one in which temporality does not temporalize itself primarily from out a retention which *awaits* (H. 354).[10]

And there are a number of reasons for thinking that Heidegger is concerned with something more fundamental than simply expanding his investigation to encompass a region of problems typically covered by anthropology or cultural philosophy. First, the use of signs in the fetishism and magic of the mythical world point toward phenomena that are not explicable on the basis of Divisions I and II of *Being and Time*. The existential analytic takes as its starting point an *ontical* and *existentiell* conception of worldhood, the work-world of *our* historical Dasein. As we saw in the previous chapter, while the existential analytic signals the necessity for working out the full *a priori* or *existential* structure of worldhood in general which "may have as its modes whatever structural wholes any special 'worlds' may have at the time" (H. 65), it does not carry out this task.[11] It is Cassirer's research into the world of mythical Dasein that makes manifest the limits of the account of worldhood in the existential analytic as the latter does not provide us with the conceptual resources for interpreting "a being-in-the-world which is *'immediate [unmittelbaren]'*" (H. 81).

Second, this immediacy points toward a temporal problematic that is neither readily assimilable to the analyses of fallen everydayness nor of authenticity. Heidegger himself points this out when he writes that "even primitive Dasein has possibilities of a being which are not of an everyday kind, and it has a specific everydayness of its own" (H. 51). If for mythical Dasein the "use of signs is completely absorbed [*geht ... auf*] in what is indicated," then this absorption not that of the fallenness everydayness of our historical Dasein analyzed in *Being and Time*, but rather is "a primordial absorption [*Aufgehen*] in 'phenomena' (taken in the pre-phenomenological sense)" that is of positive help in bringing out basic ontological structures (H. 82, H. 51). Mythical Dasein has *something like* everyday and non-everyday possibilities of being and it is characterized by *something like* fallenness. But an account of what makes its world possible—and more importantly its existential-temporal basis—remains outstanding.[12]

Third, in *Being and Time*, Heidegger insists that anthropology presupposes an existential analytic as its *a priori* basis (H. 45, cf. H. 16, H. 45–52). Yet the passages there that deal with mythical Dasein also point toward basic difficulties concerning the relation between the *a priori* and temporality. As was argued in Chapter 2, the analyses of world and equipment in §§14–24 of *Being and Time* and in §11 of *The Basic Problems of Phenomenology* show the existential origin of the traditional conception of the *a priori* in dealings with the ready-to-hand and ultimately in a particular and derivative mode of the temporalization of temporality. This means that this conception of the *a priori* has its origin in a specific understanding of the being of entities—namely as ready-to-hand—that belongs to the work-world of *our* historical Dasein but does not belong to Dasein as such, as the mythical world shows.

In other words, by introducing the problem of a phenomenological interpretation of the mythical world, Heidegger implicitly admits that the analysis of the worldhood of the work-world in *Being and Time* not only remains preliminary but also that it *may well be relative to our specific historical situation* and lacking significance for an ontology of Dasein as such. Further, given that the notion of the *a priori* that has dominated philosophy from Aristotle to Kant is itself existentially rooted in the givenness of entities within this specific and historically contingent world that may have "*nothing* to contribute as ontological clues" to understanding the world of primitive Dasein (H. 82, my emphasis), this again raises a basic question of what the *a priori* can mean in the context of Heidegger's work. And as Heidegger's work aspires to an *a priori* status, this problem again points toward the task of reconceiving the *a priori* on a more basic and original basis than on the experience of beings as πράγματα (H. 68).

Fourth, as noted above, Heidegger refers to "*an* [*ein*] understanding of being that is constitutive for primitive Dasein and the primitive world in general." The use of the indefinite article here is remarkable. It introduces the possibility of a *plurality* of different understandings of being, raising the question of what makes this plurality possible, how they are interrelated, and how they become modified. A close reading and comparison of the general introduction to *Being and Time* and the introduction to Division II with respect to this issue is illuminating. The former consistently refers to *the* meaning of being [*der Sinn von Sein*]. At the end of the latter, however, Heidegger claims that "within the horizon of time the projection of *a* [*eines*] meaning of being in general can be accomplished" (H. 235, my emphasis).[13] This phrase is significant because the context, namely an outline of Division II, Chapter 6, suggests that "the horizon of time" does not refer to the primordial temporality unveiled in Division II, Chapter 3 but rather to "an even more primordial temporalizing of temporality" that "the understanding prepares itself for" (H. 235). This suggests that this passage not only refers to a mode of temporality that remains outstanding in the first two Divisions but also, given that the mythical world is characterized by its own "immediate" temporality, to the primal time mentioned in the opening to this chapter.[14]

A fifth, related issue is that on Heidegger's account mythical Dasein is incapable of *conceptualizing* its understanding of being, because it is incapable of an objectification and identification of many under a unifying one. Can the understanding of being that underlies the mythical world be brought to light and conceived at all? A number of interpretative possibilities suggest themselves here. (1) Mythical Dasein has a non-conceptual understanding of being that we, but not it, can conceptualize or (2) it has a non-conceptual understanding of being that cannot be conceptualized at all but can perhaps be indicated in a non-conceptual fashion or (3) the understanding of being that belongs to mythical Dasein is completely inaccessible to us, either conceptually or otherwise, or (4) that the problem of the mythical world demands that we rethink the existential-temporal conditions for concept formation and indeed the problem of the self-showing of original phenomena on the basis of a fuller investigation of temporality and truth as unconcealment (cf. H. 349). In the following, I will argue (4) is the option most consistent with Heidegger's overall approach.

The preceding considerations also allow us to answer, at least in part, an objection Matthias Wunsch raises to Heidegger's interpretation of Cassirer. Wunsch notes that in the 1928 Cassirer review Heidegger proposes appropriating Cassirer's phenomenology of the mythical world and carrying out a radical ontology of Dasein in the light of the problem of being, specifically in terms of the existential of thrownness. Wunsch notes that Heidegger's starting point in the existential analytic is the "average everydayness" of our historical Dasein and he assumes there are "essential" structures of everydayness "which in *every* kind of being that factical Dasein may possess, persist as determinative for the character of its being" (H. 17, my emphasis). The problem Wunsch detects here is a kind of anachronism in Heidegger's approach: It is implausible to think that we can illuminate the mythical world starting from the average everydayness of 1920s Germany. Underlying this, Wunsch claims, is a methodological problem upon which Heidegger has not sufficiently reflected: that of the historicity of his attempts to disclose universal existential structures.[15]

However, Heidegger's interpretation of the world of mythical Dasein is more methodologically reflected than Wunsch allows. For when Heidegger emphasizes that mythical Dasein has everyday possibilities and "a specific everydayness *of its own*" (H. 51), he recognizes that the everyday world of mythical Dasein is in important respects different from that of our historical Dasein, not least in its experience of the environing world. Further, to interpret mythical Dasein out of its thrownness is not to interpret it in terms of the fallen everydayness of our historical Dasein, even though both this way of being and mythical Dasein are characterized by kinds of absorption in the world. Specifically, "thrownness" in the context of the Cassirer review is not the fallen everydayness of our historical Dasein[16] nor even the disclosure of "the pure 'that-it-is' of one's ownmost individualized thrownness" in anxiety (H. 343) but a phenomenon that exists between the two: The fallenness of mythical Dasein is distinctive, it seeks shelter from overwhelming by identifying itself with it rather than the surrounding totality of significance. For these reasons, I think the significance of Heidegger's engagement with Cassirer lies in its indicating the provisional and incomplete nature of the analysis of world in *Being and Time*, in pointing beyond the existential analytic, and thereby facilitating access to a mode of temporality that remains unthematized therein.

2 Birth and the Darkness of Facticity

Central to understanding Heidegger's critique of Cassirer and indeed the further elaboration of his own project is the temporality of thrownness or of birth. In §15 of the 1928–9 lecture course *Einleitung in die Philosophie*, Heidegger treats the "*Faktum* of birth," developing his account of temporality beyond the fallen present and authentic being-toward-death thematized respectively in Divisions I and II of *Being and Time* and providing the key to interpreting the mythical world. As we saw in Chapter 1, Dasein constantly finds itself stretched along between its beginning and its end, its birth and its death. Heidegger had stressed that instead of being an event that belongs to our past, we exist as having-been born, thus indicating that birth is constitutive of being-in-the-world in a manner quite distinct from being-toward-death (H. 374).[17]

When Heidegger takes up this topic anew in §15 of *Einleitung in die Philosophie*, it is in the context of a discussion of the difficulties of gaining phenomenological access to the Dasein of the earliest stages of humankind (mythical Dasein) and to the Dasein of infants. At first glance, this seems to suggest that Heidegger is just sketching out how fundamental ontological insights can be applied to the regional disciplines of anthropology, child psychology, and pedagogy.[18] However, a closer reading shows that the analysis of birth here has wide-ranging implications for seeing how Heidegger develops his earlier account of temporality and thus cannot be regarded as merely an addendum to research in the ontic sciences.

Einleitung in die Philosophie, §15 begins by revisiting claims made in *Being and Time*: Heidegger reminds us that birth is not to be seen simply as the other end of Dasein and that it cannot and should not be treated in the same constellation of problems. And just as death is not a future event but Dasein exists as dying, so too the fact of birth is not absolutely behind us: Dasein exists as born (GA 27 124–5, cf. H. 372–5). How does birth become phenomenologically accessible to us? It cannot be simply the inversion of being-toward-death as time is not potentially reversible sequence of nows (H. 425–6). This means the temporality of birth must be worked out in terms of what is peculiar to it as an existential movement (GA 27 124). Heidegger's account of new-born Dasein is thus not just a foray into anthropological, psychological, or pedagogical speculation (GA 27 125) but bears directly upon what he calls the enigma of temporality and motion.

The beginning of Dasein's existence shows it cannot be conceived as a self-encapsulated entity. Screaming, wriggling, reaching out without a determinate aim, turning toward food, warmth, and sleep, it is in relation to the world from the first, albeit while in an obscure, semi-consciousness condition. Its screaming expresses its sensitivity [*Empfindlichkeit*] to disruption by what is other to itself. It is a way of letting something shocking and disrupting be [*ein Verhalten des Seinlassens von etwas*], a letting-be very distinct from the letting be involved [*Bewandenlassen*] that is the ontological condition for equipmental engagement (H. 86). The shocking does not approach it from a definite direction but the "from which" of the shocking is concealed: It is the strangeness of the world as such. It affectively finds itself [*Sichbefinden*] in the world, exposed, delivered over (GA 27 125). What shocks it is the world-entry of beings. In shock, the newborn has no hold on things. What prevails in its relation to beings is a fundamental obscurity:[19]

> "The twilight state in which such an early Dasein is does not imply that there is yet no relationship to beings, but only that this self-relation towards … does not yet have a determinate aim. Being alongside beings is, as it were, still nebulous, not yet illuminated, such that this Dasein cannot yet make a determinate use of the beings alongside which it always already essentially is."[20]

The infant's turning toward rest, warmth, and sleep is at the same time a "turning from [*Abkehr*]" and recoil before beings in their alienness. This turning has "a quite peculiar negative character [*ganz eigentümlichen negative Charakter*]" (GA 27 125, cf. H. 297) that lies in its turning from the disquieting event of the world entry of beings.

This analysis of the temporality of birth has striking structural similarities to the accounts of anxiety in *Being and Time* and especially in "What Is Metaphysics?" In the peculiar temporality of anxiety [*der eigentümlichen Zeitlichkeit der Angst*] (H. 344), Dasein finds itself threatened, but the threatening is nowhere, it is disoriented, faces the strangeness of beings as such (H. 343, PM 88 [GA 9 111–12]). Moreover, the clarification of the phenomenon of birth clearly draws upon and employs the ontological structures of Dasein treated in the existential analytic and in subsequent texts. However here, as in other texts in which Heidegger develops the metaphysics of Dasein, the discussion foregrounds the moment of Dasein's being brought before the hiddenness of beings, before a darkness and a strangeness that precedes significance.

The use of the terms *Ausweichen*, evasion, and *Abkehr*, turning away, in this context provides an excellent example of this shift in emphasis. In *Being and Time*, the moods of everydayness disclose Dasein's thrownness "in the manner of an evasive turning away [*in der Weise der ausweichenden Abkehr*]" such that Dasein "evades [*ausweicht*] its very self" (H. 136, 139). Ultimately such an evasion seeks to look away from being-toward-death by turning to everyday concerns (H. 253). And in §15 of *Einleitung in die Philosophie* too *Ausweichen* is employed in its phenomenological interconnections with turning from, *Abkehr*, and fleeing, *Fliehen*. The turning from is a flight before the unknown and indeterminate strangeness of beings themselves:

> "Thus, the primary interpretation must first of all begin to indicate how the child's mere turning from [*Abkehr*] distinguishes itself from a fending off [*Anwehr*]. Turning from [*Abkehr*] is a mere evasion [*Abweichen*] of ...., but in evasion there is already a determinate fending off [*Abwehr*], a rejection [*Abweisen*] of ... Fleeing [*Fliehen*] before something is already a stance of being opposed [*Dagegen*] that is not yet active; from turning from and fending off we have to distinguish the mustering of an opposition [*Gegenwehr*] in which the authentic counter-movement [*Gegenbewegung*], the assumption of an opposed position [*Entgegenstellen*], sets in. All these intentional phenomena are at the same time such that they work themselves out in their being realised in the first situation in which such a Dasein finds itself, in the originary state of being helplessly delivered over to the world."[21]

While the existential analytic focuses on Dasein's evasion of its being-toward-death, §15 of *Einleitung in die Philosophie*, like "What Is Metaphysics?," emphasizes Dasein's evasion of its thrownness, its being born and delivered over to beings so long as it is. Just as Dasein can either seize hold of or seek to flee from its ownmost being-toward-death, so too it can let itself be brought back to or try to evade its having been born, its factical situatedness amidst beings. We will see in the following section how the temporality of birth or thrownness provides the phenomenological basis for Heidegger's interpretation of the mythical world and his critique of Cassirer.

3 A Phenomenology of the Mythical World

In the first section of this chapter, I argued the question of a phenomenological interpretation of the mythical world was connected to a cluster of problems concerning temporality, historicality, and possibilities of ontological understanding. More specifically, I identified five groups of problems: (1) a temporality of "immediacy," (2) the problem of the "how" of the world of mythical Dasein (and the problem of signs therein), (3) the problem of the relation between the *a priori*, historicality, and temporality, (4) the problem of the understanding of being that belongs to mythical Dasein (and of the apparent plurality of such understandings), and (5) the problem of conceptualizing an understanding—or understandings—of being and the associated problem of the temporality of concept formation. In what follows, I will show how these problems are at the heart of Heidegger's more sustained engagement with phenomenology of the mythical world.

(a) The Mythical Understanding of Being and Temporality

In his review of the second volume of *The Philosophy of Symbolic Forms*, Heidegger credits Cassirer with laying out a phenomenology of mythical consciousness and showing that myth is "an original possibility of human Dasein, which has its own proper truth" (KPM 180 [GA 3 255]). But he also claims that Cassirer fails to push forward to the problem of Dasein's transcendence.[22] Instead of carrying out the interpretation of mythical Dasein in the constitution of its being, Heidegger argues that Cassirer's account has neo-Kantian presuppositions that themselves need to be interrogated. Cassirer "begins with an analysis of the mythical consciousness of objects, the form of its thought, and the form of its intuition" (KPM 187 [GA 3 266]). And his work on mythical *thought* moves within the horizon of a particular understanding of thinking: "Thought here means nothing less than an 'attending and intending' ['*Sinnen und Trachten*']" (KPM 180 [GA 3 255]). Heidegger's claim is that although for Cassirer "myth is its own spiritual 'creative principle of world formation [*Weltgestaltung*]' (p. 19)" (KPM 180 [GA 3 256]), Cassirer fails to push through to the temporality specific to this world formation, specific to the showing itself of the world. The retrieval of this more original problematic requires calling into question Cassirer's understanding of thinking, intuition, and the *a priori*.

To understand these claims, we need to consider some of the key features of Cassirer's interpretation of the mythical world. Cassirer regards the mana-representation, a term inspired by the *mana* of Melanesian and Polynesian cultures, as the core of mythical thinking.[23] The term "*manitou*" of the Algonquin is the expression of astonishment at the new and strange, the "*orenda*" of the Iroquois, the "*wakanda*" of the Sioux are similar such interjections.[24] *Mana* expresses this sense of the extraordinary that can erupt at any moment and is not bound to any particular sphere of objects. It is closely affiliated with the notion of taboo, which denotes on the one hand the restriction of the will and the drives and on the other acts as the precondition for other fundamental directions of consciousness.[25] It lifts mythical consciousness out of the everyday and the common, opening up other possibilities, measures, and means of acting.²⁶ Cassirer further claims that it is the "ground [*Grund*]" of mythical and religious consciousness in that it expresses a fundamental affect. It is the basis of the wonder, θαυμάζειν, that belongs to philosophy and to scientific knowledge.²⁷

According to Heidegger, the merit of Cassirer's analysis lies in indicating that the mana-representation is "the 'how' of everything that is mythically actual, namely, the being of those beings" (KPM 188 [GA 3 266]). It is not an object, not a pre-established ontological domain, but rather occurs between self and world. In the mana-representation, Heidegger claims, "what becomes evident is nothing other than the *understanding of being* that belongs to *every* Dasein as such [*zu jedem Dasein überhaupt*]" (KPM 188 [GA 3 267], second emphasis mine). This understanding "illuminates in advance thought and intuition" and is a basic way of being in which they are both rooted. Hence what becomes manifest in the mana-representation is a structural feature of Dasein as such that can undergo "specific transformations according to each basic way of Dasein's being" (KPM 188 [GA 3 267]).

Heidegger's critique of Cassirer's interpretation of myth focuses on the ambiguous place of the mana-representation within what he claims is the neo-Kantian architectonic of Cassirer's work. The mana-representation "is not dealt with among the forms of thought, and yet it is also not developed as a form of intuition" but in the transition between these. This, Heidegger claims, is "more an expression of a predicament" or of a fundamental problem than a "structural determination ... from out of the whole structure of mythical Dasein as such" (KPM 187–8 [GA 3 266], cf. GA 27 357, 362).²⁸ Like the transcendental imagination in Heidegger's interpretation of Kant, the mana-representation is homeless,²⁹ being situated neither in the understanding nor in intuition. It is neither a spontaneous power of the understanding nor is it a form of receptivity (cf. KPM 95–6 [GA 3 135–6]). This itself indicates that the framework of neo-Kantianism—and, more broadly, the underlying conception of the *a priori*—is not adequate to the grasping of this phenomenon.

A properly phenomenological interpretation of the mythical world, on Heidegger's account, would foreground the mana-representation rather than interpreting it in the light of a neo-Kantian framework. What is required is an ontology of Dasein, of how Dasein comports itself in the world. This would include a phenomenology of "the basic way of mythical 'life,' such that within this life precisely the mana-representation can function as the leading and illuminating understanding of being" (KPM 188 [GA 3 267]). Heidegger characterizes the underlying understanding of being directly: "In all mythology being [*Sein*] means nothing other than overpowering, powerfulness" (GA 27 358).³⁰ On

Heidegger's analysis, there are two aspects essential to the elucidation of this basic way of life: first, the consideration of *the mode of temporality* that makes this understanding of being possible and, second, consideration of how Dasein enacts its existence. The very terms that characterize the mana-representation—it overwhelms [*überwältigt*] Dasein, it is overpowering [*Übermächtigkeit*], instantaneous [*Augenblichlichkeit*], and extra-ordinary [*überraschende Außerordentliche*]—show that it is the moment of Dasein's being brought back to its facticity that is essential to the mana-representation. Being-overpowered can only occur to a being that is delivered over to the world, that is thrown. It is in being turned toward its thrownness that "any and all uncovered beings have ... the Being-character of overpoweringness [*Übermächtigkeit*] (mana)" (KPM 188 [GA 3 267]). Heidegger claims that because Cassirer moves within the horizon of the ordinary conception of time,[31] the temporal significance of the mana-representation cannot come into view.

> "If the ontological interpretation were to push forward to the specific 'temporality [*Zeitlichkeit*]' that grounds thrownness, then it could be made ontologically understandable *why* and *how* what is actual as mana always makes itself evident in a specific 'instanteousness [*Augenblichlichkeit*]'. In thrownness there is a proper being driven here and there [*Umgetriebenwerden*] that is open from out of itself for what is always and in each case the suddenly extraordinary [*überraschende Außerordentliche*]. The specific 'categories' of mythical thought must then be 'deduced ['*deduziert*']' by following the guiding thread of the mana-representation."[32]

A sense of beings as a whole as overpowering permeates the world of mythical Dasein and it is constantly open for the extraordinary and incomparable. Its everydayness is "within the horizon of the overwhelmingly uncommon." Dasein stands "between the sacred and the profane" (KPM 181–2 [GA 3 257]). This is key to understanding the immediacy that characterizes the being-in-the-world of mythical Dasein: "What is actual as mana always makes itself evident in a specific 'instantaneousness [*Augenblichlichkeit*]'" to the Dasein open for "the suddenly extraordinary" (KPM 188 [GA 3 267–8]).

Heidegger's critique of Cassirer implicitly emphasizes the parallels between the mana-representation and his own account of anxiety. The term *Augenblick* was used in "What Is Metaphysics?" to refer to the possibility, at any moment, for anxiety to erupt, significance to recede, and beings as a whole to turn toward Dasein in their strangeness. This temporality of thrownness or birth, as we saw in the previous section, is characterized by the shock of being brought before the actual, before beings as a whole (GA 27 125, cf. KPM 188 [GA 3 267–8]).

Mythical Dasein too constantly stands within the possibility of the extraordinary and the sacred breaking in at any moment upon the ordinary and the profane. And like infant Dasein, mythical Dasein exists in a kind of twilight state, neither fallen into the public world nor taking over its ownmost being:[33]

> "A basic feature of the mythical consciousness of Objects lies in the fact that a demarcated boundary is lacking between what is dreamt of and what is experienced while awake, between what is merely imagined and what is perceived, between image and the object that is formed in the image, between word (meaning) and thing, between what is merely wished for and what is actually possessed, and between what is living and what is dead. Everything remains on one uniform level of being that is immediately present, by which mythical Dasein is dazed [*benommen*]."[34]

Heidegger proposes what can be loosely characterized as a kind of transcendental deduction—or, better, a deduction from Dasein's transcendence—of the basic concepts of the mythical world from this primal, immediate temporality: "The specific 'categories' of mythical thought must then be 'deduced' by following the guiding thread of the mana-representation" (KPM 188 [GA 3 268]), more precisely from the temporality of thrownness. The everyday world of mythical Dasein is one in which the extraordinary can break in upon it at any moment and one in which Dasein responds to this possibility by identifying itself with the power of beings as a whole. It is against this background that we can understand Heidegger's claim in *Being and Time* that mythical Dasein "has a specific everydayness *of its own*" and "possibilities of a being which is not of the everyday kind" (H. 51). Its world is neither that of our fallen everydayness where we are "completely fascinated [*benommen*] by the 'world' and by the Dasein with of Others in the 'they'" (H. 176) nor is it that of an anxiety in which Dasein is betaken or "fascinated [*benommen*]" with its sheer being-there (H. 344). Like the former, mythical Dasein does not make a "conceptual difference [*begrifflichen Unterschied*] between its own manner of being and the manner of being of things towards which it comports itself" but the "identification" here is with beings as a whole, with nature, and not with whatever role Dasein has assumed in the public world (PIK 17 [GA 25 24] translation modified, cf. BPP 120–1 [GA 24 170–1]). Like authentic Dasein, mythical Dasein lets itself be taken to the uncanniness of its facticity but unlike authentic Dasein it does not see itself as distinct from the power that permeates all beings. The "conceptual difference"—and clearly an outstanding problem here concerns what kind of a concept this is—"between the mode of being of human Dasein and the mode of being of things" does not come into view. This means the fallenness constitutive of mythical Dasein is of a peculiar kind: It identifies itself with the beings as a whole, with nature as an overwhelming power. Hence for mythical Dasein "everything"—including itself—"remains on one uniform level of being that is immediately present, by which [it] is dazed [*benommen*]" (KPM 181 [GA 3 256], cf. PIK 17 [GA 25 24], MFL 88, 138 [GA 26 109–10, 174], cf. BPP 120–1 [GA 24 170–1]).

The categories of mythical thinking expressing how beings come to presence are derived from this temporality of thrownness. For instance, the space of the mythical world is partitioned into a "'common ['*gemeinen*']'" region "accessible at all times to everyone" and the sacred, "extraordinary, appropriately preserved, and protected." Dasein sees the order of time, the seasons, and life and death as cosmic and destinal powers and dedicates cults and rituals to them. Different numbers have magical powers owing to their "belonging to a determinate region of the uncommon [*Ungemeinen*]" such as the phases of the moon, the four regions of the sky, and familial triad (KPM 182, 183 [GA 3 258, 260]). Cult and ritual mediate between the sacred and the profane, between "the power and uncommonness of the divine [that] primarily and thoroughly dominates mythical Dasein" and the everyday world (KPM 185 [GA 3 263]). The non-separability of word from thing and signifier from signified in fetishism and magic, which Heidegger mentions in *Being and Time* and which Cassirer analyzes in detail in the second volume of *The Philosophy of Symbolic Forms*, arises from this sense of being bound to all beings and sharing in a life or force common to them all.

(b) The Mana-Representation, Dasein's "How" and the Wish

Heidegger's sketch of a "deduction" of the categories of the mythical world begins not simply with the temporality of thrownness (KPM 188 [GA 3 267]) but also takes into account the peculiar fallenness of mythical Dasein. Dasein identifies with the overwhelming power of beings through ritual, sacrifice, fetishism, and magic with a view to releasing itself from its subjection to these forces and powers. It thereby attempts to control or harness them. This leads to the second point of Heidegger's critique of Cassirer, namely "the question concerning mythical Dasein's basic comportment and its comportment to itself" (KPM 188–9 [GA 3 268]). And we find that Heidegger's discussion of the "how" of mythical Dasein draws upon and repeats the analyses of wishing, fallenness, and conscience in *Being and Time*. But the repetition takes place in terms of the recursive moment back to facticity. How does this repetition take place and to what extent does it parallel and differ from the existential analytic?

Cassirer claims that the first force in which human beings come to themselves "is the force of the *wish* [*die Kraft des* Wunsches]."[35] Mythical Dasein knows of no clear line of demarcation between an "inner" and an "outer" world nor between willing, wishing, and possession. Wishing is both the beginning and the end of the process of actualizing something: There is no medium separating the wish and its fulfillment. Mythical consciousness on this level does not know of tools or equipment as such. Even when the transition from a magical to a "technical" relationship to nature has occurred, Cassirer argues tools themselves are still experienced as having an innate daemonic power and as needing the accompaniment of magical rituals and the cooperation of magical forces in order to be efficacious.[36]

In keeping with his attempt to ground Cassirer's account of the mythical world on the analysis of Dasein, Heidegger claims Cassirer passes over what is essential here: an existential interpretation of wishing. The analysis should show, he contends, how wishing is rooted in Dasein's thrownness. Specifically it should discuss "how the (mere) wish [*bloße Wunsch*], on the basis of a peculiar non-survey [*eigentümlichen Nichtüberschauen*] of its many possibilities can have the force of this efficacy" and why it is bound to mana-representation (and hence to Dasein's thrownness) (KPM 189 [GA 3 268]). In this Heidegger is clearly alluding to his own existential interpretation of wishing in *Being and Time* (H. 194–6). He there interprets wishing in terms of a "non-survey of Dasein's many possibilities": Fallen Dasein is so enthralled by the "actuality" of the public world that it is blind to its being-possible (H. 195). There too wishing reveals, in an oblique fashion, fallen Dasein's "independence" or ownmost being: Fallen Dasein's "being towards possibilities shows itself for the most part as mere *wishing* [*bloßes* Wünschen]" (H. 195). Yet the analysis of *Being and Time* also sees wishing as a symptom of an inertia or an unwillingness to take over possibilities, thus as a self-evasion and not as a self-manifestation.

And the analysis of the phenomenon of wishing in the mythical context moves in precisely the opposite direction to that of the analysis of Dasein's fallen everydayness. *Being and Time* prioritizes the authentic future—and treats wishing as the evasion of this—but in the Cassirer review the interpretative accent lies on Dasein's thrownness. This accounts for the most striking difference between the two accounts of wishing, namely that concerning the *efficacity* of the wish. Far from being merely an escapist fantasy born from resignation to the "actuality" of everyday world, for mythical Dasein the wish is a force or a power in the face of the overwhelming actuality of beings as whole that enables action.[37] In wishing, mythical Dasein comes toward itself: Wishing enables action and brings it into the situation.

This inversion or turnaround in meaning is entailed by what I earlier described as a recursive temporal movement. The temporality of mythical Dasein is primarily one of *thrownness* and it is in this mode of temporality that wishing can bring Dasein to itself. In the face of the overwhelming power of beings as a whole, wishing, and phantasy are the first expression of Dasein's independence and autonomy and reveal its potentiality. Wishing awakens a capacity to act and expresses a limited independence from an overwhelming actuality. Yet the wish, the fantasy, seems not to come from Dasein itself but from a protective magical force. Only at later stages of culture does Dasein see this power as its own:

> "In its being threatened by magical powers, mythical Dasein's 'own' soul stands as an 'alien' power [*'fremde' Macht*] over and against it. Even where the representation of protective spirits is awakened, one's own self is still a power, as it were, which protectively takes up the individual I. Only first at higher levels does the magical daemon become *daimonion* and genius, in such a way that Dasein in the end comes to determine itself not as an alien power but rather from out of that for which it is freely *capable* [vermag], from itself and for itself as an ethical subject."[38]

This characterization of mythical Dasein's awakening to its own power and capacity to act has marked similarities to the analysis of conscience in *Being and Time*. The phenomenon of conscience is often interpreted, Heidegger notes, as having a possessor other than Dasein itself. It is seen as "an alien power [*fremden Macht*] by which Dasein is dominated" (H. 275). It is an "*alien* voice [fremde *Stimme*] voice" that "*passes over* [*übergangen*]" Dasein's everyday self-interpretation (H. 277, H. 273).[39] Interpreted existentially, conscience is understood as calling Dasein back to the uncanniness of its thrown being-in-the-world. Yet in the world of mythical Dasein, which is characterized by the identification of itself with the power of beings as a whole, there is no clear distinction between the self and the alien: The surrounding world of beings is alien to it and it is alien to itself. Mythical Dasein knows nothing of an ontological demarcation between an inner and an outer world—waking and dreaming, imagination and perception, image and object, word and thing, the living and the dead—a demarcation that seems self-evident to our historical Dasein. Consequentially, mythical Dasein cannot understand itself as an individual and thus is also incapable of the individualization that is required for raising the question of being (cf. H. 39).

(c) The "Factical Ideal of Dasein" and the Problem of Historicality

At this point we can bring the various strands of Heidegger's understanding of the mythical world together so as to see how it differs from our world. First and most importantly, mythical Dasein feels itself "bound to all beings" through an "'indeterminate life-feeling'" (KPM 184 [GA 3 261]). This identification of itself with the overpowering all means it experiences everything "on one uniform level of being" (KPM 181 [GA 3 256]).[40] The part is the whole; each thing is permeated by the magical forces that belong to the whole. Yet it is precisely mythical Dasein's tendency to *identify* itself with the all that, on Heidegger's analysis, constitutes an *evasion* of the movement of transcendence.

As we saw, Heidegger claims that the merit of Cassirer's work lies in its attempt at "a 'phenomenology of mythical consciousness'" which shows myth is "an original possibility of human Dasein, which has its own proper truth" (KPM 180 [GA 3 255]). The truth proper to mythical Dasein thus lies in its identification with the power of beings as a whole. Heidegger's discussion of a phenomenology of the mythical world outlines a way of being characterized by an immediacy and "a primordial absorption [*Aufgehen*] in 'phenomena' (taken in the pre-phenomenological sense)" that is positive help in bringing out basic ontological structures (H. 81, H. 51). Yet it is precisely this absorption in the phenomena that prevents the disclosure of the ontological difference and of Dasein's temporal transcendence.

Toward the end of the 1928 Cassirer review, Heidegger turns to the question of how Dasein can be explicitly brought before its transcendence. This question, as we saw previously, is the question of how Dasein can be brought before the ontological difference, of how it can let this emerge. Although mythical Dasein is primarily determined by the thrownness which permeates its understanding of the world, its self-understanding suffers from an essential limitation. Wishing and other comportments of mythical Dasein "are always only ways according to which the *transcendence* of Dasein is *unveiled* [*enthüllt*] and not first produced [*hergestellt*]" (KPM 189 [GA 3 268]). Underlying this distinction between unveiling and producing or bringing forth Dasein's transcendence is Heidegger's concern with how the ontological difference can emerge. He broaches this problem in the second half of *Einleitung in die Philosophie*. Heidegger claims that there are two basic possibilities of relating to the revelation of beings as a whole: *Bergung* (oriented toward rescue, salvation) and *Haltung* (the philosophical stance) (GA 27 367).⁴¹

Mythical Dasein's stance is *Bergung*, a seeking of shelter from the overwhelming, an attempt to protect itself from it. The experience of everything as on one level of being is a flight from the overwhelming, the identity thinking of magical cults and fetishism an attempt to escape the overwhelming, the threatening actuality of the world (GA 27 359–60).⁴² A kind of concealment belongs to this: It prevents Dasein's individuation as the self that is exposed to the overwhelming as such and prevents Dasein from understanding death as its ownmost possibility.⁴³ Thus, while mythical Dasein lives *within* the temporality of thrownness, this temporality does not become manifest in its own right.

We saw earlier that Heidegger claims the *mana*-representation reveals "the *understanding of being* that belongs to *every* Dasein as such [*zu jedem Dasein überhaupt*]" (KPM 188 [GA 3 267] second emphasis mine). And *Bergung*, which seeks shelter from a disquieting and overpowering otherness, is not a primitive way of being that belongs to our pre-history. Religion, science, and technology are also ways in which our Dasein seeks shelter before beings as a whole and evades the ontological difference.⁴⁴ The turn from the ontological difference becomes manifest in attempts at the technological "conquest of nature" "which rages about in the 'world' today like an unshackled beast ... [and] is the real proof for the metaphysical powerlessness of Dasein, which can only attain its freedom in its history" (MFL 215 [GA 26 279]) and that is among the most prominent of "those idols everybody has and to which they are wont to go cringing" (PM 96 [GA 9 122]).

Bergung and *Haltung* are two fundamental ways of being in the truth and the weight can shift from one to the other in Dasein's factical existence as it moves from seeking deliverance to facing the strangeness of beings (GA 27 367). The philosophical stance, *Haltung*, designates Dasein's holding itself in the original strangeness of beings prior to the occurrence of truth. It is thus the counterpart and complement to the seizing of its ownmost truth thematized in *Being and Time* and constitutes a fuller working out of the factical ideal referred to therein (H. 310). In *Being and Time*, hiddenness and untruth were for the most part considered in the light of the fallen present. The discussion of *Haltung* in *Einleitung in die Philosophie* also displays the reversals or about-turns of the metaphysical period: What characterizes Dasein there is a willingness to let the strangeness of beings be unconcealed (GA 27 338–41, 366–70). As in "What Is Metaphysics?," the interpretative accent falls on Dasein's non-evasion of the strangeness of beings as a whole. This turn to facticity, as we saw in the previous chapter, is a turn to the origin of truth, to the enigma of facticity, to the darkness and powerlessness which repels the Dasein intent on security. *Haltung* is a holding fast to this existential insecurity (GA 27 338–41).

Conclusion

In the preceding, we saw how the movement back to facticity allows Heidegger to interpret two phenomenological limit cases mentioned in *Being and Time*: birth and the world of mythical Dasein. Both the scream of infant Dasein and the astonishment of the mana-representation, the fundamental mythical affect, are responses to the immediacy and strangeness of beings as such, they originate from a kind of twilight state in which lines of distinction are erased and they react to what is prior to the formations of productive consciousness: the sheer strangeness of the world. Neither is primarily to be interpreted as belonging to a chronological past, be it personal or historical, but rather point toward a constitutive and basic feature of Dasein, its having been born or thrown. Perhaps most importantly, both indicate how we can maintain the philosophical *Haltung* where the ontological difference can explicitly emerge.

However, one very important problem remains outstanding, the problem of historicity. As already noted, mythical Dasein has an understanding of being but is unable to conceptualize this understanding and, it turns out, is unable to conceptualize itself as a self, as distinct from beings as a whole. This suggests that, at best, disclosing the temporal conditions for modes of understanding being and for the ontological difference is a possibility that belongs not to Dasein as such, but to our historical Dasein. Are the notions of historicality and the seeking of transcendental conditions incompatible? It is to this issue that we now turn.

Notes

1 This chapter develops, considerably expands, and to some degree implicitly critiques my earlier treatment of these themes in two short papers: Aengus Daly, "Zeitlichkeit und Geburt in Heideggers Auslegung der mythischen Umwelt," 267–78 and "Heidegger's Metaphysics of Objects: A Reply to Graham Harman," 228–38.

2   MFL 209 [GA 26 270].
3   My goal here is not to defend Heidegger's claims as an interpretation of Cassirer but instead to pursue the more limited aim of shedding light on how Heidegger's engagement with Cassirer is central to the unfolding of his overall problematic in this period.
4   Heidegger also claimed that he and Cassirer agreed on the need for an existential analytic (H. 51, xi). I am not aware of any independent corroboration of this claim.
5   See Heidegger, "Aufzeichnungen zur Temporalität," 11–23, here: 19 and Chapter 2 for a discussion of the relations between the ready-to-hand, the εἶδος and "always already."
6   In *Being and Time* Heidegger refers to primitive rather than mythical Dasein while in texts from 1928 onwards he uses the term "mythical Dasein." At times, Heidegger seems to see the two terms as roughly equivalent, for example in his reference to "primitive, mythical Dasein [*des primitiven, des mythischen Dasein*]" (MFL, 138 [GA 26, 174]). I use the term "mythical" as it avoids the pejorative overtones of "primitive"—which are misleading as "primitive" can also mean closer to the phenomena (H. 51)—and because *Bergung*, the basic stance mythical Dasein takes toward the world, does not simply belong to prehistory but also to the religion, science, and everydayness of our Dasein.
7   As we will see in what follows, mythical Dasein lacks the reflective distance to perform these operations of reflection and objectification. This is not to be considered so much a defect as the investigations of mythical Dasein provide significant indications concerning an original mode of temporality and thereby aid in shedding light on the problem of the temporality of ontological concept formation (cf. H. 349).
8   See Ernst Cassirer, *Philosophie der Symbolischen Formen, 2: Das Mythische Denken* (Darmstadt: Wiss. Buchgesellschaft: 1964), 50–61, cf. 245, 284–6. English translation: *The Philosophy of Symbolic Forms Volume 2: Mythical Thinking*, trans. Steve J. Lofts. (Abdington: Routledge, 2021), 48–56, cf. 244–6, 288–90.
9   And this is only raised as a possibility, for Heidegger refers to this understanding of being hypothetically: "*if* [*Wenn aber*] an understanding of being is constitutive for primitive Dasein" (H. 82, my emphasis). It becomes clear from writings in subsequent years that Heidegger does indeed think that mythical Dasein has an understanding of being and one that is made possible by a particular mode of the temporalizing of temporality. However, the hesitation is telling. Mythical Dasein, like infant Dasein, is a kind of limit case of Dasein. For Cassirer, mythical consciousness stands at the threshold between the human and the non-human. Yet the distinction between Dasein and non-Dasein is not equivalent to the distinction between the human and the nonhuman, as we will see in the next chapter. For a

discussion of mythical consciousness as the lower limit of the human, see Wunsch, *Fragen nach dem Menschen*, 185–200.

10 Moreover, as being-toward-death, Dasein's being is constituted by a fundamental "not yet." As we will see below, mythical Dasein is incapable of understanding death as its ownmost possibility.

11 See Chapter 3, Section 1 and Wunsch, "'Welt' in Heideggers metaphysischer Periode" and his *Fragen nach dem Menschen*, 18–29.

12 Lofts has rightly stressed the parallels between average everydayness and mythical Dasein, claiming that "access to this everydayness is facilitated through an analysis of the mythical life-world." The mythical world is of particular help in this regard because its self-interpretation is not distorted by inappropriate theorization. See Steve Lofts, "Cassirer and Heidegger: The Cultural-Event. The *Auseinandersetzung* of Thinking and Being" in *The Philosophy of Ernst Cassirer: A Novel Assessment*, eds. J. Tyler Friedman and Sebastian Luft (Berlin: De Gruyter, 2017), 233–58, here: 241. Yet what also must be borne in mind is that the absorption and the fallenness of mythical Dasein have a peculiar nature as mythical Dasein identifies itself with the power of beings as a whole and not with the surrounding referential totality of significance. Whereas our historical Dasein tends to think of itself as a "what," in the distinctive fallenness of mythical Dasein beings as a whole are understood as alive, as a "who" or a plurality of "whos." As we will see, this has implications for the historical possibility of raising the question of being: Because everything is understood on one level of being in the mythical, the ontological difference cannot emerge (KPM 181 [GA 3 256]).

13 In his 1936 commentary on *Being and Time*, Heidegger interprets the shift from speaking of "'the' meaning of being ['*der*' *Sinn des Seins*]" to "*a* meaning [ein *Sinn*]" as "the first essential insecurity [*die erste wesentliche Unsicherheit*]" in the work (GA 82 125). I will argue in the following section that the understanding of being underlying the givenness of beings in the mythical world—beings as a whole as overwhelming—is a non-understanding or a privative mode of understanding, one in which Dasein's thrownness and not its projective understanding has a priority. The ontological difference, as we saw in the previous chapter, refers to different, co-original, and reciprocally conditioning ways of (not) understanding being.

14 On this reading, the questions raised at the conclusion of Division II (H. 436–7) are questions the subsequent phenomenological investigation of this primal temporality broaches.

15 See Wunsch, *Fragen nach dem Menschen*, 42–3.

16 For example, as Heidegger uses the term at H. 179.

17 On birth in *Being and Time*, see Ó Murchadha, *The Time of Revolution*, 28–38. Ó Murchadha does not discuss the account of birth in *Einleitung in die Philosophie* or its role in Heidegger's interpretation of the mythical world.

18 Yet even this would be to ignore what Heidegger sees as the anthropological implications of the existential analytic in "laying bare that *a priori* basis which must be visible before the question of 'what man is' can be philosophically discussed," a task "hardly less pressing than the question of being itself" (H. 45). See Wunsch, *Fragen nach dem Menschen*, 21.

19 This turns around or inverts the emphasis placed on the light of the understanding in *Being and Time* (H. 133, 170, 350). That we lack the light or clarity for interpreting early Dasein and the Dasein of the earliest humans is no deficiency (GA 27 123) because what is at issue is a mode of temporality in which Dasein faces the darkness of its facticity.

20 GA 27 126. The original German text reads: "*Der Dämmerzustand, in dem ein solches frühes Dasein ist, besagt nicht, dass noch kein Verhältnis zum Seienden da wäre, sondern nur, dass dieses Sichverhalten zu … noch kein bestimmtes Ziel hat. Das Sein bei Seiendem ist gewissermaßen noch umwölkt, noch nicht aufgehellt, so dass dieses Dasein noch keinen bestimmten Gebrauch machen kann von dem Seienden, bei dem es immer schon seinem Wesen nach ist.*"

21 GA 27 126. The original German reads: "*Die primäre Interpretation muss zunächst dabei beginnen zu zeigen, wie sich die bloße Abkehr des Kindes unterscheidet von einer Abwehr. Die Abkehr ist ein bloße Ausweichen vor …, aber im Ausweichen ist schon eine bestimmte Abwehr, ein Abweisen von … In Fliehen vor etwas ist schon ein Dagegen, aber noch nicht ein Aktives; von der Abkehr und Abwehr müssen wir die Gegenwehr unterscheiden, bei der die eigentliche Gegenbewegung, das Entgegenstellen einsetzt. Alle diese Phänomene der Intentionalität sind zugleich derart, dass sie in ihrem Vollzug die erste Situation, in der sich ein solches Dasein in der anfänglich hilflosen Auslieferung an die Welt befindet, ausarbeiten.*"

22 See Jaran, *La Métaphysique du Dasein*, 193–200.

23 Cassirer, *Philosophie der Symbolischen Formen 2*, 94–6. English translation: *The Philosophy of Symbolic Forms 2*, 94–6.

24 Cassirer, *Philosophie der Symbolischen Formen 2*, 98–9. English translation: *The Philosophy of Symbolic Forms 2*, 96.

25 Cassirer, *Philosophie der Symbolischen Formen 2*, 97–100. English translation: *The Philosophy of Symbolic Forms 2*, 96–100.

26 Cassirer, *Philosophie der Symbolischen Formen 2*, 98. English translation: *The Philosophy of Symbolic Forms 2*, 97–8.

27 Cassirer, *Philosophie der Symbolischen Formen 2*, 99. English translation: *The Philosophy of Symbolic Forms 2*, 98, cf. H. 172, PM 95 [GA 9 121].

28 For instance, Cassirer both stresses that mythical consciousness lives in an "immediate *impression*"—"*lebt in unmittelbaren Eindruck*"—that grips and overwhelms it while also referring to the *mana*-representation, in the context of a reference to Codrington's anthropological work, as the core concept [*Kernbegriff*]

of mythical thinking. The first expression refers to how mythical consciousness is given pre-conceptually to itself, the second to how it is *conceived* in interpretations of the mythical world. See Cassirer, *Philosophie der Symbolischen Formen 2*, 93, 96. English translation: *The Philosophy of Symbolic Forms 2*, 94, 96.

29 More precisely, Heidegger claims the transcendental imagination is "*heimatlos*" (KPM 95 [GA 3 136]), a term whose political connotations were noted in Chapter 2. See Chapter 6 for a discussion of the political overtones of Heidegger's terminology and political implications of his philosophy.

30 My translation. The original German reads: "*In allen Mythologien bedeutet Sein nichts anderes als Übermacht, Mächtigkeit*" (GA 27 358).

31 Taking this in the context of Heidegger's interpretation of Kant and Cassirer in this period, I interpret this as referring to the understanding of the *a priori* in Cassirer's work, that is, as one which originates in the world of the ready-to-hand. The phenomena of mythical thinking are, on Heidegger's interpretation, to be understood in terms of another mode of temporality, a mode which must be *a priori* in a sense different from that of the tradition.

32 KPM 188 [GA 3 267–8].

33 Yet an important difference lies in the fact mythical Dasein is more alert to its being delivered over to its thrownness than new-born Dasein. The rituals and cults of mythical Dasein make manifest "the specific wakefulness to the being-delivered over to the overpowering [*der spezifischen Wachheit des Ausgeliefertseins an das Übermächtige*]" (GA 27 359).

34 KPM 181 [GA 3 256], cf. GA 27 126 on the twilight state of the new-born.

35 Cassirer, *Philosophie der Symbolischen Formen 2*, 187–8. English translation: *The Philosophy of Symbolic Forms 2*, 192 (translation modified), cf. KPM 189 [GA 3 268].

36 Cassirer, *Philosophie der Symbolischen Formen 2*, 253–5. English translation: *The Philosophy of Symbolic Forms 2*, 252–4.

37 I also read this as the basis for the connection Heidegger makes between anxiety and creativity (PM 93 [GA 9 118]).

38 KPM 185 [GA 3 262], cf. GA 27 357–8.

39 Yet conscience is not just alien but also "the voice of the friend whom every Dasein carries with it" (H. 163), and thus is a kindred phenomenon to "one's own self … [as] a power, as it were, which protectively takes up the individual I" (KPM 185 [GA 3 262]).

40 A point already made in BPP 120–1 [GA 24 171].

41 Crowell suggests translating *Haltung* with self-control. I argued in Chapter 1 a kind of self-control or, better, self-restraint is an existentiell condition for existential analysis in *Being and Time*, namely, a refraining from giving oneself over to the interpretative tendencies of the "they." And there can be no doubt here that

Heidegger is here taking up anew the problem of the factical ideal mentioned in the existential analytic (H. 310) and that self-restraint is essential to this. Yet the self as such is not at issue here and the term "control" risks to my mind obscuring the correlation between this stance, the experience of the overwhelming, and the creativity or play that is essential to Dasein's being. For these reasons, I prefer the wider term "the philosophical stance" as it ultimately concerns a specific and distinctive movement in which disclosure takes place, a movement that is both definite but lacking any determinate content. See Crowell, "The Middle Heidegger's Phenomenological Metaphysics," 229–50, here 236. I discuss Crowell's reading of Heidegger's metaphysics in the following chapter.

42 See Crowell, "The Middle Heidegger's Phenomenological Metaphysics," 236–7.
43 Again, mythical Dasein is pre-individual because it is incapable of grasping itself as ontologically distinct from the surrounding world and because it does not and cannot draw distinctions between the world of the living and the world of the death (KPM 181 [GA 3 256]).
44 Again, see Lofts (2015) 233–58, especially 241.

5

Transcendental Philosophy and Historicism?

We saw in the preceding chapter that Heidegger's venture into a phenomenology of the mythical world has two central features that bear on the further development of the project begun in *Being and Time*. First, he uses the temporality of thrownness, a key concept in the metaphysics of Dasein, to interpret the animism and sense of unity with all that, following Cassirer, he takes to be characteristic of earlier mythical cultures. Second, and correlated with this, Heidegger claims that Cassirer's own interpretation of the mythical world remains too indebted to a Kantian-transcendental framework.

Heidegger's treatment of this topic thus supports one of the major contentions of the present work, namely that Heidegger is engaged in a critique of the temporal presuppositions of Kantian transcendental philosophy in this period. We saw in Chapter 2 how the 1927 lecture course *The Basic Problems of Phenomenology* raises a basic difficulty for Heidegger: His investigation lays claim to an *a priori* status but also problematizes the relation between the traditional conception of the *a priori* and temporality. Heidegger tries to show that the Kantian *a priori*, which refers to a prior or "earlier" condition for understanding, is a time determination but that it is not based on a metaphysically original conception of time. It is, Heidegger claims, incapable of thinking how nature and history are originally given.

Yet this reading also runs counter to a widespread and long-standing interpretation that in *Being and Time* Heidegger extends Kant's question of the conditions of the possibility for understanding nature over to the meaning of being in general. This chapter takes up a challenge to my preceding arguments from this perspective, namely the critique of historicism and the variety of Kantian transcendental philosophy robustly defended in Steven Crowell's interpretation of Heidegger's work. Crowell's reading argues for a phenomenological conception of the *a priori* grounded in the consideration of concrete facts. He develops a notion of the *a priori* based on Dasein's practical identity, that is, one that does not simply use or take over an ontological paradigm grounded in dealings with the ready-to-hand.

Despite its sophistication, I argue this account of Heidegger's transcendental philosophy fails because it is based on an incomplete understanding of temporality, one that emphasizes our having a future and neglects our thrownness, and it oversimplifies the problems posed by the historical conditions for the manifestation of essential structures of Dasein's being. These findings have implications for understanding Heidegger's politics, which problem I will examine in more detail in the following chapter.

1 Historicism or Transcendental Philosophy?

Crowell provides a highly developed interpretation of Heidegger's *Being and Time* as a transcendental philosopher and makes a trenchant critique of historicist readings of his work. He locates Heidegger's phenomenology in this period firmly within the transcendental tradition: "phenomenology transforms transcendental philosophy by expanding its scope to embrace all experience, not just the cognitive, axiological, and practical 'validity spheres' addressed in Kant's three *Critiques*." It thus "accomplishes a universal generalization of the transcendental turn."[1] Yet he also emphasizes that this universalization does not involve simply importing a framework from Kant but entails a rethinking of the nature of the transcendental. Instead of focusing on purely formal possibility conditions, transcendental philosophy in the phenomenological vein "clears the space between formalism and empiricism."[2] This understanding stresses the phenomenological character of the *a priori* as grounded in the given rather than in extra-phenomenological or metaphysical dogmas.

Crowell explains both the collapse of the project of *Being and Time* and Heidegger's politics in the 1930s as resulting from Heidegger's falling prey to a quasi-Kantian transcendental illusion in which properly phenomenological concerns are run together with metaphysical-ontic considerations. He detects this most especially in the metaphysics of Dasein of the late 1920s but sees it as already present in the discussion of historicality in *Being and Time*. On this reading, "the collapse of *Being and Time* has less to do with phenomenology than with what proved to be a transitory positive evaluation of metaphysics."[3] In the following section I first focus on Crowell's critique of historicist readings of *Being and Time*[4] in *(a)*, then I turn to some of the key characteristics of the variety of transcendental philosophy he defends through his reading of Heidegger's work in *(b)*, before finally detailing why he sees Heidegger's metaphysics as linked to his *völkisch* metapolitics, both of which he interprets as separable from the properly phenomenological-transcendental concerns of *Being and Time*, in *(c)*.

(a) Crowell's Critique of Historicist Readings of Heidegger

Although Crowell locates Heidegger within the Kantian tradition of transcendental philosophy, he foregrounds an essential difference between the phenomenological and the Kantian *a priori*. He stresses that the former begins from a *given fact* and reflects on the essential characteristics of experiences we *happen to have*. This means the kind of necessity claimed by phenomenology differs from both metaphysical necessity and the necessity that Kant claims is supposed to hold of the structures of subjectivity as such. For phenomenological necessity is conditional: "given such and such a thing, it must have these and those features."[5] And although phenomenology starts from a given historical reality and is conditioned by it, this does not mean the claims it makes are simply contingent. Rather, by starting from a given and contingent fact—Crowell uses the example of the fact of memory—phenomenological analyses seek eidetic insight into what memory is. Such insight does not become undermined by the thing itself, memory, changing because it would then simply cease to be memory and would be something else (say, imagination, perception, etc.).

Such phenomenological insights are in principle capable of translation into other linguistic and conceptual schemes, that is, they are not simply relative to a given culture. Engagement with other conceptual schemes can lead us to amend and refine our initial analyses. But this does not entail a cultural relativism for, as Crowell points out, "nothing in the sheer existence of different cultural practices rules out the possibility of grasping trans-cultural universals." Even if the language, practices, and schemes of one culture make some things easier and others more difficult to access or understand, "mere fallibilism of this sort cannot by itself undermine the very possibility of *a priori* insight."[6]

Heidegger's phenomenology too starts from a contingent fact: the existence of Dasein. From this fact, phenomenological analyses can uncover the essential features of what it is to be Dasein. For example, because "understanding and emotional attunement are both necessary structures of Dasein, the being who dwells in a world of meaning,"[7] if a being were entirely affectless, it would simply no longer be Dasein. Hence although Heidegger's hermeneutics of facticity is concerned with "things that can always be otherwise," it "still aims at essential, theoretical truth" and grasps the essential features of Dasein's being.[8]

Crowell points out that historicist positions[9] emphasize the changes in meaning and understanding over time and use this fact to argue against the possibility of *a priori* insight. They claim that because truth claims are historically and culturally conditioned, they are also historically and culturally relative. It would follow from such a "Voluntarist metaphysical faith in the alchemy of time" that statements about what Dasein essentially is, such that we find in Heidegger's work, cannot make any claim to *a priori* insight. The fact of linguistic and historical change, on this view, puts any claim to transcendental, immutable, or timeless truth into question. It entails that "for all we know Dasein could develop into a creature who inhabits a world of meaning, yet is entirely affectless."[10] Crowell argues that such an extreme skepticism would entail that nothing intelligible can be said as everything is possible. Much like the "voluntarist theology of the fourteenth century," it ends up with the claim that "any order or necessity we grasp in the world is unreliable."[11] Further, the status of this claim itself undermines its own claim to coherence: "… if the point is that *things themselves* change in such a way as to rule out any genuine trans-historical necessities, what sort of claim is that? If it is an essential phenomenological insight, it refutes itself and is contradicted by other essential insights; and if it is an empirical generalization (or sceptical induction) it begs the question."[12]

However, if we remain within the bounds of the given, "the hermeneutic exploration of our factic situation suffices for insight into necessary connections." "Temporal distance is just difference," in other words, the deep historical past does not undermine claims to *a priori* insight.[13] Even if we cannot say *why* Dasein is or claim to know the ground that brought it into being, we can nonetheless identify, beginning from the contingent fact *that* it is, what essential features any Dasein must have.

In confusing historicality with empirical historical change, Crowell contends, the historicist falls prey to a quasi-Kantian transcendental illusion. At the heart of the historicist argument is "a tendency to equivocate on two separate concepts of facticity, or perhaps two aspects of a single concept": facticity in the strict sense, that which is "*unavailable* to reflection," and facticity in the broader sense of the term, which refers to our situated embodiment in a social and historical situation.[14] The former refers to the radical otherness prior to reflection which we face in anxiety, the fact of our essential thrownness into the world. The latter encompasses phenomena like "embodiment, history, language and social practices" that, although culturally and historically conditioned, are in principle capable of being investigated and intuitively unfolded through phenomenological reflection.[15]

Crowell argues that when these two different senses of facticity get run together, one aspect of the subject's facticity is "singled out and given quasi-metaphysical status": history, tradition, power, language, the flesh, or, in the case of the Heidegger of the metaphysical period, nature or the overpowering.[16] But he claims these cannot "be identified with the factic ground of the subject in the strict sense, since they are all available to phenomenological reflection." Facticity in the strict sense is radically other to reflection while these "are in fact 'constituted aspects of transcendental subjectivity,'" "can be intuitively unfolded, or made explicit, in reflection," and thus cannot "shed any *light at all* on Dasein's facticity in the strict sense."[17] Such quasi-metaphysical claims arbitrarily project what are in fact constituted aspects of transcendental subjectivity into the unknown, beyond the scope of any possible phenomenological evidence. For facticity in the strict sense is precisely that which resists insight and explanation.

Crowell thus argues we cannot claim "that facticity is equivalent to something like embodiment or history," that "the surreptitiously metaphysical appeal to an absolute notion of historical change is illicit, [and that] the mere existence of this or any 'radically other' factic ground cannot render otiose a claim of insight into essential truth."[18] In fact, we lack any criterion for opting for one rather than another of these quasi-metaphysical absolutes—for deciding between Gadamer's tradition, Foucault's power, Merleau-Ponty's flesh, or Heidegger's overpowering or nature. Because such claims have moved beyond the bounds of any phenomenological evidence, they stray into a quasi-Kantian antinomy.[19]

(b) Transcendental Philosophy and Normativity

On Crowell's interpretation, the transcendental project must be rethought in the face of Dasein's facticity rather than abandoned. The first step in "appreciating Heidegger's revision of transcendental philosophy is to break the assumed identification between facticity and historicality." The historicist misses this because they fall prey to "an understandable but fatal interpretative slide that equates a moment of Dasein's original temporality with a dimension of historical time."[20] Historical time is *das Vergangene*, the bygone or what has been, whereas the moment of Dasein's original temporality is *das Gewesene*. The latter is not the chronologically prior but refers to Dasein's essential alreadiness, its being-already-in-the-world. Drawing on the analyses of Thomas Sheehan, Crowell argues:

> "*Gewesenheit* indicates not a tense but an aspect: the '*a priori* perfect' or the perfect tense in an *a priori* 'aspect'—not 'that which has been and still is, but that which is always prior to and beyond our determination.' Corresponding to the Aristotelian term often translated as essence (*to ti en enai*), *Gewesenheit* has nothing to do with what I am 'in the process of becoming" or 'what has occurred in the past and continues to impact in the present.' It is what I *always* already am."[21]

There is thus an essential difference between on the one hand the historical past, what has been, that we draw upon in understanding ourselves and the world (explicitly when we authentically acknowledge our factical *historicality*) and on the other our essential alreadiness, our essential thrownness into the world, our *facticity*, a basic and necessary aspect of being-in-the-world disclosed in anxiety.

And this double sense of Dasein's facticity—its *that-it-is* and its *having-to-be*—entails, Crowell claims, both "philosophical autonomy" and a "concern with reason and truth."[22] Anxiety does more than make manifest the meaningless of the world, it also reveals that we must take over a possibility of being in the world, that we have to take up reasons for one possibility rather than another in the space of the world. In other words, "... what anxiety reveals is not the nihilistic absence of normativity but my *responsibility* for it" and "doing so means I turn grounds (in the sense of givens) into *reasons*."[23] Turning grounds into reasons implies a discursive practice concerned with "'grounding,'" that is, reason-giving, "an interest in truth," and in "getting it right about something." On Crowell's interpretation, "in the very same movement" where Dasein discovers its autonomy in responding to the call of conscience, it also discovers the world as a normative space and therewith "the project of reason-giving." This self is "a being defined by a concern for normativity." Transcendental philosophy is ultimately "nothing but the factic subject's authentic self-understanding."[24]

Crowell develops these claims further in his 2013 work *Normativity and Phenomenology in Husserl and Heidegger*. On this interpretation, Heidegger's phenomenology in *Being and Time* uncovers the conditions for the possibility of responsiveness to the normative as such. Central here is Heidegger's account of conscience as the call of care. Conscience is the condition for the possibility of making factical *grounds* into justifying *reasons* for certain actions. Responding to the call of conscience occurs in the moment Crowell aptly describes as "possibilizing."[25] When the significance of the social space withdraws in anxiety, all grounds are brought back to one (primal) ground, which is the sheer fact of my being-in-the-world, and I am opened to different possibilities that make a claim upon me and to my own agency and answerability in taking up a practical identity.

Crowell highlights a key claim in the discussion of conscience and guilt as indicating this movement to responsibility and answerability. Heidegger writes: "The self, which as such has to lay the ground for itself, can never get that ground into its power; and yet, as existing, it must take over being-a-ground."[26] Crowell notes that Heidegger here plays on the double meaning of "*Grund*" as both "ground as *facticity* and ground as *reason*," elaborating that "the notion of ground is twofold, thanks to the two equiprimordial aspects of Dasein's being: thrownness and projection."[27] In the first sense, factical grounds means things I am subject to as thrown into the world—nature, my inclinations, social roles that it is possible for me to assume, etc. But these are not just givens or brute facts but are *possibilities* that I *can* be claimed by. Understanding that some are to be preferred to others is to enter the space of reasons. This is the condition for being able to make the diverse claims of facticity, nature, inclination, language, and history my own.

It is important to underscore that Crowell understands the *a priori* constitutive of Dasein in terms of responsible, practical identity rather than in terms of an equipmental paradigm. He insists on the temporal distinction between striving to live up to a practical identity (atelic and ongoing) and finishing a piece of work (telos-oriented, anticipating its future completion).[28] For example, completing a task—for example preparing a seminar—is an undertaking that makes sense against the background of a larger context of significance and ultimately my sense of who I am and my trying to live up to the norms inherent in the practical identity I have taken up—for instance, of a university teacher. While completing the task is a short-term project, the underlying social role is ongoing, prescriptive of goal-oriented action rather than a goal capable of being fulfilled. For the practical identity whose norms I implicitly recognize is not telos-oriented but rather atelic and ongoing.

These claims obviously pose a major challenge to the theses on the *a priori* in Heidegger's project developed in the previous chapters. For there I argued that Heidegger rejected the traditional conception of the *a priori* because it was rooted in the experience of poesis, in making, and that this conception was incapable of taking into consideration the temporality peculiar to Dasein's being. Yet if the reading defended by Crowell is correct, the type of *a priori* perfect that belongs to Dasein is in fact rooted in its own kind of being, where its response to the claim of the normative and its taking up of a practical identity is at issue.

(c) Heidegger's Metaphysics and Metapolitics

Crowell's understanding of what he designates the "middle Heidegger's phenomenological metaphysics" also underpins his analysis of Heidegger's *völkisch* politics. For on his interpretation, this metaphysics not only has nothing genuinely phenomenological about it but also highlights the philosophical error—seeking an ontic ground for ontology—that underlay Heidegger's endorsement of National Socialism. This reading has the advantage of allowing a clear line of demarcation between Heidegger's purportedly genuine philosophical accomplishment in *Being and Time* and his disastrous politics. Crowell reads this metaphysics as attempting to provide an ontic ground for ontology and thereby a bridge between truth disclosing Dasein and the factical human being that each of us in each case is, in other words, for bringing together the transcendental and the empirical.[29]

I will focus on three central claims that Crowell makes: first, that Heidegger's account of the conditions for Dasein's normative responsibility are existentially neutral, factically and politically, second, his critique of Heidegger's account of the play of transcendence as making possible the space of norms and roles, and third what he contends is Heidegger's illegitimate shift from the phenomenology of individual self-responsibility in *Being and Time* to a "we intentionality" of the people or *Volk*.

The movement of Dasein's transcendence does have a place on Crowell's interpretation: It opens Dasein to the claim of the normative and enables authentic responsibility. "The world formed in this way [in transcendence] is normatively ordered, not by an implicit telos of reason but by freedom's capacity, as self-control, to pass beyond the totality of entities toward what is *epekeina tes ousias, ta agathon*, toward a norm or measure [*Vor-bild*] (1998a: 123–4)." It is what allows Dasein to submit itself to the claim of a norm [*Vor-bild*]: for example, not just doing what teachers do, what is common practice, but striving to realize the good in this social practice. "The way of world-forming in which this orientation toward a norm comes to prominence" is one that concerns "the human being's responsibility for its understanding of what it means to be *whatever* it is trying to be."[30]

Heidegger's attempt to provide an ontic ground for ontology inevitably introduces grounds, conditioned by factors like politics, history, embodiment, and sexuality that are ultimately contingent, unlike the neutral and formal conditions that existential analysis seeks to disclose. Once these factors are brought in, the problem becomes that of how we cross over from the ontically conditioned empirical human being to Dasein in its neutrality as having the transcendental capacity for disclosing truth. The metaphysical notion of play as characterizing Dasein's world-forming is, on Crowell's reading, supposed to bridge this gap. He writes:

> "The ontic ground of ontology would thus lie in 'life's' capacity for world-forming, and the paradox of human subjectivity would be resolved by showing how the worldview of self-control[31] develops (transcendental) philosophy—acting for the sake of being a philosopher—as one of its possibilities, one in which world-forming itself is thematized as the condition for grasping the being (*truth*) of things."[32]

Heidegger thus attempts to bridge the gap between the ontic and the ontological on the level of individual possibility. World-forming is the condition for grasping the being of things, it is in this that anything like norms, rules, and social roles take form [*sich bilden*] (GA 27 309–14), that is, become meaningful to Dasein. One of these possibilities open to Dasein is grasping this as such.

Yet Crowell contends this attempt is unsuccessful as "Heidegger provides no epistemic justification for the metaphysical conception of life as play," it is not tied to any specific way of being which "leaves it unclear how acting for the sake of being a philosopher connects with truth," and, correlatively, because of the gap between this understanding of the play of life and "'neutral' Dasein's transcendental capacity for disclosing the truth, that capacity will only be *contingently* connected to the world forming essence of the human being." Indeed, as conditioned by contingent factors like politics, sexuality, bodiliness that belong to the specific factual situation of the philosopher, it can only yield *doxa* and can be no more than an individual and arbitrary attempt at world-formation.[33]

Crowell does not deny that such ontic grounds are mentioned in the existential analytic, but he does deny they are needed. This is the background to his claim we can afford to ignore the *völkisch* claims of the chapter on Dasein's historicality, maintaining it is essentially an excursus that brings nothing new methodologically and does not fit with the project of disclosing existentially neutral structures. Crowell allows that individual action implies a community, co-historicizing, and a confrontation with a given heritage, but this differs depending on which rule-governed social practice Dasein is involved with, for instance "a community of teachers, a community of physicians, of parents, of baseball fans." And he claims a fundamental difficulty here lies in providing phenomenological evidence for identifying the community with the *Volk* as that which transcends any particular heritage.³⁴ Following Marion Heinz, he sees this tendency in the historicality chapter as exacerbated in the 1930s "because Heidegger [then] ascribes the ontological characteristics of neutral Dasein to the *Volk*, the whole analysis of resoluteness from *Being and Time* is carried over to the 'we', the first person *plural*," an endeavor goes together with a critique of the atomism of liberal societies.³⁵ The metapolitical notion of the *Volk* forms the bridge between the formal neutral structures of existential analysis and the factically and historically existent human being. This shift, Crowell claims, is phenomenologically illegitimate and overlooks that "the empirical and the transcendental do not belong together in this way." Crowell pulls no punches in his assessment of this metaphysical and metapolitical project: "... Heidegger's metapolitical form of passage does away with the transcendental claims of phenomenology altogether, leaving nothing in its place but a chauvinistic historical worldview that he himself will soon abandon, and with it the incoherent idea of an ontic ground of ontology."³⁶ On this interpretation, the incoherent project of metaphysics, which introduces ontic grounds for what should have remained a formal transcendental analysis, does not impinge upon the validity of the latter, but is a departure from the properly phenomenological in Heidegger's work.

2 Transcendental Philosophy and Dasein's Temporal Transcendence

Despite significant differences, there are similarities between the interpretation of Heidegger developed in the preceding chapters and Crowell's interpretation. I agree that in *Being and Time*'s break with historicism "we glimpse the existential roots of transcendental philosophy"³⁷ and also with Crowell's insistence on the double sense of Dasein's facticity—its "that it is" and its "having to be"—his detection of essential ambiguities in Heidegger's use of the terms *Grund*,³⁸ and his stress on the movement of possibilizing at the heart of Heidegger's account of temporality.³⁹

However, I will argue in the following that Heidegger's account of temporality impacts his understanding of concept formation at a deeper level than Crowell recognizes. Further, Heidegger's understanding of nature as the overpowering is not an arbitrary metaphysical presupposition but is given in the experience of the withdrawal of significance in anxiety where Dasein finds itself overwhelmed, overpowered, unable to get a grip on things. It thus has a genuinely phenomenological basis. Moreover, the underlying movement of temporality here provides the phenomenological justification for the notion of play (*(a)* and *(b)*). I then contend that Dasein's historicality runs deeper than Crowell allows: It is that which grants or denies possibilities of understanding and so provides contingent openings onto necessary structures. This thesis does not, I argue, imply that these structures are themselves contingent (*(c)*). The transcendental philosophy Heidegger develops thus encompasses both Dasein's historicality and its factical situatedness in nature. Acknowledging this, however, also makes the relation of Heidegger's philosophy and politics more complicated than Crowell recognizes (*(d)*).

(a) The Essential Equivocations in Ontological Concepts

I argued in the preceding chapters that we can detect the original and distinctive movement of temporality in the peculiarities of ontological concept formation in Heidegger's work. And Crowell's analyses testify to this point: When he diagnoses an essential weakness in the historicist's position as rooted in "a tendency to equivocate on two separate concepts of facticity, or perhaps two aspects of a single concept,"[40] this diagnosis itself equivocates on the notion of facticity. Is it a single concept or are there two separate concepts at play? Heidegger's texts seem to support both readings. On the one hand, the facticity of Dasein's sheer being-in-the-world is distinct from the facticity of language, tradition, history, social practices. On the other hand, both senses are interrelated, referring to the "that-it-is" of Dasein's thrownness and the "having-to-be" of its ahead-of-itself respectively. This hesitation as to whether there are one or two concepts at play here has its basis in the peculiar structure of Dasein's being as thrown projection.

The ambiguities in Heidegger's use of the term *Grund*, to which Crowell draws our attention, also bear witness to this. Heidegger writes: "The self, which as such has to lay the ground for itself, can never get that basis into its power; and yet, as existing, it must take over being-a-ground [*Das Selbst, das als solches den Grund seiner selbst zu legen hat, kann dessen nie mächtigwerden und hat doch existierend das Grundsein zu übernehmen*]" (H. 284[41]). What is of particular interest here—as Crowell recognizes—is that the different senses of term "ground" itself reflect the back-and-forth character of the call of conscience and the "possibilizing" movement of temporality that enables any responsiveness to the world. Dasein is called forth to take over reasons in the space of the world as the being that it has to be by being called back to the Dasein it is already, in its facticity. This accords,

Crowell notes, two "*equiprimordial* aspects of Dasein's being: thrownness and projection."[42]

These distinct meanings are thus correlated with different temporal ecstaces. In this light of the preceding analyses, this finding is not unexpected: The distinctiveness of Heidegger's ontological concepts lies precisely in their multi-dimensionality, their taking on different senses in different modes of temporalization. As we saw, other key Heideggerian terms (for example *Welt*, *Augenblick*, *Verweisung*) also exhibit an essential polysemy that resists reduction to a single meaning. This multi-dimensionality is entailed by the peculiar temporality underlying ontological concept formation.

Yet despite recognizing this equiprimordiality with respect to the term "*Grund*" and the ambiguities in Heidegger's conception of facticity, Crowell's interpretation focuses almost exclusively on the "forth" movement of Dasein's temporality, its taking over of grounds as reasons. Dasein's being turned back to its facticity in anxiety does indeed appear as an essential moment in this, but it is a *preliminary* to the taking over of a finite possibility. This reading neglects those moments in the analyses of *Being and Time* where Heidegger signals that his analyses are incomplete because they have yet to fully consider the difficult problem of Dasein's facticity (H. 56).

We see this especially in §63, which provides an outline of the overall (projected) trajectory of Heidegger's investigation: (1) The "preparatory analysis of everydayness" leads to (2) "the first conceptual definition of 'care'"[43] and (3) the "more precise grasp of existence and its relations to facticity and falling." This stage has been attained in the analyses before §63. These allow (4) "defining the structure of care" on the basis of temporality (§§64 and 65),[44] thus grasping the "formal idea of existence." A projected stage (5), which distinguishes between the idea of existence and "the idea of Reality,"[45] was to be followed by (6) showing how both "'presuppose' an idea of being in general" because in both the ideas of existence and the Real "what we have in view is *being*" and that it is "within the horizon of *this* idea of being [in general]" that "the distinction between existence and Reality is accomplished [*vollziehen*]" (H. 314). We find much the same distinction in §77 where Heidegger claims that "the idea of being embraces both the 'ontical' and the 'historical'" and "*this idea* ... must let itself be 'generically differentiated'" (H. 403).[46] This so-called "'generic differentiation'"[47]—is to be elaborated "by bringing both the 'ontical' and the 'Historical' into a *more primordial unity*" (H. 403). And precisely this is the theme of the metaphysics of Dasein.

Crowell's focus on the "forth" movement of Dasein's temporality is explained by his desire to elaborate a phenomenology of the normative inspired by

Heidegger rather than by concern with Heidegger exegesis as such. Yet the above considerations suggest that the metaphysics of facticity is more closely intertwined with the project of *Being and Time* than this reading acknowledges, not least with respect to the formation and the nature of the concepts Heidegger employs.

(b) Facticity and a Priority

Yet we also saw that on Crowell's interpretation the attempt to make metaphysical claims about the nature of Dasein's facticity is doomed to failure: We can say nothing about facticity in the strong sense of the term, he claims, because it is that which is totally other to reflection. Any attempt at a metaphysics of facticity ends up arbitrarily selecting one aspect of Dasein's facticity—history, tradition, power, language, the flesh, or, like the Heidegger of the metaphysical period, nature or the overpowering—and absolutizing it by projecting it upon an ontological void. Hence even if the problem of a metaphysics of facticity was a crucial but backgrounded part of Heidegger's project in *Being and Time*, as I have argued, this would not pose any real difficulties to the position Crowell defends if such a metaphysics of facticity is itself a senseless nonstarter.

However, there are good reasons to believe Heidegger's position on facticity is more sophisticated and better grounded in the phenomena than Crowell's characterization acknowledges. When Heidegger refers to the overpowering or nature as the basic sense of Dasein's facticity in *The Metaphysical Foundations of Logic*, this is not, as Crowell claims, an arbitrary metaphysical presupposition about what lies beyond the scope of givenness. It characterizes the experience of our limits or of our finitude: We run up against these in the experience of finding ourselves unable, overwhelmed, overpowered. We are then faced with what is totally other to reflection and resistant to conceptualization, the inherent strangeness of beings as a whole. This understanding by privation is a positive phenomenological finding. Our concepts do not hold, we find ourselves at a loss before the oppressive strangeness of beings, and faced with the enigma of being-in-the-world. This sense of being overwhelmed and "in the dark"—conceptually, emotionally, and practically—is at the same time an insight into the limitations of practical and theoretical capability.

This is why, in contrast to the preliminary characterization of the phenomenon of phenomenology in *Being and Time*, §7, the darkness of facticity belongs to the *Evidenz* situation in the metaphysical period (GA 27 339–40). This is essentially linked to the thematization of the ecstasis of temporality that remained in the background of *Being and Time*: the temporality of thrownness. The experience of *meaninglessness* in this mode of temporality is a positive finding and it comes into view through the *withdrawal* of our possibilities of understanding and of any possible horizon of meaningfulness.[48]

This undercuts the potential objection to my position noted earlier, namely, that the *a priori* that belongs to Dasein's being is not the *a priori* perfect that is rooted in production but rather that belongs to the distinctive, atelic temporality of living up to a norm-governed practical identity. The latter cannot provide us with the last word on the *a priori* constitution of Dasein's being because it is but *one* aspect of the temporalizing of authentic temporality and one *conditioned by* Dasein's having previously come face to face with its facticity as such. In other words, if we are seeking the *a priori* that is constitutive of Dasein's being, we cannot prioritize *one* mode—not even a fundamental mode—of temporality over others. Dasein's possibilizing—the movement in which Dasein discovers its autonomy—is also conditioned by its having encountered the strangeness of beings and the sheer "that-it-is" of its being-in-the-world. While the latter could perhaps remain a secondary or preliminary moment in a phenomenology of normativity, it cannot be backgrounded in a full treatment of Dasein's being and in bringing out the distinctive sense(s) of the *a priori* that belongs to it.

Read against this background, the notion of play in Heidegger's work also appears as having a phenomenological legitimacy. It is not surprising that Crowell singles out the passages in *Einleitung in die Philosophie* on play specifically for critique because it is here that Heidegger claims that the notions of norms, rules, and practical identity, that is, phenomena central to Crowell's own normative phenomenology, depend on a metaphysical conception of play. Yet his claim that Heidegger's analysis of this point lacks any epistemic justification seems to me implausible. For Heidegger emphasizes there is play in every *Stimmung* (GA 27 312) thus suggesting that here, as at other key points in this lecture course, his analysis is to be understood from out of *Being and Time*. In the existential analytic, the primary discovery of the world belongs to bare mood, it opens the space of the world as mattering to us, makes possible meaningful engagement, allows us to take up a stance in the world, deal with projects and things, relate to others, and decide on a way of being.

So when Heidegger contends that play belongs to the *metaphysical* essence of human beings, the qualification "metaphysical" highlights that the notion of transcendence and the temporal movement it implies is the key issue here. This is why it is especially important that the analysis of play ascribes joy, *Freude*, a particular privilege (GA 27 312). In *Being and Time* Heidegger had referred to the need to give existential analysis an ontic basis and referred to a "definite ontical way of taking authentic existence, factical ideal" as a presupposition to be unfolded at a later stage. But he initially characterizes it as "a sober understanding of what are factically the basic possibilities for Dasein" accompanied by both a taking action "without illusions" and with an "unshakeable joy [*Freude*]" (H. 310).

The world, as a meaningful totality, forms itself in the back-and-forth movement, the play of transcendence. The notion of play, then, belongs to how Dasein's temporality temporalizes itself, its possibilizing, to use Crowell's term. With the collapse of meaning in anxiety, Dasein cannot anticipate how the world will show itself as meaningful anew, how it will speak to it. There is an essential unpredictability to the appearing of the world as a meaningful space. This creative re-configuration of the space of meaning belongs to the essence of transcendence. What is at play therein is what Dasein will respond to, what possibilities—including the possibility of thematizing this transcendence—will emerge from this nihilative-creative movement. This movement of possibilizing thus provides the phenomenological justification for Heidegger's conception of play. It rounds out a crucial aspect of the unfinished existential analysis of *Being and Time*.

(c) Contingency, Necessity, and Factical History

Taking into account the temporality of thrownness also suggests a more complicated picture of the relation between identifying the essential constituents of Dasein's being, its historicality, and empirical history. On Crowell's reading, Dasein's having-being is distinct to the contingent constituents of empirical history, the bygone or the past.[49] For just as a phenomenological analysis of the contingent fact of memory reveals the criteria for what memory is, so too existential analysis brings out the essential constituents of Dasein's being. A being without attunement and understanding, who did not dwell in a world of meaning, would simply not be Dasein.

Yet the two borderline cases discussed in the previous chapter—the Dasein of the mythical world and of infants—suggest this separation is not so readily made and that the relation between the universality and necessity of existential structures and the historical conditions for their manifestation is more complicated than this. For mythical Dasein does not have characteristics that are essential to our historical Dasein. Central to Heidegger's interpretation of the mythical world is the *immediacy* of this Dasein's being-in-the-world, its sense of itself as bound to all things or to the all as a living whole. Because it sees no separation between meaning and thing—the ontological difference in the restrictive sense that Crowell emphasizes—it cannot understand meaning as meaning and so cannot raise the question of the conditions for the possibility of meaning. Mythical Dasein is incapable of the individuation that is a precondition for raising the question of being or even for understanding itself as "in each case mine" (H. 42). Further, it does not even understand tools as tools or things as individual things: *Things* do not matter to it. In other words, unlike our historical Dasein, the Dasein of the mythical world does not understand meaning as meaning, tools as tools, things as things, and is not even capable of understanding itself as "in each case mine," as the being for whom being is an issue, or even as distinct from the surrounding all.

This means at least some phenomenologically revelatory moods, such as anxiety, are historically conditioned, that is, they are not possible for all Dasein-like entities. The showing itself of Dasein's being in the world as such—Dasein's givenness to itself as Dasein—has historical, hermeneutical conditions for its possibility. This problematizes the separation between the two senses of facticity to which Crowell calls our attention: the contingent facticity of culture, tradition, empirical history on the one hand and the brute facticity constitutive of Dasein's being as such. For access to the essential structure of Dasein's sheer facticity is itself historically conditioned. Our facticity, our being in the face of beings as a whole, can only come into view as such in a specific mood, anxiety. The limit cases of the mythical world and infancy, where Dasein has not and cannot have a sense of itself as an individual, show that this is a possibility that *our* historical Dasein has and not Dasein as such. In other words, the attunement crucial to the disclosure of Dasein's being is not a possibility in the mythical world or the world of infants. There are historical conditions for the possibility of the self-manifestation of certain original phenomena.

The two borderline cases of the mythical world and infancy also suggest that there is no necessary incompatibility between transcendental philosophy and historicism. Both mythical Dasein and infants are part of the human species. Both are exposed to the strangeness of beings and the condition for this lies in ecstatic temporality, a universal constituent of Dasein as such. Neither, however, is capable of either bringing into view or thematizing this openness to beings as such. Both limit cases also show that the possibility of grasping and seizing hold of one's finitude does not belong to the human as such but is granted in a given historical time and a given period of life, that is, where

Dasein has grown up in possibilities but has not yet been "disintegrated and been used up" (H. 244) and where the "rare" event of anxiety occurs (H. 191). Both limit cases show that openness to the truth of existence has its occasion, it is not there for all time, be this time either historical or a lifetime. Dasein can respond to this historical and temporal openness through an existentiell seizing hold of the task of existential analysis but this openness itself must be granted or *geschickt*.

The disclosure of basic existential structures has as its enabling conditions an occasion and a historical site. These are contingent in the sense of not always being available but are *also* necessary features of that specific hermeneutic situation from which existential structures are brought into view. These latter, in other words, have historical conditions for their manifestation but they show themselves as universal and necessary structures of all Dasein-like entities in that situation. This means that the showing themselves of these structures as universal and necessary is a historical possibility that we can seize hold of, that belongs to a specific historical situation.

Crowell rightly insists that the fact that access to basic structures is culturally conditioned does not exclude our being able to grasp trans-cultural universals.[50] However, nothing in bringing into view and thematizing universal structures implies that these are accessible at all times and to everyone nor that they are universally translatable into other times and places. If such openness to existential truth is contingent, this does not mean that what is thereby given is therefore relative, rather that its becoming accessible in its universality and necessity has its occasion, its time and, Heidegger would contend, its site or place in which it can show itself as universal. It is from this perspective that we can conceive a historical transcendental philosophy that does not fall into a self-refuting relativism. It is one that takes account of the historical and temporal contingency of the possibility of disclosing necessary structures. These structures are given from out of and to a privileged site.

(d) History and Politics

If the arguments of the preceding sections are correct, then the line of demarcation Crowell proposes between the transcendental-phenomenological project of *Being and Time* and the turn to facticity and ultimately to politics cannot be drawn. The proximity between Heidegger's philosophy and his politics is the topic of the next chapter, the aim of the present section is to show that the arguments Crowell marshals to separate them are not successful.

As mentioned above, Crowell contends of Dasein's transcendence that "[t]he world formed in this way is normatively ordered, not by an implicit telos of reason but by freedom's capacity, as self-control, to pass beyond the totality of entities toward what is *epekeina tes ousias, ta agathon*, toward a norm or measure [*Vor-bild*] (1998a: 123–4)." Yet when we turn to the pages Crowell refers us to in the discussion of this point, we find Heidegger stresses the *political site* of self-responsibility.[51] Heidegger contends the "problem of the ἀγαθόν is merely the culmination of the central and fundamental possibility of the *existence of the Dasein* in the polis … For the ἀγαθόν is the ἕξις (sovereign power) that is sovereign with respect to *the possibility (in the sense of the enabling) of truth, understanding, and even being, and indeed of all three together in their unity*" (PM 124 [GA 9 160], my emphasis). The space of norms is that of the polis, there is already in this a return to an enabling political space. In his treatment of the passage cited from the *Republic* in his 1926 seminars on ancient philosophy, Heidegger claims the enabling good is the πόλις which acts as the "soil and domain of the problem of being [*Boden und Umkreis der Seinproblematik*]" (BCA 197, cf. 81 [GA 22 254 cf. 99]). Heidegger's treatment of Aristotle in 1924 makes a similar point, stressing that "the πόλις is the being possibility, the φύσει, that itself lies enclosed and traced out in advance in the human being's genuine being," the shared political space "is grounded in a having-with one another of something, in the specific sense of a κοινωνία of συμφέρον and ἀγαθόν" (BC 35 [GA 18 49]).

This issue is also central to the chapter on Dasein's historicality in *Being and Time*: It concerns the enabling conditions for Dasein's authenticity. The community and the *Volk*'s shared heritage of possibilities appear *in* authentic being-toward-death *as* the "'goodness' [that] lies in making authentic existence possible" (H. 383, cf. GA: 26 137–8/184–5). Although Heidegger is interested in disclosing existential conditions, his concern is not with "the human being's responsibility for its understanding of what it means to be *whatever* it is trying to be"[52] but first and foremost with the distinctive existentiell possibility in which these structures become manifest. The Dasein carrying out existential analysis is not neutral and the analysis of existential structures has factical, historical conditions: "the roots of the existential analytic, on its part, are ultimately *existentiell*, that is, ontical *[Die existenziale Analytik ihreseits aber ist letztlich existentiell, d. h. ontisch verwurzelt]*" (H. 13). This enterprise presupposes not just any heritage, any society, or any set of social practices but the heritage that is taken up in seizing hold of this existentiell possibility of existential analysis. For such analysis is rooted in an inherited language and conceptuality. Without the work of Kant, Aristotle, Husserl, Cassirer, and numerous others, an existential analytic would be quite literally inconceivable. There is, I contended previously, no inherent contradiction in the claim that universal existential structures are to be disclosed at a privileged site and time. However, when taken together with Heidegger's emphasis on Dasein's rootedness, especially when read together with his claim that the πόλις acts as the "soil and domain of the problem of being [*Boden und Umkreis der Seinproblematik*],"[53] this suggests Heidegger's phenomenological-transcendental inquiry in *Being and Time* and his *völkisch* politics are not mutually exclusive.

Further, Crowell's contention that there is a shift from the individual self-responsibility described in the existential analytic over to the first-person plural or the *Volk* in later texts also seems to me questionable. The concern with the historically situated first person plural is present on the first line Heidegger himself wrote in *Being and Time*: "Do *we today* [wir heute] have an answer to the question of what we really mean by the word 'being'?"[54] (H. 1, my emphasis, translation modified). He had already stressed in 1925, so prior to *Being and Time*, that "Each is not only his self, but his generation. The generation precedes the individual, is there before him and determines his Dasein [*Jeder ist nicht nur er selbst, sondern seine Generation. Die Generation geht vor dem Einzelen vorweg, ist vor ihm da und bestimmt sein Dasein*]" (GA 801. 173). This critique of liberal atomism, which Crowell sees as among the disastrous innovations of the 1930s, is also very much present in the Dilthey-Yorck correspondence, which Heidegger takes up in §77 of *Being and Time*.

Conclusion

This chapter took up a challenge to the preceding arguments, namely the variety of transcendental philosophy defended in Crowell's interpretation of Heidegger's work. In terms of this chapter's positive findings, I argued that Crowell's understanding of temporality, responsibility, and answerability presupposes the reciprocally conditioning movement between thrownness and projection and that key points in Crowell's own analysis testify to this more original domain. This movement also provides the context for understanding the concept of play. Further, I contended Heidegger's discussion of facticity is not an unfortunate excursion beyond the bounds of givenness and his conception of the overpowering is not a metaphysical projection of a constituted aspect of Dasein's experience upon an ontological void. Rather it is a phenomenologically apt description of its running up against the limits of its understanding.

An openness to the truth of existence and the bringing to light and thematizing of basic existential structures respond to an occasion where this possibility is given and can be seized upon. Such structures are accessible for a time in the double sense of certain privileged moments in historical existence and at a certain period of life. The corollary of this is that there are also historical periods and times of life in which these universal structures are inaccessible. The contingency of this opening on to existential truths—its site—belongs to their givenness, even though the structures disclosed are given as universal and necessary. This suggests a conception of historical transcendental philosophy that is not formally self-refuting nor collapses into relativism.

I will argue in the following chapter that we need not, however, accept the political conclusions Heidegger drew from these insights and I agree with Crowell that the notion of the *Volk* is phenomenologically problematic, albeit for different reasons. My view is that Heidegger overstates the specificity of the site from which existential-temporal structures become accessible and misconceives what is an unknown hermeneutical background as a native or national space.

Notes

1 Crowell, *Normativity and Phenomenology in Husserl and Heidegger*, 10.
2 Crowell, "Facticity and Transcendental Philosophy," 105.
3 Crowell, *Husserl, Heidegger, and The Space of Meaning*, 227.
4 I rely especially on the presentation of his arguments in Crowell, "Facticity and Transcendental Philosophy."
5 Ibid., 108.
6 Ibid., 108.
7 Ibid., 109.
8 Ibid., 104.
9 Crowell cites specifically the positions of Alexander Nehemas, Hans-Georg Gadamer, Charles Taylor, David Carr, Alasdair McIntyre, and Charles Guigon. Ibid., 102.
10 Ibid., 109.
11 Ibid., 107, 109.
12 Ibid., 108.
13 Ibid., 109.
14 Ibid., 110.
15 Ibid., 111.
16 Ibid., 110.

17 Ibid., 111.
18 Ibid.
19 Ibid., 120, note 41.
20 Ibid., 113.
21 Ibid., 114. The citations are from Thomas Sheehan, "Heidegger's New Aspect," 219, 217.
22 Ibid., 113.
23 Ibid., 116.
24 Ibid., 117.
25 Crowell, *Normativity and Phenomenology*, 208, 210, 277.
26 "*Das Selbst, das als solches den Grund seiner selbst zu legen hat, kann dessen nie mächtigwerden und hat doch existierend das Grundsein zu übernehmen.*" (H. 284). I follow Crowell in translating "*Grund*" as "ground" and not "basis" as Macquarrie and Robinson here render it.
27 Crowell, *Normativity and Phenomenology*, 199, 206.
28 Ibid., 272–3. Cf. 28–9, 162, 217–9, 244, 267–8, 287–8.
29 Crowell, "The Middle Heidegger's Phenomenological Metaphysics," 239.
30 Ibid., 239. He also connects this with the movement of possibilizing in Crowell, *Normativity and Phenomenology*, 208–9, 277.
31 As mentioned in Chapter 4, note 41 "self-control" is Crowell's translation of *Haltung*.
32 Crowell, "The Middle Heidegger's Phenomenological Metaphysics," 238.
33 Ibid., 238–9.
34 Ibid., 242–3.
35 Ibid., 244. I argue these themes are already well-present in Heidegger's work in the 1920s in 2. (d) below and in Chapter 6.
36 Crowell, "The Middle Heidegger's Phenomenological Metaphysics," 247.
37 Crowell, "Facticity and Transcendental Philosophy," 114.
38 Ibid., 110.
39 Crowell, *Normativity and Phenomenology*, 208, 210, 277.
40 Crowell, "Facticity and Transcendental Philosophy," 110.
41 I follow Crowell in translating "*Grund*" as "ground" and not "basis" as M and R have it.
42 Crowell, *Normativity and Phenomenology*, 199, 206, emphasis mine.
43 This definition is given in §41 as "ahead-of-itself-being-already-in-(the-world) as being-alongside entities encountered within-the-world" (H. 192).
44 Heidegger describes his account of temporality as "the unity of a future which makes present in the process of having-been" in §65 as "rough" (H. 326, 327). It is also provisional as it characterizes the mode of temporality in which

Dasein is brought essentially to itself. This and the temporality of the Real in which the world-entry of beings occurs are distinct but reciprocally implying.

45 "Reality" refers to the totality of beings that do not have the character of Dasein, that is, the present-at-hand as such or, as he deems it in the metaphysical period, nature, or the overpowering (H. 183, 211, 436–7).

46 I say "much the same" because it concerns the difference between Dasein and non-Dasein-like entities. The terminological change reflects the focus in the second passage on the problem of historicality. "The question of historicality is an *ontological* question about the state of being of historical entities," that is, entities with the character of Dasein who exist, and "the question of the ontical is the *ontological* question of the state of being of entities other than Dasein—of what is present-at-hand in the widest sense," that is, of the Real.

47 The citation is from Erich Rothacker, ed. *Briefwechsel zwischen Wilhelm Dilthey und dem Grafen Yorck v. Wartenburg 1877–1897* (Halle (Saale): Verlag Max Niemener, 1923), 191. The scare quotes also indicate that "generic differentiation" is not really generic as being is not a genus. The differentiation is instead carried out in the movement of Dasein's transcendence.

48 The published version of "What Is Metaphysics?," unlike the original version, accordingly drops any talk of a horizon. It is in the collapse of horizons of meaningfulness that the sheer strangeness of beings emerges. See Heidegger, "Was ist Metaphysik? Urfassung," 733–51.

49 Crowell, "Facticity and Transcendental Philosophy," 109.

50 Ibid., 108.

51 Crowell, "The Middle Heidegger's Phenomenological Metaphysics," 237. Crowell's discussion of the good and the movement of possibilizing in *Normativity and Phenomenology*, 208–9, 277 also does not mention the πόλις, but the omission is more surprising in an article devoted to the connection between Heidegger's metaphysics and his metapolitics. For this reason, his thesis "for Heidegger, the for-the-sake-of-which (*Worumwillen*) is the ultimate source of *all* particular norms" (*Normativity and Phenomenology*, 287) stands in need of qualification by considering the enabling role of the site and the historicality of these norms.

52 Crowell, "The Middle Heidegger's Phenomenological Metaphysics," 237.

53 BCA 197, cf. 81 [GA 22 254, cf. 99].

54 It is preceded by the famous citation from Plato's *Sophist*.

6

The Native Soil or Historical Basis of Heidegger's Transcendental Philosophy

In the previous chapter I argued that the essential correlation between the systematic and the historical aspects of philosophy is at the heart of the methodological problematic of *Being and Time*. This topic is explicitly addressed in the chapter on Dasein's historicality. This chapter is also at the heart of the controversies on the politics of Heidegger's work. For the notion of site or place is correlated with much-disputed terms in Heidegger's work such as *Gemeinschaft, Volk,* and *Kampf*[1] as well as with his polemics against *bodenlos* thinking (baseless thinking or thinking without a native soil) and against *Verwurzelung*, uprootedness, and his corresponding stress on the *Boden* of philosophical concepts and the need for them to be *verwurzelt*, rooted. We find such discourse even in Heidegger's interpretation of the obscure depths of Kant's first *Critique*: The transcendental imagination, the root of both sensibility and understanding, is ultimately homeless or without a homeland (*heimatlos*) (KPM 95 [GA 3 136]).

Leo Strauss has stressed the political implications of this terminology, claiming that for Heidegger "philosophy can have the task of contributing toward the recovery or return of *Bodenständigkeit* or rather of preparing an entirely novel kind of *Bodenständigkeit*" which "beyond the most extreme *Bodenlosigkeit* [is] a being at home beyond the most extreme homelessness."[2] Charles Bambach suggests a more immediate political context, writing "*Bodenständigkeit* is a term that will employed by the *völkisch* right after the Great War to signify a deep spiritual bond between the *Volksgemeinschaft* and the soil, landscape, homeland, and native earth."[3] Emmanuel Faye and Sidonie Keller have emphasized the anti-Semitic connotations of these terms, connotations that Heidegger himself was well-aware of and drew upon.[4] These terminological choices and the underlying philosophical and political issues raise the question of whether *Being and Time* lays the ground for Heidegger's political commitment to National Socialism in the 1930s.

In the first section of this chapter, I lay out the aporia concerning the politics of Heidegger's project by first discussing two seemingly opposed lines of interpretation of the notorious passage on "the historicizing of the community, of the people" (H. 384), one that foregrounds a political dimension and another the philosophical. In the following section I then consider how this historicizing is at work in the existential analytic itself and cannot be regarded as a superfluous addition. Against this background, I discuss a pivotal background text for Heidegger's account of historicality and for the genesis of *Being and Time* overall, the *Briefwechsel zwischen Wilhelm Dilthey und dem Grafen Yorck v. Wartenburg 1877–1897*. This work sheds much light on both the relation between the systematic and the historical in Heidegger's conception of philosophizing as well as on its political implications. I thus argue the aporia between philosophical and political readings of *Being and Time* can be dissolved. The price of the dissolution, however, is high: It suggests that Heidegger's work in the 1920s is implicated in the politics he committed himself to in the 1930s. I then conclude this chapter by proposing an immanent critique of Heidegger's understanding of the relation between philosophy and the political.

1 An Interpretative Aporia—Philosophy or Politics?

I want to explore the interpretative problems concerning the implicit politics or non-politics of *Being and Time* by focusing on a passage at the center of the controversy—the notorious characterization of Dasein's fate as bound up with the community and the people:

> "But if fateful Dasein [*das schicksalhafte Dasein*], as being-in-the-world, exists essentially in being-with Others, its historicizing is a co-historicizing [*Mitgeschehen*] and is determinative for it as *destiny* [Geschick]. This is how we designate the historicizing of the community, of the people [*das Geschehen der Gemeinschaft, des Volkes*]. Destiny is not something that puts itself together out of individuals fates, any more than being-with-one-another can be conceived as the occurring together of several subjects. Our fates have already been guided in advance, in our being with one another in the same world and in our resoluteness for definite possibilities. Only in communicating and in struggling does the power of destiny become free. Dasein's fateful destiny in and with its 'generation' goes to make up the full authentic historicizing of Dasein."[5]

Johannes Fritsche has emphasized that the political overtones of key terms in Heidegger's account of Dasein's historicality are obscured in the English translations of this passage. For Heidegger does not, as the Macquarrie and Robinson, refer to "the historicizing of the community, of a people," which would suggest he subscribes to a cultural pluralism, but more specifically to "the people [*des Volkes*]."[6] Moreover, he points to a structural opposition in the existential analytic between a "bad" or free-floating strangeness and a "good" strangeness that is Dasein's ownmost.[7] The former refers to "understanding the most alien cultures [*der fremdesten Kulturen*] and 'synthesizing' them with one's own" (H. 178, cf. 52), which mode of understanding is free-floating or uprooted from the intelligibility of the shared social space. The strangeness of these foreign possibilities—a distracting strangeness that lures Dasein away from itself—is distinct from the strangeness of Dasein's ownmost facticity—which brings it back to its basic possibilities.[8]

Further Dasein's authenticity is not only enabled by anxiety but by the shared heritage of possibilities whose "'goodness' lies in making authentic existence possible" (H. 383, cf. MFL 184–5 [GA 26 137–8]). Its individual *Schicksal*, fate, always takes place within a shared social space with its generation, its contemporaries and concerns the *Geschick*, the destiny of the community, the *Volk*. Even as seemingly abstract an undertaking as fundamental ontology must draw upon this background:

> "The way things have been expressed and spoken out is such that in the totality of contexts of signification into which it has been articulated, it preserves an understanding of the disclosed world and therewith, equiprimordially, an understanding of the Dasein-with of others and of one's own being in. The understanding which has thus already been deposited in the way things have been expressed, pertains just as much to any traditional discoveredness of entities which may have been reached, as it does to one's current understanding of being and to whatever possibilities and horizons for fresh interpretation and conceptual articulation may be available."[9]

We saw in the previous chapter that Heidegger's seminars on ancient philosophy also make this point with a more explicitly political focus. The πόλις, Heidegger contends in his Plato interpretation of 1926, is the "soil and domain of the problem of being [*Boden und Umkreis der Seinproblematik*]" (BCA 197, cf. 81 [GA 22 254 cf. 99]) and in his treatment of Aristotle in 1924 he contends "the πόλις is the being possibility, the φύσει, that itself lies enclosed and traced out in advance in the human being's genuine being" and this shared political space "is grounded in a having-with one another of something, in the specific sense of a κοινωνία of συμφέρον and ἀγαθόν" (BC 35 [GA 18 49]).[10] Read in this light, terms such as *Boden, bodenlos, Bodenständigkeit,* and *Bodenlosigkeit* as well as the correlated terms *Entwurzelung* and *Verwurzelung* have a clear political sense. To say Dasein is "historical in the roots of its being [*in der Wurzel seines Seins geschichtlich ist*]" (H. 396) is to say it is rooted in the political soil of the community and people.

Yet Heidegger's use of the terms *Boden* and rootedness is ambiguous. For in the most seemingly *völkisch* chapter of *Being and Time*, namely the discussion of Dasein's historicality, Heidegger repeatedly emphasizes that the roots of historicality are to be found in the soil or basis of Dasein's *temporality*, that is, in a seemingly formal existential condition stripped of any specific political connections. The opening section poses the question of whether "*temporality*, as we have exhibited it, first of all give[s] us the *basis or soil* [*Boden*] on which to provide an unequivocal direction for the existential-ontological question of this 'connectedness' [of Dasein between birth and death]?" (H. 373). The answer to this question is (at least in part) affirmative as Heidegger repeatedly speaks of historicality and how it "is rooted in temporality [*Verwurzelung in der Zeitlichkeit*]" (H. 375)[11], of history as a manner of being of Dasein that "has its roots so essentially in the future [*ihre Wurzel so wesenhaft in der Zukunft*]" (H. 386), and of Dasein's historicality and its being "rooted in temporality [*ihre Verwurzelung in der Zeitlichkeit*]" (H. 392). If we foreground these passages, it seems it is a matter of finding the "primal roots" of history in Dasein (H. 377) and not, as political interpretations would lead us to expect, Dasein's rootedness in the native soil and history of the *Volk*.

I take it that any adequate interpretation of these passages, if such is possible, should account for *both* senses of Heidegger's talk of rootedness and the soil or basis of concepts.[12] And we can find a very similar ambiguity surrounding other terms used in Division II, Chapter 5 of *Being and Time* when we contextualize them within Heidegger's courses in this period. Most striking are two comments written in the 1920s that suggest very different interpretations of how Dasein's fate [*Schicksal*] is bound up with the community and the people. In his 1928 Leibniz lectures, Heidegger uses terms familiar from the existential analytic generally (*Augenblick, Eigentlichkeit*) and that allude to §74 specifically (*eigentliche Geschehen*) when speaking of the insights of Kant and Heraclitus into the transcendental productivity of the subject: "Perhaps the authentic happening [*eigentliche Geschehen*] in the history of philosophy is always but a temporalization of such moments [*Augenblicke*] in distant intervals and strokes, moments which never become manifest as what they really are" (GA 26: 272–3/211).[13] The interpretation of Kant and Heraclitus with a view to understanding Dasein's original temporality seems to have little or nothing to do with a *völkisch* politics.

However, another use of the term *Schicksal* does suggest an interpretation of this concept that accords with the most violent expressions of Heidegger's *völkisch* politics in the 1930s. It can be found in an appendix to the 1924–5 *Plato's Sophist* lecture course, where it was placed by the editor of this text.[14] Heidegger first cites a line in the original Greek from Cleon's speech in Book III of Thucydides's *The Peloponnesian War*: "ἁπλῶς τε ἀκοῆς ἡδονῇ ἡσσώμενοι καὶ σοφιστῶν θεαταῖς ἐοικότες καθημένοις μᾶλλον ἢ περὶ πόλεως βουλευομένοις." Heidegger's translation reads "Taken as a whole: 'You are wallowing in the delight of listening (correlatively to speaking!) and are rather similar to the ones who are sitting there gaping at the sophists and who are supposed to decide about the fate [*Schicksal*] of the state.'"[15] This translation is a transposition into Heidegger's own conceptuality that first highlights the fallen speaking, listening, understanding that will be thematized a little over a year later in §35–8 of *Being and Time*, counterposing this with a decision about the fate of the state, thereby using the much-discussed term *Schicksal*, which has no direct equivalent in the Greek original.

There are, I think, a number of reasons why this short translation of a Greek phrase into Heidegger's terminology is significant. First, it is appended to discussions of Plato and Aristotle's philosophies as reactions against the influence of the sophists on Athenian public life, thus as having a factical political motivation, in the *Plato's Sophist* lecture course. Cleon's speech too is in large part a condemnation of the influence of the sophists on the public life and democracy of Athens. Second, Heidegger was in this period interested in the disclosive possibilities of political rhetoric,[16] an interest which remains in the background of the existential analytic. Third, the existentiell situation of the speech is also, given the charged political atmosphere of 1920s Germany and particularly the anti-Semitic stab in the back myth,[17] decidedly sinister. Cleon is advocating the destruction of the people of Mytilene who had revolted unsuccessfully against Athenian rule during the war between Athens and Sparta. Cleon claims they had been far better treated than other cites under Athenian control and that their revolt was in effect an act of war as they had "joined with our bitterest enemies [the Spartans] to destroy us."[18] Cleon argues in the name of a supposed justice and the realities of running an empire that all the men of Mytilene should be killed and the women and children sold into slavery. Given

Heidegger's translation emphasizes phenomena treated existentially in *Being and Time*, given further that the term *Schicksal* is also used in connection with the community and *Volk* in the chapter on Dasein's historicality that Heidegger claimed inspired his political commitment to National Socialism, I find it hard to believe this choice of example is a coincidence.

These two references highlight the interpretative dilemma regarding §74 and regarding the project in *Being and Time* more generally, namely, how we are to understand Dasein's historicality and the existentiell factical ideal underlying Heidegger's analyses. On this first line of interpretation, the factical ideal is that of an inquirer seeking the answer to the question of the meaning of being who strives to disclose ever more original horizons. Ultimately, this involves a willingness to face the ontological difference, to live through exposure to the meaninglessness of beings, and the emergence of historical meaning without taking refuge in the pseudo-certainties and comforting myths of everyday stories, religious belief, scientific certainty—"those idols everyone has and to which they are wont to go cringing" as Heidegger refers to them (PM 96 [GA 9 122]). A good deal speaks for this interpretation on the textual level, as I have argued over the course of this book.

Yet, on the other line of interpretation, the factical ideal underlying Heidegger's analysis is that of a figure like Cleon, who advocates exterminatory action in the name of safeguarding the political community.[19] What speaks for this line of interpretation is Heidegger's interest in the disclosive potential of political speech—although this potential is generally unrealized—in cutting through the sophistry of everydayness, demarcating the space of the community and what is other to it. This interpretation also takes into account the political sense of the term *Boden* as referring to the political community in Heidegger's lectures and seminars on Greek philosophy as well as the political overtones of the paragraph in §74 of *Being and Time* on fate, destiny, community, the *Volk*, and Heidegger's own appeal to his account of Dasein's historicality as justifying his support for National Socialism in the 1930s.

At first glance, these lines of interpretation seem incompatible. From the standpoint of the first, the second line of interpretation is implausible because *Being and Time* is not a political speech but a work of phenomenological hermeneutics and because it is in no obvious sense a work of political philosophy. Although it can be granted that Heidegger's use of the term *Schicksal* and other terms such as *Boden* have in some instances a political meaning, the political interpretation proposed above seems to ignore other passages that point to a philosophical interpretation of Dasein's historicality.

Further, the political interpretation does not seem to account for the project of *Being and Time* itself, namely, disclosing universal structures for Dasein's understanding of being.

From the standpoint of the second line of interpretation, the first is implausible as it ignores Heidegger's political use of the term *Schicksal* in translating a phrase from a demagogic and violently inflammatory speech from Greek antiquity, the political overtones of some of Heidegger's terminology, not just of §74 but also in the analyses of *das man*, the community, the people, the reference to Dasein choosing its hero, and becoming "free for the struggle of loyally following in the footsteps of that which can be repeated."[20] And the "political" line of interpretation need not be purely or solely political as what arguably interests Heidegger on the phenomenological level is the temporality underlying existentiell political decisions and existential structures that show themselves therein.

2 *Gemeinschaft* and *Volk* in the Existential Analytic

I will broach this aporia by first exploring if the existential analytic itself exemplifies the movement of historizing in retrieving the heritage of a particular community, people, and language to thematize basic existential phenomena. If the community and the people are already present in the analyses of *Being and Time*, then these notions are no superfluous appendage to the work and the individual engaged in the project of fundamental ontology already implies "*das Geschehen der Gemeinschaft, des Volkes*" (H. 384).

In the background to the following interpretation are two programmatic claims made in *Being and Time*. The first is the claim that "the ultimate business of philosophy is to preserve the force [*Kraft*] of the most elemental words in which Dasein expresses itself, and to keep the common understanding from levelling them off to that pseudo-intelligibility which functions in turn as a source for pseudo-problems" (H. 222). Heidegger's use of the term force, *Kraft*, draws, as we will see in the following section, much upon Yorck von Wartenburg's understanding of becoming historical [*Vergeschichtlichung*]. The second is the claim that in so-called "'primitive phenomena'" a "way of conceiving things which seems, perhaps, rather clumsy and crude from our standpoint, can be positively helpful in bringing out the ontological structures of phenomena in a genuine way" precisely because they "are often less concealed and less complicated by extensive self-interpretation" (H. 51). The significance of such "primitive" phenomena was already underscored in Heidegger's interpretation of the mythical world, treated in Chapter 4.

I will focus here on Heidegger's discussion, informed by Jacob Grimm's linguistic research, of the sense of the "*In*" of "*In-der-Welt-sein*," a discussion in which Heidegger develops the most fundamental distinction in the entire existential analytic, that between the existential and the categorical (H. 53–6).[21] Grimm begins his article "*In und Bei*" with a general claim about words: Their concealed roots reach into a long distant past but only their stripped down, blunt tips reach us.[22] This is especially true of particles like "*in*" and "*bei*," whose contemporary use leaves little clue as to the originally sensible concepts underlying them.

It is not difficult to see why these claims would have interested Heidegger. Grimm's characterization suggests there are original experiences underlying these elementary words that are scarcely preserved in their leveled-down remnants found in present everyday language use and he does so using a metaphoric of rootedness. In Heideggerian terms, underneath superficial self-evidence and rigidified grammar that dominates our typical use of these prepositions lies the transformative potential of *Geschichte* as the realm of concealed possibilities. Retrieving these concealed experiences allows the phenomena to show themselves in a far more direct and immediate fashion, free from ontologically dubious theoretical presuppositions.

Grimm traces the preposition "*in*" back to the verb "*innan*," which means *wohnen*, to reside, abide, dwell, senses preserved in the German term "*innung*." *Innan* consists of what Grimm calls an anomalous "*ann*," which he links with *amo, diligo, faveo* (I love, I esteem, I favor) to which he claims an immediate affiliation with the German terms *gönnen* and *gunst* (to bestow or indulge and favor). So he claims: "*ann will eigentlich sagen: ich bin eingewohnt, pflege zu bauen,*" "*ann* really wants to say: I am accustomed to trust in, tend to, cultivate, build on."[23] This, Grimm notes, is connected to the Latin *colo* (I till the land, protect, cultivate, worship, honor), which characterizes both *habito* (I reside, inhabit, remain, dwell) as well as *diligo* (I esteem, price, love, have regard for or, I sunder by choosing, selecting).[24]

Grimm claims the particle "*bei*" has a similar kinship to *bauen* and *bin*. He underscores co-belonging of the notions of dwelling, essence, and being: "*ich wohne, d. i. ich bin, aus der vorstellung des wohnens ist die des wesens and seins aufgestiegen,*" "I reside or dwell, that is, I am, from the notion of residing or dwelling has arisen that of essence and being."[25] It is not just that *ich wohne*, I dwell, and *ich bin*, I am, are etymologically related to the terms *Wesen*, essence, and *Sein*, being, rather an understanding of *Sein und Wesen* arose from out of this primordial domain of dwelling or residing.

Although Grimm notes we find similar constellations of meaning in English, specifically in the old English *beon* (to become, to be, to exist) and *buan* (to live, dwell, occupy, exist) and although similar relations, because of the inner contact of these languages, can be found in Sanskrit, Greek, and Latin terms, he maintains it is German that allows us to see these roots the most closely. Comparative research can grant secure information over a variety of roots but in individual cases, like this one, ultimately "the language of one's own [namely, German] opens up the deepest view into the secrets of all [*die eigne sprache den tiefsten blick in die geheimnisse aller öfnet*]."[26]

The influence of Grimm's articles on Heidegger might seem too obvious to merit mentioning here and is familiar to most readers who have even attempted to tackle *Being and Time*. But the methodological presuppositions of this influence and how it testifies to the movement of historicizing within the existential analytic are worth reviewing. For one, such etymological research "preserve[s] the force of the most elemental words in which Dasein expresses itself" because it indicates an understanding that belongs to factical, pre-philosophical, and pre-theoretical existence. This is what distinguishes this procedure, essentially a kind of phenomenological repetition with a view to freeing up and uncovering original phenomena, from an "uninhibited word mysticism" (H. 220). Moreover, the particles "*in*" and "*bei*" preserve the traces of the original experience from which I am, being, and essence are rooted, traces that are preserved, on this account, most especially in the German language.

And it is directly after emphasizing what these older senses of the term testify to that Heidegger provides us with his formal existential characterization of being-in: "*'Being-in' is thus the formal existential expression for the being of Dasein, which has being-in-the-world as its basic state*" (H. 54). It is through the former historical "matter" that the latter formal structure shows itself in an exemplary fashion. This linguistic material can be said to be "contingent" but only in the derivative sense of the "contingency of something present-at-hand" (H. 144) but it essentially belongs to the hermeneutic situation in which an existential analysis is ventured.

Furthermore, Heidegger's critique of Greek productive metaphysics is tied back to his retrieval of the possibilities and experiences preserved in the German language. This structure of dwelling there revealed is "in principle one which cannot be grasped by the traditional ontological categories" (H. 54–5). Dwelling and inhabiting are the unthematized background conditions for the way in which entities were discovered in Greek ontology. The "disposable possessions and goods, property," "possessions, means, wealth" (BPP, 108–9, GA 21, 153), namely οὐσία in the pre-philosophical sense, form the everyday horizon within which Greek ontology moves and draws its terminology but without making this thematic, let alone its more original condition of dwelling (H. 61).

A telling ambiguity can be found in Grimm's discussion of the terms "*in*" and "*bei*." On the one hand, Grimm emphasizes the older senses of inhabiting and taking in but also of the senses of being taken in, taking up a lodging, taking shelter, so of being received into a place, senses with overtones of grace, rest, and mercy. These characteristics are all repeated on the ontological level by Heidegger in *Being and Time* especially in the middle-voiced sense of the phenomenon of phenomenology and in the basic characterization of Dasein's being as care. Heidegger also draws our attention to "in" as having "the signification of '*colo*' in the senses of '*habito*' and '*diligo*'" (H. 54). The last term means "I esteem, price, love, have regard for, or I sunder by choosing," connotations also found in Dasein's responding to the call of care, its relinquishing possibilities that count for nothing, its taking up of one possibility, and not choosing others.

As fundamental as the passages on the "in" of being-in-the-world are to the existential analytic, they are far from the only point at which Heidegger draws upon a shared history and linguistic community in the existential analytic to combat overly theorized or fallen, free-floating interpretations of existential phenomena. I will take one example[27] from the high point of the analysis of temporality in *Being and Time* in §65. The characterization of the authentic, futural temporality of Dasein reads: "'Future [*Zukunft*]' does not mean here a now that has *not yet* become 'actual' and *will be* sometime, but the arrival [*Kunft*] in which Dasein comes to itself [*auf sich zukommt*] in its ownmost potentiality for being" (H. 325, translation modified).[28] This contrasts the everyday way of talking and thinking about the future with a more original, underlying existential phenomenon that Heidegger thematizes by drawing on the archaic term *Kunft* to refer to the arrival of the future, a term that belongs in the semantic field of dwelling, taking in, being taken in, as Grimm's dictionary emphasizes.[29] This semantic field points toward phenomenological kinships between the key terms Heidegger uses to speak of the disclosures of the existential analytic that parallel those between the key terms of Greek philosophy like οὐσία, εἶδος, ἰδέα, ὁρισμός, and ὑποκείμενον whose concrete meaning refers back, on Heidegger's account, to the everyday discoveredness of things. As in the ontologies developed in the Greek world, Heidegger draws upon the *Boden* of his historical world but his inquiry claims to open up a more fundamental ontological domain as "the area of being to be disclosed [*zu erschließende Seinsgebiet*] is ontologically far more difficult than that which was pre-given [*vorgegebene*] to the Greeks" (H. 39, cf. 3).[30]

On the foregoing interpretation, Heidegger's appeal to the resources of the German language does not simply reinforce points made independently by adding a bit of local color. Rather, this heritage is precisely the enabling condition, the "goodness," underlying the existentiell project of raising anew the question of being. And by considering how repetition and Dasein's co-historicizing within a given historical community and *Volk* are at work *within* the existential analytic, we see that the separability thesis is untenable, that is, we cannot maintain the bulk of the existential analytic carries out a transcendental-phenomenological analysis but then unfortunately lapses into ontic, empirical history in the chapter on Dasein's historicality in a way that prepares the way for the errors of Heidegger's metaphysical period in the late 1920s and his politics in the 1930s. The above considerations suggest that Heidegger saw the German language as having the resources and being uniquely placed to carry out the project of raising and thinking through the question of the meaning of being and to reveal what he claims are basic existential phenomena.

This undertaking does not privilege the archaic *as such*, but the past is repeated with a view to bringing out concealed experiences and possibilities of understanding that have become leveled down. Throughout *Being and Time* there is a productive tension between the tradition, that is, especially rigidified philosophical concepts that have become common currency and thus *bodenlos* over the centuries and the *Boden* of factical, pre-philosophical life in which existential phenomena often show themselves on an existentiell level in an immediate, albeit crude, way.[31] Yet these considerations do not suggest a direct resolution to the aporia outlined in the first section of this chapter. For it is not obvious that such an undertaking need have any political implications, far less a commitment to a far-right political ideology.

3 Heidegger's Appropriation of Yorck von Wartenburg

If Heidegger's appropriation of Grimm and of the concealed possibilities of the German language shows us that the movement of historicizing and the attendant notions of the linguistic community are already at work within the existential analytic, the *Briefwechsel zwischen Wilhelm Dilthey und dem Grafen Paul Yorck v. Wartenburg 1877–1897* gives us important clues as to how this movement takes place and why Heidegger conceived it as having political implications. Heidegger ascribes this work a pre-eminent significance for the development of his own work, writing: "the preparatory existential analytic of Dasein is resolved to foster the spirit of Count Yorck in the service of Dilthey's work"[32] (H. 404). §77 of *Being and Time* consists largely of citations from Yorck's letters to Dilthey and these recapitulate and repeat key themes of the existential analytic. The question of Yorck's influence on Heidegger is also one of the disputed points about the politics of Heidegger's *Being and Time*. Bambach notes how Yorck "present[s] himself as an advocate for the life rooted in the soil, the earth, the homeland, and in history," as opposed to the rootlessness of modern existence, and claims Yorck "would provide Heidegger with a model for a way of thinking through a connection between autochthony and history" (18). Faye argues for a strong connection between Heidegger's emphasis on the *Boden* of thinking, his anti-Semitism, and his resolve to foster "spirit of Count Yorck."[33] In order to see why Heidegger accords such importance to Yorck's work, I will consider the wider context of those themes that Heidegger emphasizes in Yorck's letters (*(a)*) before considering how Heidegger himself takes these up and their political implications (*(b)*).

(a) Yorck on Becoming-Historical

Central to Yorck's understanding is the primary fact of concrete, historical life: "That the entire psycho-physical givenness [*Gegebenheit*] *is* not but lives is the germinal point of historicality [*Geschichtlichekit*]."[34] Philosophy, as a manifestation of life, is essentially historical, meaning attempts to separate the historical or historiographic and the systematic dimensions of philosophy are defective: "Just physiology cannot be abstracted from physics, so philosophy—especially when it is critical—not from historicality [*Geschichtlichkeit*]."[35] The wish to do so, Yorck contends, is a remnant of metaphysics (ibid.), by which term he means an essentially Roman way of thinking oriented toward the timeless. In contrast to Lutheran and original Christianity,[36] Yorck claims this outlook is incapable of thinking death: "In the stance of its consciousness, Rome is timeless. Hence the eternal Rome is not [just] a saying. For this reason it is the seat of metaphysics—in contrast to transcendence. Rome does not conceive of death, just as no Roman [does]."[37] Yorck's frequent criticisms of the philosophy, scientific thinking, and historical research charge them with neglecting the primary fact of historical life:

"When one grasps philosophy as a manifestation of life, not as the coughing up of a baseless thinking or a thinking without a soil [*bodenlos Denkens*], which emerges as baseless [*bodenlos ercheinend*] because sight is diverted from the basis or soil of consciousness [*Bewußtseinsboden*], then the task is as scanty in its results, as it is convoluted and arduous in its acquisition. Freedom from prejudice is the presupposition and already this is hard to acquire."[38]

Such "*bodenlosen Denken*" arises because the view is diverted from the *Boden*, basis or soil, of consciousness in present historical life. Formalistic, abstract scientific dogmas such as Darwinism have a "metaphysical" attitude because of their remove, on Yorck's view, from concrete life, an attitude that is itself a historical product that is blind to its own historicality.[39] Similarly, historians such as Leopold von Ranke also fall prey to this tendency. His approach is, Yorck argues, "seeing a history" and he contends that "Ranke is a great oracularist, for whom what has vanished cannot become actualities."[40] This attitude presents history as a drama we view and passes over the fact that we *live* history: "With history, what makes a spectacle and catches the eye [*augenfällig*] is never the main thing. The nerves are invisible just as the essentials in general are invisible."[41]

For beneath the drama of events and personages are the non-apparent, "hidden sources [*vorborgenen Quellen*]" that history in the proper sense of the term is concerned with.[42] We access this through a kind of silent heeding that allows "the arduous becoming present of the bygone [*die arbeitsvolle Vergegenwärtigung der Vergangenheit*]."[43] Yorck tells Dilthey, "I enjoy the silent self-discussion and communing with the spirit of history [*Geschichte*]."[44] Silence is the pre-condition for a dialogue with the past resonating within present life, speaking to its untapped possibilities. History in the proper sense is a source of power, an enabling possibility for present historical life: "when you are silent you will hear, that is, understand."[45]

Yorck names this heeding of the historical past that speaks to unspoken possibilities in the present, *Vergeschichtlichung*, a becoming historical. This lies in the background to his claims about the politics of education, an issue the correspondents discuss repeatedly, in both theoretical and practical terms. Yorck insists "the practical purposes of our standpoint is the pedagogical in the widest and deepest sense of the term."[46] He explains in another letter that decisive for *Gymnasium*-level education is "inward historical enrichment, … becoming historical [*innerer geschichtlicher Bereicherung, … Vergeschichtlichung*]."[47] Through education, through preoccupation with oneself in others, the student becomes historical [*Vergeschichtlichung*], becomes aware of their own historicality. This enriching occurs, however, by drawing upon the past that belongs to the student as opposed to simply gaining competence in another contemporary language, hence Yorck's praise of the study of ancient languages and utterly dismissive attitude toward learning the merely useful like French at this level of education.[48]

The task of state pedagogy is ultimately, he contends, enabling the formation of individuality and conscience instead of submitting to public opinion.[49] Hence a proper approach to historicality does not prioritize the past as such—as in the antiquitarian attitude toward history that Nietzsche and Heidegger also criticize—but begins from present historical life. The speaking of the past to the living possibilities of present historical life guards against falling into antiquarianism as letter 108 clarifies:

> "The knowledge or recognition of history that turns, starting from one's own aliveness, back to the past in appearance [*Erscheinung*], what is preserved in force [*Kraft*], would in the depiction send on ahead an analysis of the present of the past and at the same time would provide a check for the historical [*Geschichtliche*] against the antiquarian [*Antiquarischen*]. Only what is forcefully [*der Kraft nach*] in the present belongs to the domain of history [*Geschichte*]."[50]

A proper understanding of history thus moves backwards from one's own historical life to the resources of force or power the past holds. Such appropriation always and necessarily involves relinquishing other possibilities, and takes place against the dominant currents of the present. "The appropriation is at the same time an expanding relinquishment or expropriation [*Die Aneignung ist zugleich eine erweiternde Entäußerung*]."[51]

The past is not solely individual but is shared. With respect to both our contemporaries and figures from the past, we understand them with an "immediate vital belonging [*unmittelbar lebendige Zugehörigkeit*]."[52] Yorck stresses that this is not grasped by sight or by bodily presence for if Luther, Augustine, or Paul the evangelist were still alive, it would not be by seeing them and transposing our inner experience on to them that we would understand them.[53] The notion of historical effectivity, *geschichtliche Wirkung*, which takes place from person to person,[54] underscores the difference between the ontic (grasped oracularly) and the historical (a non-oracular, ontologically basic kind of interpersonal influence that we silently heed). This shared historical life also explains the resonance he detects between silent intellectual endeavor and the realm of the deed, political life, wherein the latter has a priority: "The new ways of thinking, that must come, are first manifest in and through an ingenious personality and always first in the realm of the deed."⁵⁵

Yorck claims, however, that this understanding of selfhood, history, education, and politics does not give way to sheer arbitrariness or reduce historiography to whim. Letter 140 is particularly instructive on this point. Yorck there criticizes Dilthey's claim that philosophy of history is impossible and develops a more detailed account of the relation between the historical matter that is grasped in historiography and the kind of appropriation it undergoes in the present. This involves a peculiarly historicized conception of the *a priori*.⁵⁶ The stuff or matter [*Stoff*] of history is first investigated through empirical research and brought to the highest degree of reliability. This historical-ontic material is animated or brought to life through the living engagement of the historiographer, interwoven with psychological analysis.⁵⁷ Yet while this is an indispensable stage, Yorck stresses it is also only preliminary. For it is when this threshold is crossed, its real historical quality [*geschichtliche Qualität*] takes effect. This implicitly happens in the conceiving or grasping the matter of history, which involves a kind of *a priori*: "The grasping of the matter happens to the ontic character of the stuff in an *a priori* way [*Die Ergreifung des Stoffes geschieht dem ontischen Character des Stoffs gegenüber apriorisch*]." Inherent in the act of grasping are concepts or ways of understanding that transcend the material level of the empirical facts. This is what is heeded of the past and what is ultimately grasped is not a neutral matter or stuff but is "one's own flesh and blood [*eigen Fleisch und Blut*]" and the priority in this grasping is not abstract but concrete, embodied, living.⁵⁸ For as history is always already acting upon us, always already appears in the present, past figures, and past worlds, are already present to us, taking effect upon our life.⁵⁹ And history in this sense cannot simply be a history of the present because it speaks of possibilities that the present day does not heed and that can only be grasped through heeding the past. This "higher process of the becoming historical of the human [*Ein höherer Vorgang der Vergeschichtlichung des Menschen*]" moves on a level beneath chronological time, in a between of past and present.⁶⁰

These claims could give rise to the impression that Yorck's conception of historicality is largely a defense of a kind of communitarianism centered on historically situated individual conscience. However, even allowing for the possibility of a critically appropriation of such a position from his correspondence, it also must be noted that Yorck frequently correlates his views on historical selfhood, individual consciousness, education, and politics with an anti-Semitic, nativist outlook. In the above-cited letter 108, for instance, Yorck emphasizes Spinoza's being Jewish—he was "not a Jew for nothing," adding "the Jew then was not doing historical work"[61]—to explain his purportedly dead deism, lack of feeling for life, and mechanistic psychology. And immediately after detailing his conception of historicality in letter 140, Yorck gives qualified praise to a book by a key figure in the development of nineteenth century racist pseudo-science, Arthur de Gobineau. Yorck's criticism does not concern the content of the work—he describes it a beautiful mosaic by an erudite and quick-witted man—but criticizes him for his lack of method, which, he claims, should be provided by an *Erkenntnistheorie*.[62]

The political overtones of term *Boden* are particularly evident in letter 15, from which Heidegger cites the line "All history that is truly alive and not just reflecting a tinge of life, is critique."[63] The context of this remark is a discussion of the *Boden* of republican politics, represented by Machiavelli and Napoleon, whose idea of the state, Yorck contends, is not to be solely explained from out of the *Boden* of the Renaissance but stems back to Rome, the source of timeless rather than historical thinking. He stresses that this idea fundamentally differs from that of the *Reich*,[64] whose representative is Bismarck, writing "the concept of life and the state [in the latter], more correctly the notion of the *Reich* as opposed to the state, is the fruit of the rural land in the Middle Ages."[65] This underpins Yorck's claim as to the political significance of returning to the native soil, for "with alienation [*Entfremdung*] from the soil [*Boden*] the sustaining force [*Kraft*] is lost. The status of being without soil brings about a shaky or precarious balance in a human being and his form of life that gives way to every shock."[66]

Faye emphasizes that in such letters *Boden* also means the physical soil[67] and not just a lack of a metaphorical basis for thinking. And he also stresses that Yorck appeals to this sense of the *Boden* or soil to make an argument against the employment of Jewish faculty, using the term with both a primary literal meaning—the physical native soil—as well as a metaphorical meaning—as in "baseless thinking."[68]

> "I congratulate you on every single case where you kept the thin Jewish run-of-the-mill, which lacks consciousness of responsibility for thought, just as the entire stock lacks the sense of psychical and physical soil, far from the professorships."[69]

There is good reason to think these comments more than personal asides reflecting widespread prejudices of the era. Yorck's conception of history, with its emphasis on situated historical life, presupposes a specific site within which the individual consciousness is situated and the need for historically situated consciousness to look to this *Boden*, its basis or native soil. He conceives his site as having given rise to a politics that is supposedly "the fruit of the rural land in the Middle Ages" and contends the republican forms of political organization and those of Jewish descent are alien to it.

(b) Heidegger's Appropriation of Yorck and Its Implications

To what extent does this background help us in understanding Heidegger's conception of historicality—and the question of the political in his work? We can note first that Heidegger's selection "in a provisional way" of passages from Yorck's letters (H. 399) recapitulates key moments of the existential analytic: the understanding of selfhood as thoroughly historical rather than as an abstract epistemological (and an abstract political) subject, the polemics against the dominance of publicness and *bodenlos* thinking, the corresponding stress on conscience and the need for thinking to have a *Boden*, the importance of silence in understanding, and the task of distinguishing the ontical from the historical.

Yorck's conception of becoming historical through engagement with the past also has parallels with Heidegger's approach to key figures in the history of philosophy. This does not mean reading texts arbitrarily but, as Yorck emphasizes, proceeds against the background of detailed analyses in the context of the then available research. Heidegger's interpretations of Plato, Aristotle, Augustine, and Kant and treatment of philosophical issues in the late 1920s, perhaps more than any other period of his works, show a great sensitivity to what is revealed in object-historical research. And Heidegger's own emphasis on ancient languages, particularly old German and Greek, stresses, as we saw, preserving the force, *Kraft*, of the most elemental words but does so by drawing upon scholarly linguistic research. A key point in Yorck and Heidegger's conception of historicality is that object historical research is always already responding to the force of concealed possibility, otherwise the thematic object would not impress itself upon us or matter to us.[70]

Moreover, lived or existential historicality breaks with what we can call—in a broad sense—an oracular conception of the *a priori*, including that of models, norms, or standards. At the heart of the movement of repetition is a response to what appeals to us in the past, beneath tradition, a response to the suppressed or concealed possibilities of the present, hidden sources of understanding. This is not the subordination of the past to some present purpose, what addresses us from the past is what wants or needs to be thought today despite the dominant current of the today.

Yorck's understanding of the essential relation between the historical and the systematic in philosophy and of the historical *a priori* clearly informs Heidegger's attempt to develop a historicized transcendental philosophy and his reading of the history of philosophy. It is from this movement of repetition that we find the core of Heidegger's historized conception of the *a priori*. The more basic task he undertakes is not describing our access to the living past as such, but the very movement of Dasein's historicizing itself and thinking this movement in its *a priori* conditions.

Although the historicality chapter stresses the rootedness of history in temporality and temporality as the *Boden* of history, the foregoing suggests this cannot be simply read unidirectionally, as signaling that historical awareness is rooted in the formal condition of temporality. It rather refers to a back-and-forth movement that encompasses both aspects: Authentic temporality presupposing the *Boden* of the community and the people and Dasein's historicality becoming manifest as *Geschehen* through temporality. Each becomes manifest as what it is through the other. In this respect, the term *Boden* functions like other key Heideggerian concepts, encompassing different but reciprocally implying meanings that refer back to different but co-original modes of temporality.

If the foregoing suggests a strong philosophical influence of Yorck on Heidegger—as the praise of the former in *Being and Time* would lead us to expect—what does this suggest concerning the aporia outlined in the first section of this chapter about the philosophical and the political in Heidegger's work? I wanted to broach this question through an anti-Semitic passage in Heidegger's correspondence that Faye has emphasized.[71] The letter in question is from October 2, 1929, and is addressed to Victor Schwoerer, ministerial councilor in Baden. The passage reads:

> "… we are faced with the choice between either leading German spiritual life back to forces and educators from the native soil [*echte bodenständige Kräfte und Erzieher*] or handing it over irrevocably to the growing Jewification in the wider and the narrower sense. We will find the way back only if we are capable of unfolding fresh forces [*Krafte*] without agitation and unfruitful confrontation."[72]

Are these claims the expression of a personal prejudice on Heidegger's part or are they connected with his philosophical outlook? Several considerations speak in favor of the latter interpretation. For one, as Faye has stressed, the passage in question here strongly echoes Yorck's own anti-Semitic education politics.[73] And although Heidegger does not directly refer to Yorck's anti-Semitic educational politics in *Being and Time* or other philosophical texts, he does cite Yorck's claim that "the practical purposes of our standpoint is the pedagogical in the widest and deepest sense of the term" (H. 402). While Heidegger's polemics against atomism, urbanity, and statism are developed in the 1930s, these themes are already present in passages from Yorck's letters.

We also saw that the concept of *Boden* does not refer simply to the historical background to philosophizing but in passages in Heidegger's lectures on ancient philosophy also to the possibilities opened up by the space of the political community. That Heidegger, like Yorck, saw an isomorphism between the philosophical and the political is suggested by his interest in the disclosive power of political speech generally in the 1920s. On a more sinister level, his translation of a phrase from Cleon's speech in Thucydides's *The Peloponnesian War* advocating the massacre of a people accused of a war-time betrayal into his own idiom supports the interpretation that one of the possibilities informing Heidegger's ontological analyses is that of extreme violence in a concrete political situation.

Taken individually, each of these points might seem negligible. But taken together in their wider social and political context, they provide a strong indication that Heidegger conceived his philosophical project as bound up with a nativist, anti-Semitic political outlook open to extreme possibilities of political action. I would suggest this is not a historical contingency or a temporary aberration that can be ignored by readers of *Being and Time*.

4 The Political and the Alien

On the foregoing interpretation, Heidegger's phenomenology is implicated in his politics as shown on the terminological, substantial, and existentiell level. To have misgivings about Heidegger's politics can go further than a moral repulsion although they are certainly an element of such a repulsion. Such repulsion can indicate an unthought that seeks to be thought. The key philosophical question, it seems to me, is whether the site and heritage of philosophizing can be equated with that of political decision and whether it can be regarded as akin to an actual or potential national space.

I argued in the foregoing that a kind of *völkisch* understanding implicitly runs through Heidegger's philosophy in this period. In *Being and Time*, §34 we read the claim: "Among the Greeks, their everyday existing was largely diverted into talking with each other, but at the same time they had 'eyes' to see" (H. 165). Who are "the Greeks"? Not the Spartans, who on Herodotus's account, were notoriously adverse to the spoken word.[74] Nor does Thucydides's account of the demagoguery, social breakdown, war fever, and mass hysteria in Athens and in the Greek world more widely give the impression of a people with "'eyes' to see."

From the perspective of the ordinary concept of time and history, we can say that Heidegger's claim about "the Greeks" is an unwarranted generalization. But the passages in question refer to the founding figures of an ontology and the philosophical logic that developed primarily based on their ontology of the present-at-hand. This inaugural moment, on Heidegger's interpretation, found its enabling conditions within, responded to, and was bound back to the factical form of life in the πόλις. The "Greek" world was one in which "everyday existing was largely diverted into talking with each other," an everydayness of a political and social order that gave precedence to the spoken word, where "man shows himself as the entity which talks" (H. 165). The horizon of this everydayness was modified in philosophical discourse by addressing things in their presence, sighted as having-been produced, and asking after what constitutes this. This discourse had, Heidegger claims, a factical political motivation: It responded to a situation where the political ideal of the sophists dominated Athenian public life and it responded with a concern for seeing, for addressing what is spoken of.

The term soil as enabling possibilities of being has a place not only in Heidegger's interpretation of the Greek world and Greek conceptuality but also in the movement of thinking Heidegger describes. In the light of the for-the-sake-of-which, one draws on the dark background, the obscure depths of history, one cultivates its possibilities to articulate what is going unsaid. When Heidegger uses the Latin term "condition," from *condo*, I build or establish, we can read this as a translation back into *colo*, and ultimately *bauen*, cultivating. This movement needs both the light of the for-the-sake of which and the dark ground or soil of history.

This manner of speaking has a certain justification in the matter spoken. The Kantian analytic of finitude speaks of founding, of establishing a territory and boundaries for understanding, and securing ground (A 235–6, B 294–5). For establishing the territory of the understanding presupposes, on his view, a more basic sense of dwelling or residing in the world that Kant does not thematize, hence the claim that the time-forming power of the transcendental imagination is *heimatlos*, without a homeland. The kinship of terms like *wohnen*, *bauen* with *wesen* and *sein* provides Heidegger with indications for thinking the existential of dwelling.

Yet an example from Heidegger's discussion of Dasein's being-toward-the-end illustrates what is meant by a return to the soil from which basic philosophical concepts are formed as well as the philosophical problems with equating the historical background of philosophical thought with a homeland. Heidegger cites, or rather glosses, a phrase from Chapter 20 of Johannes von Tepl's *Der Ackermann*, a work of early high German which reads: "As soon as a man is born, he is at once old enough to die [*Sobald ein Mensch zum Leben kommt, sogleich ist er alt genug zu sterben*]," adding that "Death is a way to be, which Dasein takes over as soon as it is" (H. 245). The former saying retains an authentic understanding of being-toward-the-end and contrasts with the everyday evasion of this, "as if to say, 'One of these days one will die too, in the end; but right now it has nothing to do with us [*man stirbt am Ende auch einmal, aber zunächst bleibt man selbst unbetroffen*]'" (H. 253).

The text of the *Ackermann* does more than illustrate an existentially appropriate or authentic way of being toward death. For, as Peter Atterton has argued, Heidegger's phenomenological variation of Dasein's being-toward-death draws on images from the text: debt, inheritance, and ripeness.[75] Existential analysis does not simply take over these images and this understanding of death and, as Atterton points out, it entirely dispenses with its wider theological framework.[76] Hence Dasein's being-toward-death does not mean that death is akin to an outstanding loan ["*Schuld*"] (H. 242) that must be repaid but rather that "*indebtedness* [Verschuldung] *becomes possible only 'on the ground of'* ['auf Grund'] *a primordial being-guilty* [Schuldigseins]" (H. 284), that is, Dasein's constantly having to take over the ground of its thrown facticity that it can never get into its power. Inheritance does not refer to a factical inheritance or hereditary sin (H. 180, 306 note ii) but to Dasein's taking over "a possibility which it has inherited [*ererbten*] and yet has chosen" (H. 384). The ripeness [*das Reifen*] of a fruit is "formally analogous to Dasein" but the latter does not fulfill itself with death (H. 244). Instead, temporality "*temporalizes or ripens* itself [zeitigt sich]" in Dasein's authentic being-toward-death and brings it to itself essentially (H. 328, cf. H. 323).[77]

The existential analysis takes these themes and imagery up, subjects them to phenomenological variation with a view to characterizing Dasein's kind of being. There is a return to the "soil" of history but this is appropriated in an elaborate conceptuality. Heidegger no more takes over the ordinary meanings and resonances of these terms and images but seeks to uncover an implicit and basic existential phenomenon, a possibility that is presently forgotten or obscured. The very act of philosophical conceptualization removes the philosopher from the everyday and from the historical possibilities it has already taken up unawares, that is, displaces them.

Do this displacement and appropriating return of history entail a return to the *native* soil? Staying with Heidegger's example, do we find in the text of *Der Ackermann* a primitive phenomenon, uncomplicated by excessive theorization, a primordial understanding that springs from the soil of the German rural culture of the Middle Ages? In fact, we do not. The phrase glossed by Heidegger is from Death's reply to the Ackermann, the titular ploughman, who is mourning the death of his wife. Death reproaches him for his lacking of understanding, saying he should not grieve and lament:

> "Have you not heard of the sage who wished to die in the bath, have you not read in his books that nobody should complain about the death of mortals? If you didn't know, then know it now: as soon as a human being is born it has drunk from the chalice, and so it must die … If you lament your wife's youth, you are wrong to do so; as soon as a human being comes to life, it is old enough to die."[78]

Death is reproaching the ploughman not simply for his lack of acceptance of the fundamental fact of human morality but also for his lack of acquaintance with Seneca, whose work would have remedied this defect. The phrase Heidegger cites is a sentiment found in several of the works of the philosopher eminently responsible for the Latinization of Greek philosophical concepts.[79] The existentiell testimony of folk wisdom is not autochthonous but has more tangled roots in Latin, in the late medieval, and the early Renaissance.[80]

The assumption that this dark unknown whose possibilities can be cultivated could be akin to a potential or actual political space or territory is also belied by the movement of thinking in *Being and Time* and related texts themselves. Some skepticism is already aroused by the fact that the linguistic relations that Heidegger detects between *wohnen*, *bauen*, and *sein*, and *wesen* are not only found in German but also, as Grimm notes, in English and other languages. Further, an elemental word which retains the force of an original experience is *mana*, a term that makes manifest an astonishment before the sheer fact of thrownness. This term is the central point of Heidegger's immanent critique of Cassirer, specifically of the latter's indebtedness to a neo-Kantian architectonic. This term *mana*, which is no doubt both elemental and forceful, is also a term drawn from, on Heidegger's way of conceiving, a highly exotic culture. There can be little doubt that something there shows itself in an exemplary fashion that is "positively helpful in bringing out the ontological structures of phenomena in a genuine way" (H. 51). Finally, given Heidegger's considerable indebtedness to German-Jewish thinkers, the discriminatory educational politics expressed in the letter to Victor Schwoerer amounts to a negation of the factual conditions that made his own work possible.

What philosophical point does this imply? The heritage that belongs to the movement of philosophical thinking is not the same as that of a community or a supposed people. Speaking of what is one's own or foreign here is already to be making an unwarranted presupposition about a background which is dark, hidden, and whose roots are more obscure and tangled than they seem. The deep past heeded in philosophical thinking is not only arduous and other to the today but all but inaccessible and incomprehensible on a collective level. If what is to be thought, what appeals to one, cannot be determined in advance of pursuing its disclosure, the clear corollary of this is it cannot *a priori* be included at the outset.

Yet we saw that certain passages in Heidegger's work suggest he saw the political and philosophical domains as exhibiting a kind of parallelism, both containing the possibility of responding to the historical moment. The conception of thinking that emerges from his work is essentially antinomian, it finds itself with and for others only against the everyday, through struggle. Following on from Heidegger's conception of providing a phenomenological basis for different areas of being, can a conception of the political be derived from the temporalizing of temporality, one formally characterized also by a movement of nihilation-creation that transforms previously instituted social structures? Would not especially a time of political crisis call for this? And if philosophical thinking is always already bound up with the world of others and has a venture character, specifically a venturing against, then does it not call for a politics of venturing against established institutional senses? And, inversely, could not the realm of politics as the realm of the deed be the first site of manifestation of new ways of thinking?[81]

Although I would acknowledge that a political crisis can, at least in principle, call forth possibilities of thoughtful response, Heidegger does not seem to me to provide the resources for thinking of political responses to such crises. Heidegger's conception of the historical which gives such weight to the acoustic, to heeding what speaks to unthematized possibilities also seems to me to have limits when carried over to the political. Heeding the hidden, non-apparent sources of the essential, of meaning that can become manifest in the present, however appropriate to silently communing with the spirit of history in one's study, risks obscuring the often senseless and accidental character of events, a senselessness that does not just belong to the breaking in upon life of accidents and natural disasters but inescapably to the accidents and short-sightedness that goes together with living and acting in a world with others.

And despite Heidegger's insistence that his analyses of fallen everydayness are purely formal and far from any moralizing judgments, he tends to characterize the social world by appealing to the reader's experience of jealousy, gossip, small-mindedness, and personal insecurity, rather than, say, friendly co-operation, good-willed discussion, and magnanimity. The pejorative overtones of such descriptions undoubtedly serve a methodological role in that they help in warding off everyday interpretative tendencies. Underlying such phenomena is Dasein's tendency to turn from a basic existential insecurity, which suggests we can expect these tendencies of flight to be aggravated in times of legitimacy crises in politics: a blind and bewildered seizing-hold of possibilities nearest to hand, much like inhabitants fleeing a burning house, reality denial through disappearance into a wish-world and fantasy projection, discursive emptiness, mutual suspicion, an I-thou relation of *ressentiment*, and strident claims to false certainties. In other words, we can expect an intensification of attempts to close off the movement character of existence and a seeking of security. The demagogue Cleon, as Thucydides depicts him, presents us with such a spectacle, as do Heidegger's political claims. They present us with the spectacle of one whose claims to be heeding essential insight into the realm of political decision are actually little more than an aggravation of the tendencies of fallen everydayness, driven by a furious sense of grievance, rather than an authentic counter-movement to that everydayness.[82]

Conclusion

Stressing the need to avoid one-sided reductionist readings of *Being and Time*, the complexities of the underlying issues and context, and the philosophical character of this work has long since become commonplace in debates about Heidegger's politics. I hope it is clear to anyone who has had the patience to read the preceding chapters that I do not deny the philosophical character of Heidegger's work. Yet I also believe that the contextualization and discussions of Bambach and many of the core interpretative claims made in Heidegger-critical scholarship such as that of Faye, Fritsche, and Kellerer are well-founded. The thesis that Heidegger's philosophy in the 1920s is implicated in his politics is not only plausible but far more convincing than a de-politicized interpretation and less simplistic than attempts to draw a ready demarcation between his philosophy and his politics. For it is precisely Heidegger's critique of the ontological limitations of transcendental philosophy that leads back to the question of the historical place or site of philosophy. Some of his key philosophical influences, his terminology and claims in his philosophical work and his correspondence indicate he conceives this site in an explicitly nativist, anti-Semitic sense and that his conception of Dasein's *Schicksal* foreshadows the most violent expressions of his politics in the 1930s.

I also proposed an immanent critique of this aspect of Heidegger's philosophical approach, arguing that it involves presuppositions incompatible with his conception of historical thinking. The concepts in the existential analytic and the historicizing at work therein have a complex and tangled genealogy, indicating that the historical background against which philosophizing takes place resists identification with an actual or potential national space. The latter is, on this view, a leveled-down, oversimplified interpretation that conceals the positive possibilities of a historicized transcendental philosophy.

Of enduring philosophical interest in this transcendental philosophy, I suggest, is its awareness of both how the past is formative of our possibilities of understanding while being formed by them, which interplay is central to Heidegger's work in this period. The account of temporality in Heidegger's work is one in which we are put at a remove from the present and can bring out the untapped possibilities of the past as it removes us not only from the familiarity of the surrounding world but also from how the past was present in it. This de-familiarization of the past, this sense of its strangeness makes possible rather than excluding object historical research. The effort made in Heidegger's texts is to think through this movement of de-familiarization itself using the philosophical and conceptual resources open in his situation. The *a priori* of temporality is the underlying "how" of historical appropriation, that is, how it occurs or temporalizes itself, and it shows through in the different, reciprocally implying senses of the concepts used.

Notes

1   Although this latter group of terms only occurs in one paragraph of *Being and Time*, this does not mean they are of only marginal significance. Other key concepts in the existential analytic are scarcely mentioned—for example, that of *Temporalität*—but cannot be neglected in any serious attempt to understand this work.
2   See Leo Strauss, "Philosophy as Rigorous Science and Political Philosophy" in his *Studies in Platonic Political Philosophy* (Chicago: University of Chicago Press, 1986), 29–37, here 33. I owe this reference to Peter Trawny's *Heidegger und der Mythos der jüdischen Weltverschörung* (Frankfurt am Main: Vittorio Klostermann, 2014), 37.

3   See Charles Bambach, *Heidegger's Roots: Nietzsche, National Socialism, and the Greeks* (USA: Cornell University Press, 2003), xix, note 6.
4   See, for example, Emmanuel Faye, *Heidegger: The Introduction of Nazism into Philosophy in the Light of the Unpublished Seminars of 1933–1935*, trans. Michael B. Smith (USA: Yale University Press, 2009), 12, 34–8 and "Das Sein als Mythos oder als Begriff: Heidegger und Cassirer," 67–112 and "Thomas Sheehan: The Introduction of Insults into the Heidegger Debate," 831–57, Sidonie Kellerer, "Philosophy or Messianism?" in *Confronting Heidegger*, ed. Gregory Fried (London: Rowman & Littlefield, 2020), 179–208.
5   H. 384–5.
6   Johannes Fritsche, *Historical Destiny and National Socialism in Heidegger's "Being and Time"* (Berkeley: University of California Press, 1999), 37.
7   Fritsche, *Historical Destiny and National Socialism*, 53. See also Faye, *Heidegger*, 16–7.
8   However, the return to Dasein's ownmost strangeness can provide the existential basis for interpreting the Dasein of even very remote cultures, as we saw in Heidegger's treatment of the mythical world, a peculiarity that will be discussed later.
9   H. 168.
10 Lee has rightly emphasized the political dimension of the term *Boden* in this lecture course but neglects the wider context of Heidegger's critique of Greek everydayness. See Jaehoon Lee, "Heidegger en 1924: l'influence de Yorck von Wartenburg sur son interprétation de Descartes" in *Heidegger, le sol, la communauté, la race*, ed. Emmanuel Faye (Paris: Beauchesne, 2014), 25–48, especially 38–42.
11 Note that the factical ideal mentioned at H. 310 is referred to in a footnote to this passage. Cf. H. 394.
12 Sheehan stresses the philosophical sense of the terms, claiming "*Bodenlosigkeit* refers to the 'groundlessness' of an argument, its lack of any reasonable foundation" and *Boden* means a "basis" for philosophy, thus a "ground." He describes Faye's translation, which reads these terms are referring to a rootedness in the native soil, as a "grotesque misreading" and opts for "'grounds' and 'lack of grounds' (*Boden* and *Bodenlosigkeit*)." See Sheehan, "L'affaire Faye: Faut-il Brûler Heidegger? A Reply to Fritsche, Pégny, and Rastier," *Philosophy Today*, Volume 60, Issue 2 (Spring 2016): 481–535, here 506, and "Emmanuel Faye: The Introduction of Fraud into Philosophy?" *Philosophy Today*, Volume 59, Issue 3 (Summer 2015): 367–400, here 383. Cf. Faye, *Heidegger*, 12. Faye argues these terms are ambiguous but that the primary, literal meaning is a nativist sense of the soil. See his "Das Sein als Mythos oder als Begriff," 67–112 and "Thomas Sheehan," 831–57.
13 I have here slightly modified the Heim translation, which reads: "Perhaps the true happening [*eigentliche Geschehen*] in the history of philosophy is always but

a temporalization of such 'moments' in distant intervals and strokes, moments which never become manifest as what they really are." The original German reads: "*Vielleicht ist das eigentliche Geschehen in der Geschichte der Philosophie immer nur eine in weiten Abständen und Würfen aufbrechende Zeitigung solcher Augenblicke, die nie in dem, was sie eigentlich sind, wirklich offenbar werden.*" (MFL 211 [GA 26: 272–3]).

14 This and the following paragraph summarize the argument of my article "Deciding the Fate of the State: Heidegger, Thucydides and the Boden of Ontology" which contains a fuller discussion of this citation. What remained unexplored there is the connection between this political understanding of "*das Geschehen der Gemeinschaft, des Volkes*" and other passages in Heidegger's text that suggest philosophical interpretation of his conception of historicality.

15 PS 437 [GA 19 629]. The German text is: "*Im Ganzen genommen: 'Ihr schwelgt im Genuß des Zuhören (Korrelativ zu Reden!) und gleicht eher solchen, die dasitzen und Sophisten begaffen als solchen, die über das Schicksal des Staates sich entscheiden sollen.*" I have modified the English translation by rendering "*Schicksal*" as "fate" rather than destiny here in order to make the terminology consistent with *Being and Time*.

16 See Kisiel, "Situating Rhetorical Politics in Heidegger's Protopractical Ontology: 1923–5: The French Occupy the Ruhr," *International Journal of Philosophical Studies*, Routledge, Taylor & Francis, Volume 8, Issue 2 (2000): 185–208.

17 Kisiel highlights a Heideggerian allusion to anti-Semitic post-war propaganda, writing: "This possibility of irresponsible gossip and chatter (*unverantwortliches Geschätz*) about nothing in particular, Heidegger remarks in phrases that are left out of the recently published edition of the course, are 'as such more dangerous than a Big Lie' ('*als solches gefährlicher al seine kräftige Lüge*': transcript of Helene Weiss, 16. XI. 23, p. 95)." He continues: "One might add that doubly dangerous is the drum-like repetition of a whopping 'powerful' (*kräfige*) lie like the 'November betrayal', the legend of the 'stab-in-the-back', 'the war-guilt-lie', 'the Langemarck lie', etc." Kisiel's article carefully situates Heidegger's lecture "*Wahrsein und Dasein,*" delivered in Cologne in December 1924, within the political context of its times, including its use of a "metaphorology both *territorial* and *militant.*" However, I cannot endorse Kisiel's claim that in the early Heidegger "the ethos of Greek civic discourse is held up as a paradigm in counterpoint to the propaganda ridden speech community of the Weimar Republic" given that in the 1924–5 *Plato's Sophist lecture* course, which Kisiel does not discuss there, Heidegger illustrates the countermovement to sophistry using the perhaps most inflammatory speech in Athenian political life that we have a record of. See Kisiel, "Situating Rhetorical Politics in Heidegger's Proto-Practical Ontology: 1923–25: The French Occupy the Ruhr," 188, 190, 189.

18 Thucydides, *The Peloponnesian War*, III.39.
19 It is clear from Thucydides's text, however, that the danger is past and Cleon himself is a power-hungry demagogue.
20 "The authentic repetition of a possibility of existence that has been—the possibility that Dasein may choose its hero—is grounded existentially in anticipatory resoluteness; for it is in resoluteness that one first chooses the choice which makes one free for the struggle of loyally following in the footsteps of that which can be repeated." (H. 385).
21 See Jacob Grimm, "In" and "In und bei," *Kleinere Schriften*, siebenter Band (Berlin: Ferd. Dümmlers Verlagsbuchhandlung, 1884), 247–50.
22 "*Alles wurzeln der Wörter sind verhüllte wesen, deren grund und beginn in einer fernen zeit ruht, aus welcher nur die letzten spitzen zu uns reichen.*" Grimm, "In und bei," 249.
23 My translation here builds on the helpful Macquarrie and Robinson translation's footnote 2 to H. 54.
24 Grimm, "In und bei," 249.
25 Ibid., 250.
26 Ibid.
27 I am taking one for the sake of brevity but checking Grimm's *Wörterbuch* for the etymological background to any of the key concepts of the existential analytic can, I think, enrich our understanding of *Being and Time*.
28 "'*Zukunft*' *meint hier nicht ein Jetzt, das, noch nicht 'wirklich' geworden, einmal erst sein wird, sondern die Kunft, in der das Dasein in seinem eigensten Seinkönnen auf sich zukommt.*" (H. 325).
29 See "*Kunft*" in Grimm's *Wörterbuch*, https://woerterbuchnetz.de/#2 (accessed 13/5/2023).
30 An additional layer of complication is added by the fact that Heidegger's "translations" of Greek terms into German are also an appropriation.
31 Heidegger underscores this point using again the terminology of rootedness at H. 21.
32 See his *Genesis*, 324.
33 See Faye, See his "Das Sein als Mythos oder als Begriff," 67–112, here 97–104 and "Thomas Sheehan," 831–57.
34 "*Das die gesammte psycho-physische Gegebenheit nicht ist sondern lebt, ist der Keimpunkt der Geschichtlichkeit.*" *Briefwechsel*, 71, cited at H. 401. All translations of this correspondence, unless otherwise noted, are mine.
35 "*Wie die Physiologie von der Physik nicht abstrahiren kann, so die Philosophie—gerade wann sie eine kritische ist—nicht von der Geschichtlichkeit.*" Ibid., 69, cited at H. 402.
36 These two terms are more or less equivalent for Yorck. It is the Christian who lives temporality.

37 "*Seiner Bewußtseinsstellung nach ist Rom zeitlos, daher das ewige Rom keine Redensart. Darum ist es der Sitz der Metaphysik—im Gegensatze zur Transzendenz. Rom begrieft nicht, wie kein Römer, den Tod.*" Briefwechsel, 120.

38 "*Wenn man Philosophie als Lebensmanifestation begrieft, nicht als Expectoration eines bodenlosen Denkens, bodenlos erscheinend, weil der Blick von dem Bewußtseinsboden abgelenkt wird, so ist die Aufgabe wie knapp in Resultate, so verwickelt und mühsam in seiner Gewinnung. Vortheilsfreitheit ist die Voraussetzung und schon diese schwer zu gewinnen.*" Ibid., 250, cited by Heidegger at H. 402.

39 Ibid., 39, partly cited by Heidegger at H. 38.

40 "*es ist ein Geschichte sehen, nicht ein Geschichte leben [...] Ranke ist ein großes Orkular, dem nicht, was entschwand, zu Wirklichkeiten werden kann …*" Ibid., 60, partly cited by Heidegger at H. 400.

41 "*Mit der Geschichte ist so, daß was Spektakel macht und augenfällig ist nicht die Hauptsache ist. Die Nerven find unsichtbar wie das Wesentliche überhaupt unsichtbar ist.*" Ibid., 26, cited by Heidegger at H. 401. I am using Macquarrie and Robinson's translation of this citation.

42 Ibid., 109, cited by Heidegger at H. 401.

43 Ibid., 26.

44 "*… dann geneiße ich das stille Selbstgespräch und den Verkehr mit dem Geist der Geschichte.*" Ibid., 133, cited by Heidegger at H. 401.

45 "*wenn ihr Stille seid so werdet ihr vernehmen, d.h. verstehen.*" Ibid., 26, cited by Heidegger at H. 401. Cf. H. 165, 395.

46 "*[d]ie praktische Abzweckung unseres Standpunkts ist die paedagogischem im weitesten und tiefsten Wortsinne.*" Ibid., 42–3 cited by Heidegger at H. 402.

47 Ibid., 101.

48 Ibid.

49 Ibid., 249–50, cited by Heidegger at H. 403.

50 "*Die Geschichtserkenntniß, welche von der eigenen Lebendigkeit aus sich rückwärts wendet zu dem der Erscheinung nach Vergangenen, der Kraft nach Aufbehaltenen würde in der Darstellung eine Analysis der Gegenwart der Vergangenheit vorausschicken und damit zugleich eine Controle bieten für das Geschichtliche gegenüber dem Antiquarischen. Nur was der Kraft nach gegenwärtig, in der Gegenwart ist, gehört zum Bereiche der Geschichte.*" Ibid., 167.

51 Ibid., 233.

52 Ibid., 192.

53 Ibid., 192–3.

54 Ibid., 193.

55 "*Die neue Denkweise, die kommen muß, manifestirt sich zuerst in und mittelst einer genialischen Persönlichkeit und wie immer zuerst im Bereich der That.*" Ibid., 65. Yorck is writing here of Bismarck.

56 Ibid., 223.
57 As Heidegger stresses, for Yorck the self is not primarily grasped through the regional discipline of analytic psychology but is historical through and through, which is a key point in his critique of Dilthey (H. 399).
58 *Briefwechsel*, 223.
59 "*Das Erkenntnißorganon aber ist und bleibt der Mensch und die Erkenntnißmittel sind in dem psychischen Capitale strukurirter Lebendigkeit beschlossen.*" Ibid., 192.
60 Ibid., 223.
61 "*war nicht umsont Jude,*" "*[d]er Jude stand damals nicht an der geschichtlichen Arbeit*" Ibid., 169.
62 "*Das Buch von Gobineau kenne ich im Originale. Eine schöne Mosaikarbeit eines unterrichteten und geistreichen Mannes. Keine Methode. Die muß eine historische Erkenntnißtheories bringen.*" Ibid., 233. As Dilthey's previous letter has been lost, it is not clear which of Gobineau's works is being discussed. The context suggests Dilthey had referred to a translation or a forthcoming translation of one of Gobineau's works. A German translation of Gobineau's main pseudo-scientific work appeared in 1898 as *Versuch über die Ungleichheit der Menschenrassen*, so one year after this letter (March 1897).
63 "*Alle wahrhaft lebendige und nicht nur Leben schillernde Historie ist Kritik.*" Ibid., 19, Macquarrie and Robinson's translation, cited by Heidegger at H. 401.
64 "*Die Politik der Republik ist Macchiavell und Napoleon. Jener läßt sich sonach nicht wie üblich nur aus dem renaissance-Boden erklären. Und wiederum die renaissance war solche noch weit mehr als gemeiniglich angenommen wird. Die städische Commune als politischer Typus ist das characterische Merkmal der neueren Zeit, in der wir noch drin stecken.*" Ibid., 19–20. Yorck later contends, in a comment cited by Heidegger immediately prior to the aforementioned citation on history as critique, that humanity after the Renaissance is ready for burial. Ibid., 83.
65 "*Ich wiederhole mich, wenn ich sage, Lebens—und Staatsauffassung, richtiger der Gedanke des Reichs gegenüber dem des Staats, im Mittelalter ist die Frucht der Ländlichkeit.*" Ibid., 20. Cf. Bambach, *Heidegger's Roots*, 17–20.
66 "*Mit der Entfremdung von dem Boden geht die haltende Kraft verloren. Der boden-los Status bewirkt im Menschen und in seinen Lebensgestaltungen das labile Gleichgewicht, welches jeder Erschütterung weicht.*" Ibid., 20.
67 Cf. Fritz Kaufmann, *Die Philosophie des Grafen Yorck von Wartenburg* (Halle a.d.S.: M. Niemeyer, 1928), 40–6.
68 See Faye, *Heidegger* 12, the sixth section of his "Thomas Sheehan" and "Das Sein als Mythos oder als Begriff," 97–104.
69 "*Ich gratuliere zu jeden einzelnen Falle, wo Sie die dünne jüdische Routine, der das Bewußtsein der Verantwortlichkeit für die Gedanken fehlt, wie dem ganzen Stamme das Gefühl psychischen und physischen Boden, von dem Lehrstuhl fern halten.*" *Briefwechsel*, 254.

70 For Heidegger this is ontologically grounded in the disclosive power of Dasein's moods, in which the world shows itself as mattering to us.
71 See Faye, *Heidegger* 33, the sixth section of his "Thomas Sheehan" and "Das Sein als Mythos oder als Begriff," 97–104.
72 Ibid.
73 Ibid and *Briefwechsel*, 254, cited above.
74 "When the Samians … reached Sparta, they gained an audience with the authorities and spoke at length commensurate with their need. The Lacedaemonian response to this first audience, however, was to say that they had forgotten the earlier parts of the Samian's speech, and could not follow the later parts. The Samians gained a second audience, however, at which they said nothing at all, except that they brought a bag with them and said, 'This bag needs gain.' The Lacedaemonians replied that the word 'bag' was redundant, but they still decided to help them." Herodotus, *The Histories*, trans. Robin Waterfield (New York: Oxford University Press, 2008), 3.46.
75 Peter Atterton. "'As Soon as a Man Comes to Life, He Is Old Enough to Die': Heidegger and Chapter XX of *Der Ackermann aus Böhmen*," *Research in Phenomenology,* Volume 52, Issue 1 (2022): 48–67. The following draws much on Atterton's analysis of Heidegger's appropriation of these images.
76 Atterton, Peter. "'As Soon as a Man Comes to Life …,'" 51–2.
77 Ibid., 61–6. Atterton denies there is any existential sense of ripening associated with death, my reading here rests on "*zeitigen*" as derived from the Middle High German term "*zītigen*," that is "*reifen* [to ripen]." See "*zeitigen*" *Das Herkunftswöterbuch: Etymologie der deutschen Sprache*, 5th edition, Vol. 7 (Berlin: Duden, 2014) and in Grimms Wörterbuch. https://woerterbuchnetz.de/#2 (accessed 14/5/2023).
78 I am here using the translation given in ibid., 53.
79 That Heidegger himself appeals to Seneca's conception of *cura* (H. 183) underscores this anti-nativist point.
80 Atterton, Peter. "'As Soon as a Man Comes to Life …,'" 52.
81 *Briefwechsel*, 65.
82 Such considerations clearly motivated early Greek historiography, especially that of Thucydides. His seeking "clarity of bygone events [τῶν τε γενομένων τὸ σαφὲς]" involves another kind of ascetics of thinking to that involved in philosophizing, but also one that counters an "impatience of labour" that sooner takes things on hearsay and "turns to the things nearest to hand [ἐπὶ τὰ ἑτοῖμα μᾶλλον τρέποντα]" or heeds what sounds "more delightfully to the ear than [is] conformably to the truth [ἐπὶ τὸ προσαγωγότερον τῇ ἀκροάσει ἢ ἀληθέστερον]." See Thucydides, *The Peloponnesian War*, 1. 20. Hobbes translation modified.

Conclusion: Metaphysics and Misgivings

If this book reads like an attempt to explain Heidegger's work in the late 1920s, it is more the record of a venture in understanding it. What I have sought to do in these interpretations is to preserve a sense of the strangeness and unfamiliarity of his thinking. Heidegger's texts are written from out of a situation and an experience alien to us, a fact easily forgotten in rereading them, writing about them, teaching them, and seeking to make them comprehensible to others. The strangeness of *Being and Time* is perhaps most evident when we first start reading it, but, through a familiarity with it and with its institutional senses, the way people at conferences and in universities talk about it, it becomes familiar and how it speaks to the alien within our experience forgotten. Yet what it speaks of is a movement in which the world becomes strange and it speaks of this movement drawing upon a strange language,[1] history, and situation.

This danger of making the alien and unsettling familiar is an inescapable aspect of any interpretation as such an undertaking involves a familiarization and domestication, a seeing it within one's own situation. The dangers involved here can be mitigated by keeping alive a sense of how strange a philosophical text is: other to what we usually think, to what we want it to say, to the important things we feel it should be talking about. Most especially with texts whose core themes are the alien in experience, one's own understanding needs to be constantly checked against this strangeness, by striving not to talk over, jump to conclusions about, or put a familiar narrative upon the matters under discussion. This applies as much to the understanding of terms that look the most familiar to readers of philosophical texts—*a priori*, condition of the possibility, the transcendental, idea, being, concept—as to words that are familiar to us in everyday life—talk, death, guilt, conscience, time, the word "is."

Retaining a sense of the strangeness of a text is to heed our misgivings about these terms. Their meaning is not clear. This does not mean becoming trapped in a fear of not understanding but opens up the text's historical dimension.

This means cultivating a sense of the situation in which it was written, with the misgivings of that situation, and with what strove to be given. Yet this also awakens the understanding that Heidegger's situation is not ours. His world, whatever parallels it may exhibit to our own, differs from it. The Dasein that is in each case mine—or yours—is not the Dasein of the author of the existential analytic. This sense of difference and of distance raises the question of Heidegger's situation. Even when we faithfully follow the injunction to "project these existential phenomena upon the existentiell possibilities which have been delineated in them, and 'think these possibilities through to the end' in an existential way" (H. 302–3), we nonetheless risk misconceiving the phenomena if we miss this historical dimension.

This historical dimension is central to the phenomenological *a priori*, that peculiar fact, the facticity of Dasein's existence. We do not seek its essential characteristics in the same way as those of a present-at-hand thing and Dasein is not a genus. Even in those limit cases where it is in question whether a being is Dasein or not—infancy and the mythical world—these are interpreted from out of the situation which is one's own. Another Dasein is given as the being-there of another and not in the way of a self to itself. And the contingency that belongs to our existence is a contingency we confront while existing: the possibility of our no longer being. This contingency is of quite a different order to the contingency of an inter-worldly entity. The fact of Dasein's existence has a factical necessity even—or especially—when it confronts the possibility of its not being, for it is precisely then that it is brought into the most concrete awareness of its situation, which is always *this* situation.

And to this situation belongs a given heritage. From a hypothetical and unimaginable view from nowhere, this heritage appears as contingent. Existential analysis does indeed try to grasp what belongs existentially to the situation as such, its formal features. But it belongs to this very attempt that it grasps what belongs to the situation from out of *this* situation drawing on *its* heritage and *these* possibilities of understanding. This venture presupposes an existentiell movement of historicizing, *this* historicizing, even when it tries to grasp the formal features of the movement of historicizing itself. The notion of repetition, which encompasses the act of interpreting Heidegger, takes place against the background of a situation that is not Heidegger's own, another "this" situation. It unavoidably opens up a temporal difference deeper than that which can be bridged by a generic unity.

It is in terms of this essential historicality that I understand Heidegger's endeavor to bring out a phenomenologically original conception of the *a priori* that belongs to Dasein as such—be it mythical, infant, Greek, or our contemporary Dasein—but that also has historical conditions for its manifestation. This tension is inherent in the initial characterization of the project of fundamental ontology: unveiling a universal horizon for the understanding of being through an analytic of a particular entity, Dasein, more specifically our historical Dasein. This tension is also indicative of *a priori* with two essentially related moments, Dasein's always already being factically situated in the midst of beings and its always already being ahead of itself.

The past is always already being taken up in the present as something that has given form to it and is formed by it. The historical is not simply the contingent and the empirical but that which provides a contingent opening onto transcendental structures—structures that are accessible to us in a historical moment. We can think here of Heidegger's existential genealogy of philosophical concepts. Their meaning is not capable of clarification purely in terms of their present meaning, which has become flattened down to a kind of false self-evidence. We need to understand the horizon—including the political and social horizon—in which they were given to understand their scope and limits. Understanding how they arose is essential to understanding what they point out. Focusing solely on the contemporary use of a concept—for example of the *a priori*—misses this historical dimension. There is a constant back and forth—a "*repl[ying] [erwidert]* to the possibility of that existence which has-been-there" (H. 386)—between the origin and sense of such concepts. They are both formative of and formed in the present moment of philosophizing. The temporality Heidegger seeks to uncover and the concepts he forms testify to this back and forth. This is also clear in his approaches to other authors. His interpretations of Kant and Greek philosophy are based on close readings of the source texts and the available scholarship while also appropriating them in terms of his own question.

Motivating this approach is a sense of misgivings with, an alienation from how we typically understand things, the ready-made phrases, and stock interpretations that enable us to cope and deal with situations. For Heidegger's texts in this period emphasize the alien or the strange within experience. And we respond to this sense of misgiving by putting our usual interpretative tendencies aside, by striving not to chatter over, jump to conclusions about, or put a facile narrative upon our experience. This action, an ascetics of thinking in which we silently heed how things stand for us, returns us to our factical situation. This, which Heidegger calls wanting to have a conscience or a readiness for anxiety, also prepares us for the withdrawal of what usually counts as significant. When this occurs, things nearest to us are put at a remove, become alien, opaque, and we faced for a time with the sheer fact of being there. From out of such an experience we are opened to other possibilities of understanding and sense-making that were previously passed over and that appeal to us from the past. They provide us with ways of articulating and understanding what went unheeded in the general situation but to which we were already factically attuned.

This awareness of the otherness of beings in themselves underlies, but without becoming manifest as such, everyday life, the attempt to control and subdue nature through technology, the rituals and cults of mythical worlds, both past and present, that seek salvation before the overwhelming power of beings, in infant Dasein's turn from the world entry of beings and the attempts, in crisis situations, to find something, anything, to hold on to. The implicit understanding of being therein is theological in the very broad sense of an awareness of what which overpowers and overwhelms. It is in-finite in the sense that all horizons of finite, historical understanding withdraw and one is simply confronted with the strangeness of things. It is the unconditioned (GA 27 360–1).[2]

Heidegger's work in this period, as I understand it, explores the conditions for a thinking attuned both to the strangeness of beings and to the historical situation. In contrast to Dasein immersed in the mythical world, religion, scientific endeavor, and everydayness, the existentiell project of philosophy strives to make explicitly manifest and thematize what makes possible the tacit awareness—a "shadowy awareness" as Heidegger puts it (PM 87 [GA 9 110])—of the split between the strangeness of beings and our historically conditioned modes of understanding. It seeks to conceptualize its temporal conditions using the resources of the historical situation. The explication of temporality is his answer to this question. It explains what makes possible our basic senses of what is—and of what is incomprehensible—and how these can become manifest. The conception of the *a priori* that develops from this investigation is one that is emergent, that is, brought forth in a way of being possible for our historical Dasein.

Heidegger's thematization of this movement of explicitly facing the strangeness of beings under the heading of the metaphysics of Dasein brought about a shift in the investigation from a concern with the meaning of being to the revelation of the ontological difference. In *Being and Time*, the idea of the Real serves as a provisional designation for the problem of Dasein's facticity (H. 314, cf. H. 403). Yet the turn to facticity takes place in the experience of the overwhelming, where its understanding no longer has a grip on things. I argued in the foregoing that this should not be read as the point at which Heidegger's project runs aground or is abandoned but rather at which it undergoes an internal transformation. The phenomenon at issue—Dasein's temporal transcendence as the condition for the revealing of the ontological difference—is shown to be incapable of being conceived in terms of an identity but instead entails a conceptual multi-dimensionality.

The movement of this thinking brings us before our being there and recreates our relation to the possible. What distinguishes this undertaking from Yorck's is that here historical thinking attempts to think its own possibility. What Heidegger calls the metaphysics of Dasein or Dasein's transcendence is the attempt to bring forth and describe the movement of this thinking in its thinking of its own conditions. The most basic words in which philosophy expresses itself are those that retain something of the force of this experience. Some of these words retain something of pre-theoretical, immediate senses of what is, such as those preserved by the kinships between the terms *in*, *bei*, *wohnen*, *sein*, and *wesen*. Others belong to the language of metaphysics. The self that stands by itself has something substance-like in its self-constancy even though it is not a substance (H. 314, 322, 114, 212, BPP 108 [GA 24 152]). In anticipating our death, we have something like an idea of our being as a whole, even though what we see is not the outward look of a thing (H. 314, 403, 61). There is something like a generic difference between our kind of being and non-Dasein like entities that becomes manifest when we are in the grip of a fundamental attunement although being is not a class or a genus (H. 314, H. 403, 3).

Past possibilities can also speak to this undertaking by showing us something of the movement character of this thinking. The Christian experience of rebirth, the transition in which the past is becoming transformed, testifies to this.[3] The Kantian transcendental imagination, in showing the belonging together of distinct ecstases, of future, having-been, and making present, beneath the conceptual unity that subsumes the differing under a unifying one, manifests this. The force of the Heraclitan fragments lies in their multiplicity of senses (MFL 210-1 [GA 26 272-3]). The very word "philosophy," read from this experience, means exposure to the overwhelming and striving for understanding of what is, that is, indicates thrownness and projection as the fundamental constituents of our being (MLF 10, 11 [GA 26 12, 13]).

It is from this movement character that I understand Heidegger's thinking in the late 1920s. The indicative character of this work, its attention to the phenomena, its care in both forming concepts and attention to how these are to be formed fully merit Heidegger's description of "the harshness of our expression, and … the minuteness of detail with which our concepts are formed" in his undertaking (H. 39). And the multi-dimensionality of his concepts, the peculiar grammar of statements such as "I *am*—as-having-been [*ich* bin-*gewesen*]" (H. 328), is grounded in their being thought from out of this temporal disunity, from out of the ontological difference.

At the heart of Heidegger's metaphysics is a kind of ascetics that brings thinking into movement and lets the world emerge anew. This creativity is always already tacitly operative within the everyday, within the shifts and displacements of the world we are concerned with. The terms freedom, joy, and creation are as essential to this undertaking as the better-known triad of anxiety, death, and guilt. To be opened for the movement of existence is to be open for a creative movement.

Notes

1   This also holds for native speakers of German. Heidegger admits his inquiry makes for awkward, inelegant, and harsh prose (H. 38–9).
2   Heidegger's description of this as "unconditioned" needs a degree of qualification. As we saw in Chapter 4, while mythical Dasein lives within an awareness of being as overpowering and the temporality of facticity is determinative for its way of being, it lacks a self-conception over against which the power of beings as a whole breaks in upon.
3   Heidegger claims "the sense of the Christian experience as rebirth [*Wiedergeburt*] is that Dasein's prefaithful, i.e., unbelieving existence is sublated [*aufgehoben*]" in the sense of being "raised up, kept, preserved in the new creation." In faithful existence, on Heidegger's characterization, an existentiell powerlessness is sublated, *aufgehoben*, but precisely this implicitly includes "*that* understanding of being that is constitutive for human Dasein as such insofar as it exists at all." The understanding of being here is of it as overpowering and ontologically speaking Dasein's powerless is essential, it belongs to it as thrown and thus it cannot be sublated, that is, definitively "raised up, kept, preserved in the new creation." The movement character of existence shows itself on the thematic level in theology, albeit ontically: theological concepts "intend a specific *transition* of existence [*Existenz*übergang], in which pre-Christian and Christian existence are united in their own way." This underlying transitional character [*Übergangscharakter*] is manifest in "the multi-dimensionality [*Mehrdimensionalität*] of theological concepts" (PM 365 and 365 note 2 [GA 9 63 note 1]).

Bibliography

Works by Heidegger

Heidegger, Martin. "Aufzeichnungen zur Temporalität (Aus den Jahren 1925–7),"
  Heidegger Studien, edited by Claudius Strube, 18 (1998): 11–23.
"Drei Briefe Martin Heideggers an Karl Löwith." In *Zur philosophischen Aktualität
  Heideggers II: Im Gespräch der Zeit*, edited by Dietrich Papenfuss and Otto Pöggeler,
  27–39. Frankfurt am Main: Vittorio Klostermann, 1990. The first two letters can be
  found in "Two Letters" in Löwith, Karl. *Martin Heidegger and European Nihilism*,
  edited by Richard Wolin and translated by Gary Steiner, 235–43. New York;
  Chichester: Columbia University Press, 1995.
Kant und das Problem der Metaphysik. Gesamtausgabe 3, edited by Friedrich-Wilhelm
  von Hermann. Frankfurt am Main: Vittorio Klostermann, 1991. *Kant and the
  Problem of Metaphysics*, 5th edition. Translated by Richard Taft. Bloomington:
  Indiana University Press, 1997.
Wegmarken. Gesamtausgabe 9, 3rd edition, edited by Friedrich-Wilhelm von Hermann.
  Frankfurt am Main: Vittorio Klostermann, 1976. *Pathmarks*, edited by William
  McNeill. Cambridge; New York: Cambridge University Press, 1998.
Zur Sache des Denkens. Gesamtausgabe 14, edited by Friedrich-Wilhelm von Hermann.
  Frankfurt am Main: Vittorio Klostermann, 2007.
Grundbegriffe der aristotelischen Philosophie. Gesamtausgabe 18, edited by Friedrich-
  Wilhelm von Herrmann and Ingrid Schüßler. Frankfurt am Main: Klostermann,
  2002. *Basic Concepts of Aristotelian Philosophy*. Translated by Robert D. Metcalf and
  Mark B. Tanzer. Bloomington: Indiana University Press, 2009.
Platon: Sophistes. Gesamtausgabe 19, edited by Ingrid Schüssler. Frankfurt am Main:
  Klostermann, 1992. PS: *Plato's Sophist*. Translated by Richard Rojcewicz and André
  Schuwer. USA: Indiana University Press, 2003.
Die Grundbegriffe der Antiken Philosophie. Gesamtausgabe 22, edited by Franz-Karl
  Blust. Frankfurt am Main: Vittorio Klostermann, 1993. *The Basic Concepts of Ancient
  Philosophy*. Translated by Richard Rojcewicz. Bloomington: Indiana University
  Press, 2008.
*Phänomenologische Interpretation von Kants Kritik der reinen Vernunft. Gesamtausgabe
  25*, edited by Ingtraud Görland. Frankfurt am Main: Vittorio Klostermann, 1991.
  Phenomenological Interpretation of Kant's Critique of Pure Reason. Translated by
  Parvis Emad and Kenneth Maly. Bloomington: Indiana University Press, 1997.

Metaphysische Anfangsgründe der Logik in Ausgang von Leibniz. Gesamtausgabe 26, 2nd edition, edited by Klaus Held. Frankfurt am Main: Vittorio Klostermann, 1990. *The Metaphysical Foundations of Logic*. Translated by Michael Heim. Bloomington: Indiana University Press, 1992.

Einleitung in die Philosophie. Gesamtausgabe 27, edited by Otto Saame and Ina Saame-Speidel. Frankfurt am Main: Vittorio Klostermann, 2001.

Feldweg-Gespräche (Erdachte Gespräche 1944/45). Gesamtausgabe 77, edited by Ingeborg Schüßler. Frankfurt am Main: Vittorio Klostermann, 1995. *Country Path Conversations*. Translated by Bret Davis. Bloomington: Indiana University Press, 2010.

Zu eigenen Veröffentlichungen. Gesamtausgabe 82, edited by Friedrich-Wilhelm von Hermann. Frankfurt am Main: Vittorio Klostermann, 2018.

"Preface by Martin Heidegger." In *Heidegger: Through Phenomenology to Thought*, edited by William Richardson. Hague: Martinus Nijhoff, 1974.

Sein und Zeit, 19th edition. Tübingen: Max Niemayer Verlag, 2006. *Being and Time*. Translated by John Macquarrie and Edward Robinson. Cornwall: Blackwell, 2000. *Being and Time*. Translated by Joan Stambaugh and revised by Dennis J. Schmidt. Albany: State of New York University Press, 2010.

"Was ist Metaphysik? Urfassung/ What Is Metaphysics? Original Version," edited by Dieter Thomä and translated by Ian Alexander Moore and Gregory Fried. *Philosophy Today*, 62 3 (Summer 2018): 733–51.

Other Texts

Allison, Henry. *Kant's Transcendental Idealism: An Interpretation and Defense*. New Haven: Yale University Press, 2004.

Alweiss, Lilian. *The World Unclaimed: A Challenge to Heidegger's Critique of Husserl*. Athens, OH: Ohio University Press, 2003.

Aristotle. *Aristotle's Metaphysics: A Revised Text with Introduction and Commentary. 1 and 2*, with introduction and commentary by William David Ross. Oxford: Clarendon Press, 1981.

Aristotle. *The Basic Works of Aristotle*, edited and with an introduction by Richard McKeon. New York: Random House. 1941.

Atterton, Peter. "'As Soon as a Man Comes to Life, He Is Old Enough to Die': Heidegger and Chapter XX of *Der Ackermann aus Böhmen*," *Research in Phenomenology*, 52 1 (2022): 48–67.

Bambach, Charles. *Heidegger's Roots: Nietzsche, National Socialism, and the Greeks*. USA: Cornell University Press, 2003.

Benveniste, Émile. *Problèmes de linguistique générale*. Paris: Éditions Gallimard, 1966.

Bernasconi, Robert. *Heidegger in Question: The Art of Existing*. Atlantic Highlands, NJ: Humanities Press, 1993.

Bernet, Rudolf. "Phenomenological Reduction and the Double Life of the Subject." In *Reading Heidegger from the Start. Essays in His Earliest Thought*, edited by Theodore Kisiel and John van Buren, 245–67. Albany: State of New York University Press, 1995.

Birmingham, Peg. "Logos and the Place of the Other," *Research in Phenomenology*, 20 (1990): 34–54.

Braver, Lee. *Division III of Heidegger's Being and Time: The Unanswered Question of Being*. Cambridge, MA: MIT Press, 2015.

Cassirer, Ernst. *Philosophie der Symbolischen Formen, 2: Das Mythische Denken*. Darmstadt: Wiss. Buchgesellschaft, 1964. English translation: *The Philosophy of Symbolic Forms Volume 2: Mythical Thinking*. Translated by Steve J. Lofts. Abdington: Routledge, 2021.

Crowell, Steven. "Facticity and Transcendental Philosophy." In *From Kant to Davidson: Philosophy and the Idea of the Transcendental*, edited by Jeff Malpas, 100–21. London: Routledge, 2005.

Crowell, Steven. *Husserl, Heidegger and the Space of Meaning*. Evanston: Northwestern University Press, 2001.

Crowell, Steven. *Normativity and Phenomenology in Husserl and Heidegger*. New York: Cambridge University Press, 2013.

Crowell, Steven. "The Middle Heidegger's Phenomenological Metaphysics." In *The Oxford Handbook of the History of Phenomenology*, edited by Dan Zahavi, 229–50. New York: Oxford University Press, 2018.

Crowell, Steven, and Jeff Malpas, eds. *Transcendental Heidegger*. Stanford: Stanford University Press, 2007.

Dahlstrom, Daniel Oscar. "The End of Fundamental Ontology." In *Division III of Heidegger's Being and Time: The Unanswered Question of Being*, edited by Lee Braver, 83–103. Cambridge, MA: MIT Press 2016.

Daly, Aengus. "Deciding the Fate of the State: Heidegger, Thucydides and the Boden of Ontology," *Journal of the British Society for Phenomenology*, 53 4 (2022): 440–54.

Daly, Aengus. "Heidegger's Metaphysics of Objects: A Reply to Graham Harman." In *Phänomenologie und spekulativer Realismus/ Phenomenology and Speculative Realism/ Phénoménologie et réalisme spéculatif*, edited by Guillermo Ferrer, Sylvaine Gourdain, Nicolas Garrera, Alexander Schnell, 228–38. Würzburg: Königshausen & Neumann, 2022.

Daly, Aengus. "Zeitlichkeit und Geburt in Heideggers Auslegung der mythischen Umwelt." In *Die Lebensphilosophie zwischen Frankreich und Deutschland/La philosophie de la vie entre la France et l'Allemagne*, edited by Olivier Agard, Gerald Hartung, Heike Koenig, 267–78. Deutschland: Ergon-Verlag, 2018.

Davis, Bret. *Heidegger and the Will: On the Way to Gelassenheit*. Evanston: Northwestern University Press, 2007.

De Beistegui, Miguel. *Heidegger and the Political: Dystopias*. London: Taylor and Francis, 2002.

De Boer, Karin. *Thinking in the Light of Time: Heidegger's Encounter with Hegel*. Albany: State of New York University Press, 2000.

Engelland, Chad. *Heidegger's Shadow: Kant, Husserl and the Transcendental Turn*. London, New York: Routledge, 2017.

Faye, Emmanuel. "Das Sein als Mythos oder als Begriff: Heidegger und Cassirer." In *Sein und Zeit neu verhandelt: Untersuchungen zu Heideggers Hauptwerk*, edited by Marion Heinz and Tobias Bender, 67–112. Hamburg: Felix Meiner Verlag, 2019.

Faye, Emmanuel. *Heidegger: The Introduction of Nazism into Philosophy in the Light of the Unpublished Seminars of 1933–1935*. Translated by Michael B. Smith. USA: Yale University Press, 2009.

Faye, Emmanuel. "Thomas Sheehan: The Introduction of Insults into the Heidegger Debate," translated by Aengus Daly, *Philosophy Today*, 66 4 (Fall 2022): 831–57.

Fritsche, Johannes. *Historical Destiny and National Socialism in Heidegger's "Being and Time"*. Berkeley: University of California Press, 1999.

Golob, Sacha. *Heidegger on Concepts, Freedom and Normativity*. Cambridge: Cambridge University Press, 2016.

Greisch, Jean. *Ontologie et Temporalité: Esquisse d'une interprétation intégrale de Sein und Zeit*. Paris: Presses Universitaires de France, 1994.

Grimm, Jacob. *Kleinere Schriften*, siebenter Band. Berlin: Ferd. Dümmlers Verlagsbuchhandlung, 1884.

Grondin, Jean. *Le tourant dans la pensée de Martin Heidegger*. Paris: Presses Universitaires de France, 1987.

Harman, Graham. *Tool-Being: Heidegger and the Metaphysics of Objects*. New York: Open Court, 2002.

Haugeland. "Letting Be." In *Transcendental Heidegger*, edited by Steven Crowell and Jeff Malpas, 93–103. Stanford: Stanford University Press, 2007.

Hegel, Georg Wilhelm Friedrich. *Werke Band 02 - Jenaer Schriften Volume: 2*. Frankfurt: Suhrkamp, 1986.

Herodotus. *The Histories*. Translated by Robin Waterfield. New York: Oxford University Press, 2008.

Jaran, François. *La Métaphysique du Dasein: Heidegger et la possibilité de la métaphysique (1927–1930)*. Bucharest: Zeta Books, 2010.

Jaran, François. *Phénoménologies de l'histoire: Husserl, Heidegger et l'histoire de la philosophie*. Paris: Éditions Peeters Louvain, 2013.

Kahn, Charles H. *The Art and Thought of Heraclitus: An Edition of the Fragments with Translation and Commentary*. Cambridge: Cambridge University Press, 2001.

Kant, Immanuel. *Anthropology from a Pragmatic Point of View*. Translated and edited by Robert B. Louden. Cambridge: Cambridge University Press, 2006.

Kant, Immanuel. *Critique of Pure Reason*. Translated by Paul Guyer and Allen Wood. Cambridge, New York: Cambridge University Press, 1998.

Kant, Immanuel. *Lectures on Logic*. Translated and edited by J. Michael Young. Cambridge: Cambridge University Press, 2004.

Kant, Immanuel. *Religion within the Boundaries of Mere Reason*. Translated and edited by Allen Wood, George Di Giovanni and Robert Merrihew Adams. Cambridge: Cambridge University Press, 2003.

Kaufmann, Fritz. *Die Philosophie des Grafen Yorck von Wartenburg*. Halle a.d.S.: M. Niemeyer, 1928.

Kellerer, Sidonie. "Philosophy or Messianism?" In *Confronting Heidegger*, edited by Gregory Fried, 179–208. London: Rowman & Littlefield, 2020.

Kierkegaard, Søren. *For Self-Examination/ Judge for Yourself*. Translated by Howard Vincent Hong and Edna Hong. Princeton: Princeton University Press, 1991.

Kisiel, Theodore. "Situating Rhetorical Politics in Heidegger's Protopractical Ontology: 1923–25: The French Occupy the Ruhr," *International Journal of Philosophical Studies*, 8 2 (2000): 185–208.

Kisiel, Theodore. *The Genesis of Heidegger's Being and Time*. Berkeley; London: University of California Press, 1995.

Kisiel, Theodore. "The Mathematical and the Hermeneutical: On Heidegger's Notion of the Apriori." In *Martin Heidegger in Europe and America*, edited by Edward G. Ballard and Charles E. Scott, 109–20. The Hague: Nijhoff, 1973.

Köhler, Dietmar. *Martin Heidegger: Die Schematisierung des Seinssinnes als Thematik des dritten Abscnhitts von "Sein und Zeit."* Bonn: Bouvier Verlag, 1993.

Krell, David Farrell. *Intimations of Mortality: Time, Truth and Finitude in Heidegger's Thinking of Being*. University Park: Pennsylvania University Press, 1991.

Lee, Jaehoon. "Heidegger en 1924: l'influence de Yorck von Wartenburg sur son interprétation de Descartes." In *Heidegger, le sol, la communauté, la race*, edited by Emmanuel Faye, 24–48. Paris: Beauchesne, 2014.

Locke, John. *An Essay Concerning Human Understanding*. Edited by Roger Woolhouse. London: Penguin, 2002.

Lofts, Steve. "Cassirer and Heidegger: The Cultural-Event. The *Auseinandersetzung* of Thinking and Being." In *The Philosophy of Ernst Cassirer: A Novel Assessment*, edited by J. Tyler Friedman and Sebastian Luft, 233–58. Berlin: De Gruyter, 2017.

McMullin, Irene. *Time and the Shared World: Heidegger on Social Relations*. Evanston: Northwestern University Press, 2013.

Müller, Max. *Existenzphilosophie im geistigen Leben der Gegenwart*, third expanded and improved edition. Heidelberg: F. H. Kerle Verlag, 1964.

Ó Murchadha, Felix. "Future or Future Past: Temporality between *Praxis* and *Poiesis* in Heidegger's *Being and Time*," *Philosophy Today*, 42 3 (1998): 262–9.

Ó Murchadha, Felix. *The Time of Revolution: Kairos and Chronos in Heidegger*. London; New York: Bloomsbury, 2013.

Plato. *Complete Works*, edited by John M. Cooper. Indianapolis: Hackett, 1997.

Plato. *Plato's Theory of Knowledge; The Theaetetus and the Sophist*. Translated, with commentary by Francis M. Cornford. New York: Dover Publications, 2003.

Plato. *Platon: Werke VI*, edited by Peter Staudacher and translated by Friedrich Schleiermacher. Darmstadt: wbg Edition, 2019.

Pöggeler, Otto. "Ausgleich und anderer Anfang. Scheler und Heidegger." In *Studien zur Philosophie von Max Scheler*, edited by Ernst Wolfgang Orth and Gerhard Pfafferott, 166–203. Freiburg/ München: Verlag Karl Alber, 1994.

Reinhardt, Karl. *Parmenides und die Geschichte der griechischen Philosophie*. Frankfurt am Main: Vittorio Klostermann, 2012.

Römer, Inga. "Zeit und Kategoriale Anschauung: Heideggers Verwandlung eines Husserl'schen Grundbegriffes," *Archiv Für Begriffsgeschichte*, 55 (2013): 251–62.

Rothacker, Erich, ed. *Briefwechsel zwischen Wilhelm Dilthey und dem Grafen Yorck v. Wartenburg 1877–1897*. Halle (Saale): Verlag Max Niemener, 1923.

Schalow, Frank. *The Renewal of the Heidegger-Kant Dialogue: Action, Thought, and Responsibility*. Albany: State of New York University Press, 1992.

Scheler, Max. "Reality and Resistance: On Being and Time, Section 43." Translated by Thomas Sheehan. In *Heidegger: The Man and the Thinker*, edited by Thomas Sheehan, 133–43. Chicago: Precedent Publishing, Inc, 1981.

Scheler, Max. *The Human Place in the Cosmos*. Translated by Manfred S. Frings. Evanston: Northwestern University Press, 2009.

Schmidt, Stefan. *Grund und Freiheit: Eine Phänomenologische Untersuchung des Freiheitsbegriffs Heideggers*. Cham: Springer, 2016.

Schnell, Alexander. *De l'existence ouverte au monde fini: Heidegger 1925–1930*. Paris: Vrin, 2005.

Schnell, Alexander. "La temporalité de l'être dans Les Problèmes Fondamentaux de la Phénoménologie de M. Heidegger." In *Recherches phénoménologiques actuelles en Roumanie et en France*, edited by Ion Copoeru and Alexander Schnell, 107–30. Hildesheim; Zürich; New York: Georg Olms Verlag, 2006.

Schürmann, Reiner. *Heidegger on Being and Acting: From Principles to Anarchy*. Bloomington: Indiana University Press, 1990.

Shapiro, Joel B. "Heidegger's Virtue Is Knowledge: Being-With and Solicitude in §26 of 'Being and Time'," *Philosophy Today*, 38 4 (1994): 400–18.

Sheehan, Thomas. "Emmanuel Faye: The Introduction of Fraud into Philosophy?" *Philosophy Today*, 59 3 (Summer 2015): 367–400.

Sheehan, Thomas. "Heidegger's New Aspect: On *In-Sein, Zeitlichkeit*, and *The Genesis of 'Being and Time'*," *Research in Phenomenology*, XXV (1995): 219, 217.

Sheehan, Thomas. "L'affaire Faye: Faut-il Brûler Heidegger? A Reply to Fritsche, Pégny, and Rastier," *Philosophy Today*, 60 2 (Spring 2016): 481–535. "Emmanuel Faye: The Introduction of Fraud into Philosophy?" *Philosophy Today*, 59/3 (Summer 2015), 367–400.

Sheehan, Thomas. *Making Sense of Heidegger: A Paradigm Shift*. London; New York: Rowman & Littlefield, 2015.

Sheehan, Thomas. "'Time and being', 1925–7." In *Martin Heidegger: Critical Assessments*, edited by Christopher McCann, 29–67. London: Routledge, 1992.

Sherover, Charles. *Heidegger, Kant and Time*. Bloomington; London: Indiana University Press, 1971.

Strauss, Leo. *Studies in Platonic Political Philosophy*. Chicago: University of Chicago Press, 1986.
Tengelyi, László. "L'idee de métontologie et la vision du monde selon Heidegger," *Heidegger Studies*, 27 (2011): 137–53.
Tengelyi, László. *Welt und Unendlichkeit: Zum Problem phänomenologischer Metaphysik*. Freiburg: Verlag Karl Alber, 2014.
Thomson, Iain. *Heidegger and Ontotheology: Technology and the Politics of Education*. New York: Cambridge University Press, 2005.
Thucydides. *The Peloponnesian War: The Complete Hobbes Translation*. Translated by Thomas Hobbes, introduction and notes by David Grene. Chicago: University of Chicago Press, 1989.
Trawny, Peter. *Freedom to Fail: Heidegger's Anarchy*. Translated by Ian Alexander Moore and Christopher Turner. UK: Polity Press, 2015.
Trawny, Peter. *Heidegger und der Mythos der jüdischen Weltverschwörung*. Frankfurt am Main: Vittorio Klostermann, 2014.
Vedder, Ben. *Heidegger's Philosophy of Religion: From God to the Gods*. Pittsburgh: Duquesne University Press, 2007.
Vogel, Lawrence. *The Fragile "We": Ethical Implications of Heidegger's "Being and Time"*. Evanston: Northwestern University Press, 1994.
Wunsch, Matthias. *Fragen nach dem Menschen: Philosophische Anthropologie, Daseinontologie und Kulturphilosophie*. Frankfurt am Main: Vittorio Klostermann, 2014.
Wunsch, Matthias. "'Welt' in Heideggers metaphysischer Periode." In *Rostocker Phänomenologische Manuskripte*, 18, edited by Michael Großheim, 3–28. Rostock: Inst. für Philosophie, 2013.

Other sources

Das Herkunftswörterbuch: Etymologie der deutschen Sprache, 5th edition, Vol. 7. Berlin: Duden, 2014.
Grimm's *Wörterbuch*, https://woerterbuchnetz.de/#2

Index

a priori 2, 12–15, 17, 18, 20, 23, 27,
    28, 34, 76, 83, 84, 87, 96, 103,
    113, 114, 124, 125, 126, 129–30,
    131–2, 134, 164–5, 167–8, 173,
    175, 183
  a priori perfect or perfect tense *a priori*
    14, 52–4, 57, 58–9, 61, 96, 134, 142
  and practical identity 135, 141–2
  as a time determination 8, 14–15,
    17–18, 19, 32, 35, 45–6, 51–75, 95,
    104–5, 107–8, 112, 129, 184–6
  of facticity 7, 32, 41, 45, 88, 141
Absens 64
absorption 107, 109, 120, 124
abstraction 41, 69, 79, 105
alien 16, 37, 38, 44, 91, 119, 126, 153, 167,
    169, 183, 185
anger 11
anti-Semitism, anti-Semitic 22, 155, 162,
    165–6, 168, 169, 175, 177
anticipatory resoluteness 39, 40, 42, 48,
    178
anxiety 5, 11, 16, 17, 26, 32, 35, 37–8, 39,
    42, 43–4, 47–9, 65, 77, 78, 82, 83,
    85, 89–94, 98–100, 109, 115–16,
    126, 133, 134, 138, 140–5, 153, 185,
    188
  peculiar temporality of 94, 111
Aristotle 14, 25, 53, 88, 98, 107–8, 146,
    153–4
attunement 16, 17, 82, 90, 143, 144, 187,
    see also mood
auf dem Sprung 85, 92, 99, 100
Augenblick, moment 18, 82, 92, 95, 99,
    100, 115, 140, 154–5, 177
authentic, authenticity 11, 17, 25, 32, 35,
    37, 38, 39, 40, 42–3, 44, 47, 48, 50,
    57, 58–9, 61, 66, 67, 70, 72, 73–4,
    84–5, 88–90, 92, 107, 110, 112, 116,
    118, 134, 136, 142, 143, 146, 152–4,
    160, 168, 171, 172, 174, 178

Being and Time 1–22, 23, 24, 25, 26, 27,
    28, 31–46, 49, 50, 51–2, 56, 57, 59,
    60, 62, 63, 64, 67, 69, 70, 71, 73–4,
    76, 78–9, 81–2, 83–93, 95–7,
    100, 101, 103–11, 116, 117, 118,
    119, 121, 122, 123, 125, 126, 129,
    131–2, 134, 136, 138, 140, 141–3,
    145, 146–7, 151–7, 159, 160–2,
    168–9, 172, 174, 176, 177, 178,
    183, 186
  alleged failure of 2, 3–5, 6, 52, 63, 101
  Division III of 2–4, 15, 17, 19, 28, 47,
    62, 69, 85, 95, 96, 104
being, different meanings of 87, 108
being of beings 15, 16, 17, 25, 46, 53–6, 59,
    61, 62, 64, 65, 74, 81, 114
beings as a whole 8, 11, 18, 24, 25, 26,
    44, 61, 63, 65, 75, 82, 84, 87, 90–7,
    100, 115–19, 120–2, 124, 141, 144,
    188
Bergung 120–1, 123
bewilderment 11, 92
birth 7, 15, 26, 41–5, 49, 50, 97, 103–4,
    110–2, 115, 122, 124, 154
  Christian experience of rebirth, 187,
    188
Boden, soil or basis 20, 22, 29, 146–7, 151,
    153–61, 162, 163, 166–9, 176, 180
boredom 16
burden of being 36, 48

care 10, 31–2, 38, 39, 41, 42, 49, 77, 134,
    140, 160
Cassirer, Ernst 19, 23, 27, 28, 103–20,
    123–4, 125, 126, 129, 146–7, 172
category, categories, categorical 21, 78,
    115–16, 158, 159
  a priori 14, 70–1, 73
  category error 52, 57
  of mythical consciousness 49, 115–17
Cleon 21, 155–6, 169, 174, 178

community, cf. *Gemeinschaft* 1, 88–9, 137–8, 173, 177
  and the *Volk* or people 21, 74, 137–8, 146, 152–61, 168, 169, 173
comparison 69, 79
concept formation 2, 23, 41, 82, 90, 123, 140
  empirical 70, 79
  temporality of 2, 14–15, 20, 47, 49, 66–74, 95, 108–9, 113, 138, 139–40
condition for the possibility 13, 45, 53, 62, 85, 90, 134, 183
conscience 48, 78, 117–18, 119, 126, 134–5, 139, 164, 167, 183
  willing or wanting to have 38–9, 48, 93, 185–6
  Yorck von Wartenburg and 165
creativity, creation 48, 113, 126, 127, 143, 173, 187, 188
Critique of Pure Reason 12–13, 14, 51, 66–74, 99
  and Cassirer 104–5
Crowell, Steven 13, 20, 24, 27–8, 76, 126–7, 129–47, 148, 149, 150

darkness, dark 49, 170, 172–3
  of facticity 86, 110, 111, 122, 125, 141
Dasein 4, 6, 7, 9, 12, 14, 16, 18, 20, 21, 24, 26, 28, 32–46, 47, 48, 49, 50, 52–6, 60–7, 73–4, 77, 78, 84, 87, 88, 90, 91–3, 100, 107, 109, 110, 113, 125, 126, 127, 129–32, 136–8, 138–47, 150, 151
  analysis of 9, 10, 22, 31–2, 81, 104, 118, 146, 162
  and transcendence 1, 2, 7, 11, 15, 18, 46, 67, 73, 77, 84, 87, 103, 113, 116, 120, 136, 138–47, 150, 187
  as such 83, 107, 114, 121, 122, 144, 184–5, 188
  authentic, authenticity of 17, 35, 38, 42, 57, 58–9, 74, 89–90, 116, 146, 153, 171
  infant 110, 111, 116, 122, 123–4, 143, 144, 184–5, 186
  mythical or primitive 47, 104–10, 112–22, 123, 124, 126, 127, 143, 144, 188

  our historical 104–9, 119, 122, 124, 143–4, 185, 186
  temporality of 4, 5, 9, 11, 15, 18, 25, 32–46, 62, 65, 73, 82, 83, 85, 95, 120, 133, 135, 138–47, 149–50, 154, 155, 160, 187
death 7, 39, 40, 41, 42, 43, 78, 110, 112, 117, 121, 124, 127, 162, 171–2, 181, 183, 187, 188
  being-towards-death 11–2, 25, 38, 39, 42, 43, 50, 100, 105, 110, 111–2, 124, 146, 154, 171–2
deduction 49, 116–17
Der Ackermann 23, 171–2
destiny 94, 152–3, 156, 177
Dilthey, Wilhelm 22, 147, 152, 161–2, 163, 165, 180
disclosure 2, 5, 13, 37, 39, 74, 94, 109, 120, 127, 144, 145, 160, 173
discourse 17, 47, 82, 83, 170
  civic 177
  counter-discourse 38
discovery 44, 46, 57, 64, 142
divine 86, 97, 117
dwelling 20, 158–9, 159–60, 171

Einleitung in die Philosophie 25–6, 28, 103–4, 110, 112, 120–1, 124, 142
elation 11, 48
Engelland, Chad 13, 18, 27–8, 57–9, 76, 78
enigma of being 10, 45
eternity 26, 86, 96
evasion 93, 111–2, 118, 120, 121–2, 171
existential and categorical, distinction between 21, 158
extra-ordinary 100, 115

factical ideal 40, 83, 104, 120–2, 126–7, 156, 176
facticity 4, 6–11, 13–15, 17, 25–6, 28, 31–46, 60, 61, 63, 65–7, 69, 73–5, 77, 78, 81–8, 92, 100, 110, 115–16, 118, 122, 125, 131–5, 138–47, 153, 171, 184, 186, 188
fallenness 10, 82, 107, 109, 117, 124
fantasy 36, 118–19, 174
fate, *Schicksal* 94, 100, 152–6, 177

Faye, Emmanuel 22, 29, 151, 162, 166, 168, 174, 176, 180, 181
fear 11, 47
for-the-sake-of-which 60, 61, 150, 170
formal indication 40–1
free-floating 33, 89, 153, 160
freedom 49, 121, 136, 146, 188
    Yorck von Wartenburg on 163

genealogy 7, 23, 44, 5, 51, 55–6, 60–1, 175, 185
Geschehen, see historicizing
Gobineau, Arthur de 166, 180
God 25–6, 86, 95–6
gods 105
Golob, Sacha 18, 27–8, 57, 59–60, 76, 77, 101
good, goodness 136, 146, 150, 153, 161
    Platonic 58, 62, 146
grammar 17, 95, 158, 188
Grimm, Jacob 19, 21, 22, 158–61, 172, 178, 181
guilt 7, 135, 171, 177, 183, 188

Haltung 120–2, 126
Haugeland, John 76
having-been 33–4, 40, 41, 45, 47, 73, 149, 170, 187, 188
    and birth 110
    and the a priori perfect 53
Hegel 87, 93, 98
Heimatlos, without a homeland 22, 74, 126, 151, 170
Herodotus 181
historical past 43, 73–4, 132, 134, 163
historicality 21, 82, 112–13, 130, 132, 133–4, 150, 151–2, 177, 184–5
    of Dasein 20, 42–5, 120–2, 137–9, 143, 146, 153–7, 161, 167–8
    Yorck von Wartenburg and 162–7
historicism 129–48
historicizing, *Geschehen*
    movement of 42, 73–4, 159, 161–2, 168, 175, 184
    of the community and the people 137, 152–3, 161–2
history, primal 88–9, 103
horizon of time 10, 62–3, 71–3, 108

idea 28, 54, 183
    of being 44–5, 60, 96, 140
    of existence 25, 46, 60, 96, 140
    of the Real 25, 46, 60, 96, 140, 186
    of world and worldhood 83, 106
    Platonic 25
imagination 119, 131
    transcendental imagination 13, 20–1, 56–7, 68–74, 114, 126, 151, 170, 187
immediate temporality 106–8, 112, 115–17, 120, 122, 125–6, 143–4
in-order-to 59–60, 106
inauthentic, inauthenticity 25, 37, 42, 61
individualize 11, 35, 37–9, 48, 109
infinite, infinity 26, 76, 82, 86, 96
inherit, inheritance 50, 86, 146, 171

Jaran, François 18, 23, 24, 28, 97, 98, 125
joy 47, 48, 142–3, 188

Kant, Kantian 1, 41, 48–9, 76, 79, 105, 107–8, 146–7, 154–5, 167, 170, 185
    and the transcendental 2, 4–5, 12–15, 18, 19–20, 26, 27, 51–74, 129–31
    and time 66–74, 77
    and transcendental ideas 100
    and transcendental illusion 130, 132
Kant and the Problem of Metaphysics 20, 24–5, 56, 72–4
Kehre, see turn
Kisiel, Theodore 13, 22, 26, 28, 76, 177
Kraft, force 21, 74, 117, 118–19, 120, 158, 164, 166, 167, 168, 172, 179, 180, 187
Kunft 40, 48, 154, 160, 178

language of metaphysics 3, 4–5, 24, 52, 95, 101, 187
legacy 43
Leibniz, Gottfried Wilhelm 13, 15, 154
"Letter on Humanism" 4–5, 24, 101
letting-be 41, 61, 76, 77, 91–2, 93, 99, 111
    and the nothing 61, 91–2
    bogus *Gelassenheit* 61
    letting-be-involved, *Bewandenlassen* 52–7, 61, 76, 111

letting-itself-come-towards-itself 40, 61
life-feeling 121
Locke, John 40-1, 48-9

magic 105, 106, 117-19, 120, 121
making-present 10
mana-representation 23, 113-18, 121, 122, 125-6, 172
meaning of being 6, 44, 51, 63, 74, 108, 114, 124, 129, 156, 161
    and the shift in Heidegger's investigation 2, 9, 11, 24-5, 45, 81, 95, 99, 186
memory 131, 143
metaphysical-ontic 4, 8-10, 23-4, 31, 35, 45, 62-3, 78
metaphysics of Dasein 1, 2-11, 16, 17, 19, 45-6, 57, 61, 63, 66, 73, 82, 86, 111, 129, 130, 140, 186-7
metapolitics 130-1, 136-8, 150
metontology 9-10, 25, 75
misgiving 52, 169, 183-4, 185
missing something 25, 64
mood 10-1, 16, 32-6, 41, 43-4, 46, 47, 48, 77, 90, 99, 111, 142, 144, 181
Müller, Max 95-6, 101
multi-dimensionality of philosophical concepts 18, 41, 73, 74, 94-6, 140, 187-8

National Socialism 136, 151-2, 156
national space 23, 148, 169, 175
nativist 165, 169, 174-5, 176, 181
nature 2, 41-5, 51, 84, 89, 101, 129
    and facticity 4, 6, 7, 31, 74, 133, 135, 138, 139, 141, 150
    and technology 49, 118, 121, 186
    Dasein's access to 9, 25, 32, 49, 55, 78-9, 81, 85
    mythical Dasein's identification with 116-17
neo-Kantian, neo-Kantianism 13, 103, 113, 114, 172
Nietzsche 164
normative, normativity 133-6, 140-2, 146
normative standard (Golob) 59
nothingness, nothing 3-4, 8, 63, 65, 88-93

Ó Murchadha, Felix 26, 42-3, 49, 50, 124
ontic condition 74
ontic foundation of fundamental ontology 7, 81
ontological difference 1, 2, 10, 12, 18, 63, 65, 75, 99, 124, 144, 156, 186-7, 188
    ancient 68
    different senses of 47, 50, 78, 83, 95-7
    pre-conceptual awareness of 91
    temporal conditions for revealing 2, 9, 11-2, 15, 24-5, 45, 83, 85, 120-1, 122
opportune moment 87
overpowering, see nature
overturning 2, 9-10, 18, 25, 90, 93

people, cf. *Volk*
Phenomenological Interpretation of Kant's "Critique of Pure Reason" 56, 66
Philosophical Anthropology 28
Plato 14, 25, 58, 59, 60, 62, 85, 97-8, 150, 153, 155, 167
play 127, 136-9, 142-3, 147
    Play-space 73
Plessner, Helmuth 16
Pöggeler, Otto 24
politics, *völkisch* 130-1, 136-7, 147, 151, 154, 155, 169
praesens 63-6, 96
primitive phenomena 21, 157, 172
productive comportment 14, 15, 60, 70
    and the *a priori* 54-6, 57

question of being 5, 12, 13, 51, 120, 125, 144, 161
    historical possibility of raising 124, 143-4
question of beings 53-4

radical ontology 81, 109
recollection
    and Plato 58
    metaphysical 75, 77
reflection 69, 123
    phenomenological 132-3
    what is totally other to 132-3, 141
religion 25-6, 121, 123, 186

repetition 7, 22, 50, 117–18, 159, 161, 167–8, 178, 184
   of Cassirer's work 104
   of fundamental ontology 8, 16, 49, 74, 81–97
resoluteness, resolute, resolution, see anticipatory resoluteness
ressentiment 174
Römer, Inga 18, 26, 28, 97
roots, rootedness 172–3, 176
   ambiguity in 154
   and linguistics (Jacob Grimm) 158–9
   and temporality 154, 168
   and Yorck von Wartenburg 162
   existentiell roots of the existential analytic 146
   of nature and history 44–5
   of sensibility and understanding (Kant) 74
   politically loaded terminology of 20–2, 74, 98, 147, 151–4, 162
   root of the "not" 3–4

Scheler, Max 7, 8, 16, 24
schematic pre-designation 64–5
schematism (Kant) 13, 14, 26, 53, 76, 79
   as authentic concept formation 72
Schmidt, Stefan 18, 24, 28, 97
Schnell, Alexander 26, 75
scream 110–1, 122
Seneca 172, 181
Sheehan, Thomas 23, 26, 27–8, 76, 77, 133–4, 149
   on Heidegger's politics 176
sleep 110–1
subsumption 18, 69–73
surprise 1, 87, 96–7

technology 121, 186
temporale 9–10, 24, 25, 31, 45, 62–5, 78
Temporalität 3–6, 8–10, 12–13, 23–4, 25, 123, 175
   and the turn to the metaphysical-ontic 62–6
temporality, derivative 14, 51, 62, 66–8, 78, 107
temporality, original 45, 62, 66–7, 72, 78, 133, 155
temporality of Dasein, see Dasein

temporality of thrownness 2, 7, 9, 11–2, 15, 19, 23, 24–5, 26, 41, 45, 82, 86, 97, 110, 115–17, 121, 129, 141–2, 143
Tengelyi, László 18, 24, 28, 46, 97, 100
   on necessary facts 31
terminological inversions in Heidegger's work 12, 97, 119
The Basic Problems of Phenomenology 3–10, 16, 23–4, 31, 51–74
   and the *a priori* 14–15, 17–18, 51–74
The Fundamental Concepts of Metaphysics 16
The Metaphysical Foundations of Logic 4, 5–6, 49, 71, 104, 141
   and the turn or *Kehre* 9–11, 23–4
   temporality in 8, 62, 71
Thucydides 21, 22, 155, 169, 170, 174, 178, 181
time, ordinary conception of 115, 170
timeless 132, 162, 166
transcendence, see Dasein
transcendental framework 12–15, 19, 51–2, 57, 129
truth
   of existence 84–5, 145, 148
   origin of 85, 122
turn, *Kehre* 26, 67, 88–93, 101
   different senses of 25–6, 35
   in Heidegger's project 3–4, 9–11, 17, 23–4, 31–45, 78, 87
   turn from [*Abkehr*] 11, 25, 32, 35–8, 90, 93, 111–2, 125
   turn toward, turning thither [*Hinkehr*] 11, 17, 32, 35–7, 45
turned around world, *verkehrte Welt* 87, 93
twilight state 111, 116, 122, 126

Umschlag, overturning 9–10, 25
understanding of being 1, 2, 3–4, 5–6, 7, 9, 10, 12, 18, 24, 31, 43, 49, 52, 55, 57, 59, 60, 62–3, 65, 67, 69, 75, 78, 87, 88, 91, 95, 98, 106, 108–9, 112–14, 121, 122, 123, 124, 157, 158–9, 185, 188
university 88, 94, 99, 135
unmeaning or meaninglessness of beings 37, 44, 134, 142, 156

Vedder, Ben 86, 98
Volk, people 136–8, 146–8, 151–61, 177

"What is Metaphysics?" 25, 81–97, 99, 115
  and *Being and Time* 18, 26, 82, 91–3, 95, 111–2, 121–2
  as a repetition 81–2
  term "horizon" dropped in the published version 99, 150
wish 48
  and mythical Dasein 47, 116, 117–20
  wish-world 36, 174
world
  cosmological conception of 84
  existential conception of 82–4

world-entry of beings 15, 88–9, 103, 111, 149–50
world-forming 136–7
Wunsch, Matthias 18, 24, 28, 97, 123–4, 125
  criticism of Heidegger's Cassirer interpretation 109

Yorck von Wartenburg, Count Paul von 19, 21–2, 147, 152, 157, 162–9, 178, 179, 180
  differences between his and Heidegger's conception of historicality 168, 187

www.ingramcontent.com/pod-product-compliance
Lightning Source LLC
Chambersburg PA
CBHW052115300426
44116CB00010B/1674